# UNDERSTANDING
# GAMES
## AND
# GAME
# CULTURES

# UNDERSTANDING
# GAMES
## AND
# GAME
# CULTURES

INGRID RICHARDSON, LARISSA HJORTH & HUGH DAVIES

Los Angeles | London | New Delhi
Singapore | Washington DC | Melbourne

Los Angeles | London | New Delhi
Singapore | Washington DC | Melbourne

SAGE Publications Ltd
1 Oliver's Yard
55 City Road
London, EC1Y 1SP

SAGE Publications Inc.
2455 Teller Road
Thousand Oaks, California 91320

SAGE Publications India Pvt Ltd
B 1/I 1 Mohan Cooperative Industrial Area
Mathura Road
New Delhi 110 044

SAGE Publications Asia-Pacific Pte Ltd
3 Church Street
#10-04 Samsung Hub
Singapore 049483

Editor: Michael Ainsley
Assistant editor: Charlotte Bush
Production editor: Martin Fox
Copyeditor: Sarah Bury
Proofreader: Rebecca Storr
Indexer: Judith Lavender
Marketing manager: Abigail Sparks
Cover design: Lisa Harper-Wells
Typeset by: KnowledgeWorks Global Ltd.
Printed in the UK

Library of Congress Control Number: 2020944086

**British Library Cataloguing in Publication data**

A catalogue record for this book is available from the British Library

ISBN 978-1-5264-9801-4
ISBN 978-1-5264-9800-7 (pbk)

At SAGE we take sustainability seriously. Most of our products are printed in the UK using responsibly sourced papers and boards. When we print overseas we ensure sustainable papers are used as measured by the PREPS grading system. We undertake an annual audit to monitor our sustainability.

# CONTENTS

# LIST OF FIGURES AND TABLES

## Figures

# Tables

# ABOUT THE AUTHORS

**Ingrid Richardson** is Professor of Digital Media in the School of Media & Communication at RMIT University. She is a digital ethnographer and phenomenologist with a broad interest in the human–technology relation, mediated embodiment and the wellbeing effects of networked interfaces. She has published on topics such as scientific technovision, virtual and augmented reality, games, mobile media and small-screen practices, urban screens, remix culture and web-based content creation and distribution. She is co-author of *Gaming in Social, Locative and Mobile Media* (with Hjorth, Palgrave), *Ambient Play* (with Hjorth, MIT Press), and *Mobile Media and the Urban Night* (with Hardley, Palgrave Macmillan, forthcoming). Over the past ten years she has taken a particular research interest in games and play as integral and significant aspects of contemporary media ecologies.

**Larissa Hjorth** is a Distinguished Professor, digital ethnographer, socially-engaged artist, and director of the Design & Creative Practice (DCP) research platform at RMIT University. Larissa has two decades' experience leading collaborative digital and mobile media projects that innovate methods to understand intergenerational and cross-cultural relationships around play, loss and intimacy. She has led 20 national and international research projects in locations such as Japan, South Korea, China and Australia. Larissa has published over 100 publications on the topic – recent publications include *Haunting Hands* (with Cumiskey, Oxford University Press), *Understanding Social Media* (with Hinton, 2nd edition, Sage), *Creative Practice Ethnographies* (with Harris, Jungnickel and Coombs, Rowman & Little) and *Ambient Play* (with Richardson, MIT Press).

**Hugh Davies** is a postdoctoral research fellow in the Design & Creative Practice (DCP) research platform at RMIT University. As an interdisciplinary producer and researcher, Hugh explores practices of playful engagement in the Asia Pacific Region. Awarded a PhD in Art, Design and Architecture from Monash University in 2014, Hugh's study of play structures and game cultures have been supported with fellowships from Tokyo Art and Space, M+ Museum of Visual Culture and the Hong Kong Design Trust.

# ACKNOWLEDGEMENTS

The authors would like to thank series editor Michael Ainsley for his guidance, support and humour in the development of this book.

The authors would also like to thank the Australian Research Council for funding the *Games of Being Mobile* Discovery Project (DP140104295). Much of the empirical work in this book draws from fieldwork conducted as part of this project.

We have also greatly appreciated the research assistance of William Balmford and the skilled copyediting of Klare Lanson.

In addition, we acknowledge the support of RMIT University and especially the Enabling Capability Platform (ECP) coordinators Esther Pierini and Adelina Onicas.

Ingrid would like to thank her daughter Zoë and son Jamie for their critical and insightful reflections on contemporary play practices. Larissa would like to dedicate this book to her son, emerging LPer Jesper.

# 1

# Introduction: Understanding Games and Game Cultures

Why do games matter in contemporary media culture?

What is meant by the 'ludification of culture' or the 'playful turn'?

Describe some of the ways that 'gamification' impacts your everyday life.

What are some examples of 'ambient play'?

Are the boundaries of the 'magic circle' of play becoming more porous? How?

> Increasingly, the ways that people spend their leisure time and consume art, design and entertainment will be games – or experiences very much like games. ... As more people play more deeply in the Ludic Century, the lines will become increasingly blurred between game players and game designers ... the 21st century will be defined by games. (Zimmerman, 2013: n.p.)

In Kyoto (Japan), 86-year-old widow Machiko loves playing the **augmented reality (AR)** game, *Pokémon GO*. *Pokémon GO* allows her to embed wellbeing into her everyday life by focusing on two things essential to ageing well – social inclusion and exercise. Every day she walks the many steps needed to hatch the best Pokémon, meeting fellow older adult neighbours on her expeditions. *Pokémon GO* invites Machiko to rediscover her local urban environment in many ways – spatially, socially and emotionally. *Pokémon GO* encapsulates the power of games for social change, especially within digital health spaces.

In the slums of Manila (the Philippines), we find 7-year-old Miguel hanging out with his friends watching **Let's Plays (LP)** in the alleyways around the videogame/internet cabinets known as *pisonet* ('piso' referring to one peso, and 'internet' piso + net). The *pisonet* reminds us of the cultural differences specific to the activity of 'watching play' across public online and offline spaces. Miguel's mother and other siblings are nearby, ambiently observing Miguel and his friends as they watch their LPs. Through the *pisonet*, informal practices of play, familial care and surveillance operate to maintain intergenerational intimacy.

In London (UK), 30-year-old Sarah uses the geolocative self-tracking app *Strava* to map her bicycle rides. The app allows her to diarize her trips, share with friends on social media and gamify her achievements with awards like King of the Mountain (KoM). It also affords Sarah a sense of ambient safety and autonomy, as she can share her location in real time with her friends and family. She names her rides with playful titles, embedding generic digital maps with her own personalized cartographies.

In New York (US), 10-year-old Reuben has been confined to his home during the COVID-19 pandemic. Each afternoon, once online school curriculum finishes, he looks forward to playing *Roblox Mad City* with his friends while chatting on Discord. Millions of school children around the world use videogames as a way to maintain sociality during a time of physical distancing – in the US, videogame internet traffic increased by 75% when COVID-19 restrictions were imposed (M.B., 2020). Even the World Health Organization (WHO), which recently added game addiction as a mental health disorder, acknowledged the communicative power and global reach of games in their support of the #PlayApartTogether initiative (Snider, 2020).

In Melbourne (Australia), 22-year-old Sam plays *Overwatch* with her friends – people she has never met face to face, but they have known each other for years and are close friends. She used to play *League of Legends*, where she never revealed her gender or sexual orientation; it was just easier that way. Now she plays as the *Overwatch* adventurer Tracer, and she and her friends are vocal in their support of the 'queering' of game characters. Sam is in her final year of a game design degree at university, and regularly shares *Overwatch* fan art on Twitter and Tumblr where she has amassed a following of thousands.

As these five opening vignettes reveal, games and game-like practices are integral to the everyday lives of many people, and involve a spectrum of socio-economic, cultural, linguistic, material, political and digital complexities. In each of these stories we see the power of games as cultural interfaces, imbricated in ways that are material, social, political and environmental. Games are always played in context – reflecting the specificities of the interface, the place of play, and the player. Games are *cultural interfaces* that occupy and mediate our daily interactions, our movement through urban and domestic spaces, our embodied experiences and our modes of communication. Games are also worlds that we inhabit, places where communities of players gather together and share common interests. The significance of game cultures today is part of the broader evolution of both gamification and the 'playful turn' in our media and communication practices – what is termed the **ludification** of culture (Raessens, 2012).

This book seeks to critically understand this playful turn in culture as the backdrop to *game practices* and their attendant *game cultures* that take place within local and global contexts. We situate games as one of the most significant media interfaces of contemporary life, and explore who makes games, who plays them, and what, how and where we play. What precisely constitutes gameplay is as ubiquitous as it is divergent, traversing digital, material, public and private spaces across generational, cultural and gender differences. This book considers the many different contexts and situations that games inhabit – being at home, in urban spaces, across networked and face-to-face contexts, and within communities of practice. Our emphasis on *situating games within culture* highlights our focus on both informal and formal practices, and the intentional and unintentional effects of games and play in everyday life.

As the title of the book indicates, we are interested in grounding games as a cultural phenomenon – a medium that expresses, reflects and mediates contemporary experiences of sociality, connection, creative practice, design and politics. Given their breadth and diversity, mapping games and their cultural effects is a complex task requiring interdisciplinary approaches and methods.

In what follows we will first explore key themes that arise throughout the book. We then turn to why studying games and game cultures is so important in contemporary research, by focusing on the significance of ludification and gamification. Finally, we provide an overview of each of the chapters.

## Book Themes

As mentioned above, game cultures today are complex, diverse and expansive. In order to frame the ways in which we are contextualizing games and game cultures, we have outlined some key themes that can be viewed as characterizing the field now. These cross-cutting themes are as follows:

1. *Mainstream and Independent*: uneven diversity and inclusion in industries and communities.
2. *Live and Social*: communities coalescing across platforms and changing modes of distribution.
3. *Ambient and Playful*: the characteristics of how games occupy contemporary culture.
4. *Mobile and Haptic*: heightening of the mobile, haptic, augmented and locative.
5. *Innovation and Intervention*: the potential of games for social and political change.
6. *Methods and Data*: emerging big and small data approaches to address game phenomena.

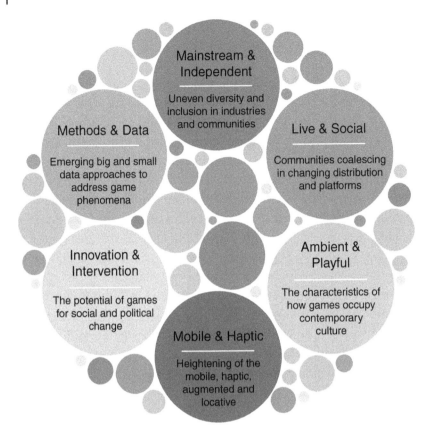

**Figure 1.1** The core themes of *Understanding Games and Game Cultures*.
Design: Adelina Onicas.

While games have become mainstream and ubiquitous through the rise of mobile devices and **livestreaming**, where we see games being played across cultures, generations and gender, we also see they are harbingers for bigger societal debates around *diversity* and *inclusion*. For example, while the opening up of mobile platforms – smartphones, tablets and consoles – has allowed independent gaming communities access into the market and thus heralded new models of diversity and inclusion, the bigger **AAA (Triple A Game)** companies are still dominated by masculine work cultures and gender stereotypes. As we discuss in Chapter 4, while it has been some time since the #GamerGate scandal, some systematic issues around the industry not reflecting the diversity of game communities remain. This phenomenon raises questions about how the games industry of tomorrow can reflect the diversity and inclusion of game communities today.

Within contemporary game cultures in which livestreaming, **eSports** and Let's Play (LP) burgeon (see Chapters 5 and 6), themes of *liveness* and *sociality* have come to the forefront. Distribution phenomena such as Twitch or the Chinese livestream service Douyu have seen communities come together in and through a game text. Livestreaming and genres such as LPs have shifted how we think about the relationship between text, audience and platform. As we explore in Chapter 6, livestreaming and Let's Plays have rewritten the boundaries between games, fans and performativity. Each platform creates and curates their own modalities of performance – what Thomas Lamarre calls *platformativity* (Lamarre, 2017). Understanding livestreaming also requires us to rethink the archive as active, which in turn requires us to recalibrate our methods.

As *data* becomes more omnipresent within everyday life, as witnessed in livestreaming, this necessitates that we rework our *methods* (Chapter 2). In this book we rethink how analysing game cultures today requires more complex deployment of mixed methods. As Lankoski and Björk (2015) note, the plethora of quantitative methods (i.e. surveys of 1,000 or more people) and qualitative methods (one-on-one interviews and focus groups) on hand for game study researchers continues to grow just like the field. Phenomena such as haptics also require us to rethink how we study the relationship between the body, interface and game, as we explore in detail in Chapters 2 and 10.

So too, understanding game cultures within everyday life requires us to acknowledge key debates around the sites, genres, practices, platforms, interfaces and contexts for games. As argued elsewhere, we define contemporary game cultures as *ambient* and *playful* (Hjorth & Richardson, 2020). We suggest that we need to take mobile games *seriously* as they expand across different public and private settings in ways that are social, ecological and even political. They are also, significantly, conduits of what we call *ambient play*, a term that conveys how games and playful media practices have come to pervade much of our social and communicative terrain, both domestic and urban. We map ambient play as part of a sensory, quotidian experience that acknowledges the complex ways in which humans and more-than-humans interact across digital, material and social environments that move across personal and public domains.

Intersecting with the ambient and playful is the role of *mobile* and *haptics*, which we discuss in Chapters 2, 10, and 11. Ambient play recognizes the ways in which contemporary haptic screens emphasize proprioception (the knowing, moving body) and diverse modes of engagement from distraction to the habitual (Hjorth & Richardson, 2020). As screens, interfaces and gameplay become more multisensorial by embracing haptics, how we experience and engage with games changes. Haptic and mobile interfaces allow for other proprioceptive attunements, especially enabling older or non-normative bodies access into the game space.

So too, the enhancements of haptics and mobile devices have seen the mainstreaming of augmented reality (AR) and locative functions that allow games like *Pokémon GO* to be accessible not only to the general public but to new demographics of players, as we saw in the case of Machiko in the opening vignette. Moreover, technologies like AR provide ways for us to reimagine familiar spaces and places in new ways, highlighting the role of play as a practice that fosters creativity, sociality and innovation.

Social innovation has a long history in the tradition of place-based games which have sought to be both innovative and interventionist. As we discuss in Chapter 8, historical movements such as Situationist International (SI) and the **New Games Movement** deployed play and games to explore political, social and environmental dimensions. Fuelled by a sense of urgency for social change, they saw games and play as vehicles for transformation. This ideology continues to be seen in more contemporary versions, such as big urban games, games for change and game jams. Here the role of games helps to develop understanding, empathy and risk-taking which can allow for *innovation* and *interventions* into social, political or environmental issues. In the deployment of multisensorial ways of being in the world, movements such as games for change have sought to provide voice for marginalized social agencies and often overlooked topics. As we explore in the next section, these themes are foregrounded by the rise of ludified and gamified practices in contemporary cultures.

## Why Games Matter: The Ludification and Gamification of Culture

As aforementioned, the playful, ludified and gamified have become mundane practices and literacies in contemporary culture globally. And yet, in each different context, these factors play out differently. As play scholar Miguel Sicart (2014) has observed, the playful has become a pivotal attitude within contemporary culture. For Frissen et al., all media interfaces could be said to be part of the 'collective playful media landscape' (2015: 29), while for games theorists Frans Mäyrä (2017) and Joost Raessens (2012) contemporary culture is undergoing a process of ludification.

In contrast to this broader interpretation of the ludic turn, which encompasses playful communicative practices on social media platforms such as YouTube, the uptake of creative apps like *Snapchat* and the proliferation of user-created content production, we have also seen the rise of gamification. Gamification – or the integration of game mechanics into non-game contexts – has become increasingly popular across many domains of life, including work, fitness and education. In this section, we explore the overlaps and distinctions between ludification and gamification in the rise of playful media, with a specific focus upon the effects of play and games upon contemporary social and media practices.

Raessens (2014) refers to the playful turn as the *ludification of culture*. For Raessens, ludification can be understood in terms of the emerging histories of game studies and media studies. In the first stage of this history, in the early 2000s, game studies emerged as an independent field of study in its own right, distinct from media studies. In the second stage, around the mid-to-late 2000s, game studies and media studies researchers collaborated, and finally, in stage three, play has been appropriated by media studies more broadly 'as a tool for the analysis of the media experience' (Raessens, 2014: 99) – a new interpretative framework for contemporary culture.

For Raessens, 'digital information and communication technologies have precisely enabled new forms of play' (2014: 103). The integration of play into media studies is evidenced by the increasing number of publications and academic courses that focus on this topic, including *Playful Identities: The Ludification of Digital Media Cultures* (Frissen et al., 2015), *Play Matters* (Sicart, 2014), *Playful Disruption of Digital Media* (Cermak-Sassenrath, 2018), and *Play, Creativity and Digital Cultures* (Marsh et al., 2009).

Ludification refers to our uptake of digital games and playful apps, the playful use of media (mods, creativity, sharing, remixing) and play competence (ludoliteracy). Raessens argues that we need a new interpretative framework with new terminologies and literacies that incorporate concepts such as playability, negotiation, gamespace, virtual affordance, immersion, ludic identity, modes of play and player-types. Playfulness is everywhere – in our media practices (e.g. user-created content and game **modding**), in our social practices (e.g. social media games and apps), in our daily work and leisure practices (e.g. games for health, finance, productivity and education) and in our political practices (e.g. hacking and activism). For Mäyrä, in this ludification process games and play will have 'more and more notable roles in informing our public and private behaviours, as well as in the practices of product and service design, work, learning, and multiple other areas of culture and society' (2017: 49). This is what he describes as the *ludic society*.

Gamification can be considered a subset of ludification comprised of particular practices, technologies and activities. Mäyrä notes that 'whereas gamification is focused on the application of game-like elements into non-entertainment applications, the focus of ludification is on the spread of play as a practice, playfulness as an attitude and the supposedly growing role of playful designs in our everyday reality' (2017: 47). Gamification principles can be applied to fitness, finance, sustainability, health, shopping, productivity (work and personal), community (prosociality) and creativity more broadly. Gamification elements may include: challenges, points, virtual currency, rewards and badges, targets and objectives, competition, reputation, leaderboards, achievements, skill development, personal mastery, social engagement and milestones that mark progression.

Gamification also identifies specific player types – killers (those who enjoy hacking, cheating and heckling other players), achievers (who are motivated to win, challenge others and compare scores), socializers (who play in order to share and help others), and explorers (those who are keen to investigate, create and discover). Gamification includes the use of game iconography (in non-game contexts) and often uses motivational design, behavioural design and persuasive design to inform gamification strategies. Gamification has become a core logic in many mobile applications, especially those related to fitness and productivity.

As we see in the case of Sarah's use of *Strava*, for example, many smartphone apps track our movements by default – storing our data in ways that gamify our experiences. Part of Sarah's quotidian use of *Strava* involves gamifying her exercise – from bike riding to running. She can keep the data for herself to reflect upon how much she exercises or she can share data with her friends or the public. When friends share, there is a tacit understanding that people show their appreciation through social kudos (e.g. likes from friends). The app also embeds game-like mechanics. These gamification mechanisms frame her experiences, memories and reflections on the data. Gamified techniques can make the data 'feel' personalized, intimate and affective. So too, for Machiko in Japan, the use of *Pokémon GO* allows her to change her relationship to her physical surroundings and, through gameplay, enhance dimensions of sociality. The app translates health benefits, such as exercise and social inclusion, into a game. It also brings a playful lens to familiar neighbourhoods – reinventing them in ways that 'ludify' urban spaces.

Reflecting upon the rise of gamification in everyday life and media, Steffen Walz and Sebastian Deterding provocatively state, 'what if every part of our everyday life was turned into a game?' (2014: 9). While gamification can motivate and engage people in different ways, it can also be deployed with datafication to coerce users. In their edited book, *The Gameful World* (2014), Walz and Deterding follow this logic of the implications of gamification's pervasiveness and the ramifications of ludified culture *par excellence*. The authors – including Ian Bogost, Bernie De Koven, Jane McGonigal and Eric Zimmerman – reflect on both the good and bad implications of a gameful world, especially in the face of automation technologies.

For game critic Bogost, gamification is not about games or gameplay – it is exploitationware that demands the 'pointsification' of everyday work and leisure practices. He laments that the purpose of gamification is to 'capture the wild, coveted beast that is videogames and to domesticate it for use in the grey, hopeless wasteland of big business' (2011: n.p.). Similarly, for Rey (2012), gamification is 'productive play'; that is, people perform free labour as play and work are brought together into the same act, or play is integrated into the process of production. Playbour, a term originally coined by Kücklich (2005) to describe the practice of game modding as a form of unpaid labour, is considered fundamentally exploitative, as it is most often the case that 'playborers obtain none of the monetary value they have created' (Rey, 2012: n.p.). But many who deploy gamification in education, workplaces and as inspiration for personal productivity, experience the positive effects; that is, play makes us feel good and is deeply social, it motivates us and makes mundane activities more fun. Play also imbues daily practices with meaning, is aspirational and prosocial in terms of engendering community and collaborative engagement. The concept and use of gamification and its principles arise in many of the chapters throughout the book.

One particularly salient example of gamification in everyday life is in the game sub-genre of social games, or games that are played on and through social media platforms. Such games have been identified by game critics as a way to leverage and gamify sociality simply as a means to make a profit – they literally commodify social relations. That is, sociality is framed as instrumental, and friends become resources, while the modalities of play depend on weak lusory goals and a diluted form of sociability, which differs from the strong lusory goals and deeper sociality of immersive gameworlds. The argument is frequently made that such games are not actual games, but rather 'cynical rule-based systems for draining time and where possible, money from players' (Balnaves et al., 2012: 2).

The rise of social media games like *Farmville* generated playful ways to connect and community-build, while also providing a revenue stream in addition to user information for social media platform companies such as Facebook. For Bogost (2010), the way social games turn friends into useful game elements leaves barely a trace of authentic sociability. The gameplay is optional, as rote play acts can be skipped or avoided by paying for immediate progression. In a very literal sense, for Bogost, they are games you don't have to play, and thus are not really games at all. They enact a persistent incursion upon our time even when we're not playing – through reminders and updates, arbitrary wait-times for recharging lives or energy, and an underlying compulsion to accumulate clicks, points or virtual currency that exemplifies the underlying motivation of gamification.

The debates around gamification and ludification of media and culture have given rise to a need to redefine how games and play operate in everyday life – especially in terms of the **magic circle**. The magic circle has long been the conceptual space that has determined the limits of a game – the rules and reality within which play takes place. It was first coined by Dutch historian Johan Huizinga in *Homo Ludens: A Study of the Play Element in Culture* (1938 [1955]) to describe the significance of play and games in human society. In later work, Katie Salen and Eric Zimmerman redeployed the term in the context of videogames (Salen & Zimmerman, 2003). However, as play pervades our everyday lives and gamification becomes quotidian, we are left to ask again – what are the limits of the magic circle?

## The Everyday Realities of Games and Play: Outside the Magic Circle

It has been argued (Bruns & Jacobs, 2006; Jenkins et al., 2013) that the evolution of the web into a meta-media platform for all networked media and communication has provided the conditions for an emergent participatory media environment – typified by dynamic interactivity, social software, web-based portals and services, and the exponential growth of user-generated and user-created content (UCC). In part, as Taylor (2009) indicates, this play turn has been generated by the infusion of gaming and 'game-like' features into our social lives – a trend that has been congruent with the merger of social media and game networks with personalized mobile media and location-based or place-specific applications. Both in tandem with and also at times resistant to the shift towards gamification, the playful or ludic attitude is at the core of an emergent 'spreadable media' culture (Jenkins et al., 2013). **Spreadable media** practices effectively blur the boundaries between production and consumption, and demand that we rethink our mediascapes in ways that are not in accordance with old 'closed' dichotomies of user and producer, gamer and creator.

Games, gaming cultures and the practices surrounding gameplay are frequently theorized as a lens through which to understand the playful turn in culture writ large. For Taylor (2009), extrapolating from Bowker and Star (1999), games are 'boundary objects', adaptive or plastic across individual contexts yet maintaining coherence and recognizability as a collective and cross-cultural experience. As boundary objects, the increasing ubiquity of games and the practices that flow through, and around, them are constituted by a cluster of complex interrelations between many factors. These aspects include, but not are limited to, the technological (platforms, systems, software and hardware), infrastructural (wired and wireless networks), institutional (domestic, legal, etc.), material (the built environment and meaningful objects within it), corporeal (the body–technology relation), social (collective habitudes, cultural specificity and communication), personal (self, gender, identity, aesthetic experience), historical (both individual and collective) and conceptual or epistemological (informed by established 'ways of knowing') (Taylor, 2009: 333).

Similarly, for Moore, as games pervade our lives – as they 'follow us in new ways' (2011: 374) through online social networks, across platforms and devices, and between public and private domains – our understanding of play must be untethered from traditional notions of immersion and 'big game' play on computers and consoles. Rather, he argues, play has become radically mobilized, not only by the mobility of smart devices such as phones and tablets, but also by the mobility of networks (logging in to our personalized media portals from any web-capable screen), and we would add, the proliferation of customized applications that extend or augment the game experience. In this way, opportunities for play are mobilized 'on our behalf' (Moore, 2011: 382–383).

Gameplay is now situated and realized within 'the contexts of gamers' common, everyday realities, rather than in opposition to them' (Kallio et al., 2011: 347). Similarly, for Lindtner and Dourish (2011), the complexities of games and gameplay must be examined beyond the frame of the game; that is, as phenomena enacted across 'sites of cultural production, imagination and identity in contemporary transnational configurations' (2011: 455). The 'meaning' of games thus 'arises at the intersections of social and material practice, cultural discourses, and the movement of ideas, people and artifacts' (2011: 455). In their analysis of game practices in China, they describe how cultural capital, aspiration, selfhood and nationhood are imbued in the way players and gamers identify themselves and their place, their 'belonging' and goals, both in the context of their actual gameplay and in their daily lived practices.

Media and game theorists have also written at length about the paratextuality extrinsic to gameplay yet intrinsic to game culture, exemplifying the underlying playfulness endemic to participatory media culture on a larger scale. It is important to distinguish here between the domain of participatory and paratexual media (including game modification, machinima, gameplay videos, walkthroughs, fanfiction and other forms of produsage) as representative of a form of cultural playfulness, and what is termed gamification. As Moore points out, the latter are defined by the translation of game principles and 'ludic structures' into social networking sites and other forms of service provision on the web (2011: 376–377). The former, on the other hand, are instances of the playful cultural turn.

Similarly, in their analysis of sociality in games, Stenros et al. (2009), for example, differentiate between the extraludic *sociability* around the game and the *social play* mediated by the game or service. Increasingly, 'game play and playful behaviours are set in more explicitly social contexts as various channels of communication are opened between users and players' (Stenros et al., 2009: 82). Consalvo and Harper (2009) describe this mobility of play in terms of how we dynamically and deliberatively 'key' between game modes (that is, by bringing the real world into the game).

As Roig et al. (2009: 99) argue, we need a more open conceptualization of play and playability so we can better understand and critique the terms as key concepts in new media. Play is a *dispersed* practice, 'scattered across social life' (exceeding specific domains such as schools, the home, etc.), and what constitutes play both transforms and is transformed by the integrated practices of gaming (Roig et al., 2009: 93). It is the dispersed nature of play that renders it potentially transformative and combinatory; that is, playfulness modifies and reshapes the way we engage with media and the manner in which it becomes part of our experience as social beings.

The social permeability of play in game and media cultures more generally means that the 'player' should take its place among other 'subjectivities' (such as the audience, the viewer, the browser, the surfer, the lurker, the gamer). In fact, as Roig et al. (2009) argue, this interchangeability of subject positions in media marks some obvious affinities with the practices of play, suggesting the idea of 'playful identities' (*pace* Raessens, 2006). As opposed to the more concrete and formal 'demarcation between playing and not playing' (Moore, 2011: 376) traditionally circumscribed by the supposed 'magic circle' of video and computer gaming, the dispersed practices of expansive and extrinsic play are more ambiguous and spontaneous, and interwoven with everyday life.

We can see covalent trajectories of this shift to cultural play across social, locative and mobile media: in the playful sociality of our networking practices and use of location-based services and game-like applications, in the small creativities of participatory social media practices such as blogging and photo-sharing, and in the very ordinariness of our mobile gameplay. Put simply, as we update our profiles on Facebook or Instagram, play *Roblox* or *Minecraft* on our mobile devices, upload and share content on social media, or engage with the numerous other modalities of play, we are in the process of rethinking (and redoing) ourselves as playful beings.

## Chapter Overview

In each chapter of this book we identify particular *contexts* and *praxes* of games, and through the experiences of our participants, describe the dynamic integration of games into our social and material lives. The structure of the book seeks to cover an ever-evolving and rapidly-changing game environment.

Chapter 2 – 'Methods in Game Studies' – begins the first part of the book, Games in Context, and provides an overview of the range of research methods that can be deployed by game studies, including both conventional and digital ethnography, practice-led research, case studies, design anthropology and approaches to big data and gamification. We challenge the separation of qualitative and quantitative methods, suggesting that to understand the diversity of game practices – mobile play, livestreaming, haptic screens, massively multiplayer games – we need to apply more integrative adaptive ways of capturing gameplay, communities and paratexts. In particular, we will explain how ethnographic approaches can be effectively combined with big data and quantitative approaches; focusing on everyday practices provides deep and granular insights into games and game cultures, which enable an interpretation of games as a cultural barometer for popular culture globally.

Understanding methods in games studies has come under radical revision. In this chapter we explore the role of datafication and gamification and how this is transforming the ways in which we conceptualize and practise methods. For example, datafication complicates qualitative methods like ethnography and vice versa. Indeed, understanding datafication and gamification requires a mixture of methods that can interpret both big data and the 'little data' of our personal lives. Moreover, the rise of livestreaming (such as Twitch and Douyu) requires us to rethink the role of the archive and liveness in the examination of game play and game cultures (Taylor, 2018b; Witkowski, 2018b; Zhang, 2019). And as societies move towards burgeoning ageing populations, the role of gamification in health becomes more apparent. The need for understanding gaming practices in terms of multisensorial ways of engaging with the screen (i.e. haptics and non-normative bodies) becomes heightened.

Therefore, in this chapter we explore a few of these key phenomena and what they represent for moving forward in game studies. Gaming cultures are as social as they are datafied, requiring us to recalibrate methods that engage with this complexity. We begin this chapter with a reflection upon the complex and often contradictory space of appification and datafication and apply ethnography to reveal the insights of our research participants. We then consider the emergence of haptic media studies as a subdiscipline that speaks to the tactile and kinaesthetic aspects of the game experience, and how we might develop methods for a haptic ethnography. Finally, we explore creative practice, practice-led research and design-based methods.

In Chapter 3 – 'Game Industries and Interfaces' – we discuss the evolution of the games industry, the range of game interfaces (e.g. console, online, mobile, multiplayer and casual) and associated developer and user practices. Turning to the contemporary context, we then provide a detailed analysis of the current crisis in the industry around gender equity and representation, the rise of indie developers and modders, and their impact upon the structure and labour practices of the creative industries. This chapter draws on a case study conducted within an international games company on best practice for diversity and inclusion.

Chapter 4 – 'Game Communities and Productive Fandom' – begins the second part of the book, Communities of Practice. Here we explore the fan cultures that surround games and game genres. It is now recognized that game-related activities go far beyond the 'magic circle' of gameplay, in the form of discussion forums and commentary, user-generated and user-created content, game guilds and both offline and online community formation. We will trace the emergence of virtual communities that gather around media content, and consider the relation between fandom and game communities.

The next chapter turns to the hybrid new media phenomena of 'eSports and Fantasy Sport'. eSports describes the broadcasting and livestreaming of competitive game tournaments (such as *League of Legends* and *Overwatch*), which draw many millions of viewers across the world and substantial prize money. Fantasy sport is a type of 'competitive fandom', where fans compete against each other as virtual managers or coaches of teams comprised of actual players across a sporting league (such as football or baseball). Both forms of play engender new ways of engaging with games and collapse the institutional and material boundaries that separate games, media entertainment and sport.

Chapter 6 concerns another form of game community-as-practice that is particular to 'Livestreaming and Let's Play'. This chapter focuses upon the increasing significance of user-generated and user-created content production around games and the rise of 'watching play' as a new form of media entertainment. We describe in detail the phenomenon of livestreaming, recording and uploading gameplay, how this has fundamentally changed the way games are accessed, played and shared, and present a case study of Douyu in China that is contextualized in relation to global livestreaming trends. The chapter also provides an analysis of the Let's Play phenomenon as a particularly robust example of game paratextuality.

In the third part of the book, Artful Interventions, in Chapter 7 – 'Between Art Games and Game Art' – we begin by considering the empowering affordances of transformative art games and investigate the way games can challenge our perceptions and assumptions. In particular, we reflect upon the relationship between game art and art games as a mode of artistic intervention, and the various ways contemporary artists deploy games as creative critical commentary on normative cultural practices and urban life. In this chapter we consider how games-as-art can provide powerful ways to mobilize publics to think differently about social and political issues. Many game studies books, while touching on game aesthetics, neglect to address the important role of games-as-art in public debates around the use of urban spaces and environments, and the place-based experience of cultural identity. We discuss exemplary works by Eddo Stern, Brody Condon, Anne-Marie Schleiner, Joan Leandre and Cory Arcangel that challenge conventional ideologies and perceptions.

Chapter 8 – 'Serious Games and Games for Change' – explores the potential of games for social change and innovation. First, we review the work of theorists and practitioners in the fields of games for change and critical and transformative design, including Colleen Macklin, Jane McGonigal and Mary Flanagan. The chapter then discusses examples of games for change workshops in a variety of contexts, including schools and tertiary institutions in Australia and Japan. Through a close analysis and evaluation of the workshop process, we articulate some effective methods through which to **codesign** games and playful intervention strategies with diverse groups of participants.

In the final chapter of this part – 'Pervasive Games and Urban Play' – we discuss the historical contexts and emerging trajectories of urban games. Fun theorist Bernie De Koven (2013) defines a contemporary trend in cultural play, one where physical games transform the urban environment into a playground, often deploying pervasive networked interfaces and platforms. These playful innovations have their history in 1960s community and political interventions such as Situationist International (SI) (de Souza e Silva & Hjorth, 2009). In the decades that followed, the New Games Movement continued to promote cooperative and creative urban play and is experiencing a revival in the present day. The chapter will provide an overview of urban play and pervasive games and discuss several interventionist game-art events that took place in central Melbourne, Australia in 2016–2017.

Chapter 10 – 'The Rise and Rise of Mobile Games' – begins the last part of the book on Mobilities. It is predicted that by end of 2020 the global revenue for mobile games will exceed that of console and computer games together. This chapter traces the emergence and proliferation of mobile games, and the way they have changed our perception of 'hardcore' and 'casual' games and gamers, transformed the economies of games and rendered games an integral part of our daily lives. The rise of mobile gaming will be contextualized in terms of the ubiquity of mobile media, social media and app-based media ecologies, and situated within current theoretical approaches in mobile media studies. In particular, the chapter will discuss the way mobile games can be considered 'ambient media', as they become thoroughly embedded in our everyday routines and communicative practices.

Chapter 11 – 'Augmented Reality Games and Playful Locative Media' – focuses more specifically on the emergence and increasing popularity of AR and locative media games, describing a number of examples, including *Mogi, Run Zombies Run* and *Geocaching*. We then provide a detailed case study of the *Pokémon GO* phenomenon in both historical and culturally-specific contexts. *Pokémon GO* could be considered a perfect storm, coalescing the transmedia success of Pokémon, the ubiquity of location-aware mobile devices, and decades of locative and AR experimentation by new media groups such as Blast Theory and artists such as Janet Cardiff. This chapter also positions mobile AR game practices in terms of debates around privacy and surveillance, and considers what we can learn from the rise and fall of *Pokémon GO*.

Finally, in the book's Conclusion we provide an overview of key themes and insights to be gained from the book and explore some of the broad issues and rubrics for future game studies. We reflect upon how phenomena, such as the COVID-19 pandemic, have transformed how we think about the role of games for sociality and wellbeing (especially in a time of physical distancing). The discussion will then turn to consider some of the potential implications for everyday communicative and playful media practices.

In this introductory chapter we have sought to explore some of the ways in which games and game cultures can be understood today. As we have suggested, the rise of gamification and ludification in everyday life has seen a recalibration of the positionality of games across our material, social and environmental spaces. This requires us to re-examine the limits, aims and boundaries of game studies as an inherently interdisciplinary field that is embedded with the logic of contemporary digital media. As society becomes more datafied and gamified, understanding games will become a core literacy.

Each chapter is an exploration of games *in situ*, across different spaces, places and bodies, and through various practices and performances, providing new insights into how games and play work as barometers for social interaction and media dynamics more broadly. As we face a challenging future in which the 'new normal' has recalibrated expectations around the role of the digital and games in our lives, work and play, it is our hope that the power of games and playful practices can fuel innovative forms of care, mindful engagement and ethical sociality.

## Further Reading

Bogost, I. (2016). *Play Anything: The Pleasure of Limits, the Uses of Boredom, & the Secret of Games*. New York: Basic Books.

Frissen, V., Lammes, S., de Lange, M., de Mul, J., & Raessens, J. (2015). *Playful Identities: The Ludification of Digital Media Cultures*. Amsterdam: Amsterdam University Press.

Hjorth, L., & Richardson, I. (2020). *Ambient Play*. Cambridge, MA: The MIT Press.

Payne, M. T., & Huntemann, N. B. (2019). *How to Play Video Games*. New York: NYU Press.

Raessens, J. (2012). *Homo Ludens 2.0: The Ludic Turn in Media Theory*. Utrecht: Utrecht University Press.

Sicart, M. (2014). *Play Matters*. Cambridge, MA: The MIT Press.

# Part I
## Games in Context

# 2
# Methods in Game Studies

Why did media studies and game studies scholars engage in a debate between 'narratology' and 'ludology'? How was the debate resolved?

Why does the study of games need diverse methods?

In what ways is haptic media studies relevant to the study of games?

What are some of the advantages of practice-led research?

Understanding games and their gaming cultures requires interdisciplinary approaches. Games are media texts, but they are also different from much screen-based media, as they are *enacted* by players in a dynamic and often collaborative process. The study of games and modes of play tackles this complexity by drawing on a variety of disciplinary perspectives beyond the now established field of game studies – including media and cultural studies, a broad spectrum of social sciences, design, usability and human–computer interaction. Correspondingly, a range of quantitative, qualitative, practice-led, codesign and innovative mixed methods approaches are applied to the analysis of game play, game texts, industry, design and player cultures. As Lankoski and Björk (2015) note in *Game Research Methods*, the plethora of *quantitative* and *qualitative* approaches on hand for game study researchers continues to grow alongside the field.

For example, qualitative methods such as interviews, participant observation and focus groups draw on ethnographic techniques that ask participants to reflect on their practices; that is, revealing player motivations and the significance of games in people's everyday lives. Game ethnography gives researchers deep insights into situated understandings of play, and can also be used as a lens for interpreting broader practices, such as the 'playful turn' in contemporary culture. Quantitative methods that collect statistical data can track changing demographic trends in game uptake across devices and platforms, and data visualizations of network analysis can provide insights into some of the dominant behaviours and attitudes within gamer cultures as well as identify who plays what games and when. Visualizations can shape how we interpret, value and experience the data (Engebretsen & Kennedy, 2020).

Over the past decade, game studies, game analysis and game design have been at the forefront of the development of a range of innovative methods. As Mäyrä notes in the preface of *Game Research Methods: An Overview*, 'game scholars need to be active in evaluating, adapting, and re-designing research methodologies so that the unique characteristics of games and play inform and shape the form research takes in this field' (Lankoski & Björk, 2015: xii).

With the rise of mobile games, **livestreaming**, gamification, **appification**, haptic screens and various forms of datafication, the divisions between *quantitative* and *qualitative* methods have become heightened. As we suggest in this chapter, in a period of **gamification** (the implementation of game mechanics into non-game contexts such as education and fitness – see Chapter 8) and **datafication** (the representation of our social interactions and everyday lives as datasets that inform predictive analytics) – big (quantitative) and small (qualitative) methods become multidisciplinary and mixed, as 'deep' qualitative ethnographies of small groups of players are used to inform game practices and motivations behind the statistical representation of large data samples (Nafus, 2016). Furthermore, as we discuss in Chapter 6, with burgeoning ephemeral practices such as livestreaming, the dialectics of 'liveness' versus 'archiving' as part of methodological considerations has taken on new dimensions (Taylor, 2018b; Witkowski, 2018b; Zhang, 2019). Moreover, the increasing predominance of haptic interfaces and mobile touchscreens as ubiquitous game devices has seen the emergence of new disciplinary subfields and methods such as haptic media studies and haptic ethnography (Richardson & Hjorth, 2017).

In this chapter we provide an overview of the somewhat unwieldy spectrum of methods that can be applied to the study of games. We begin with a brief discussion of the 'ludology versus narratology' debate between game studies and media studies scholars; while this conflict is now largely regarded as *passé*, it marked an important moment in the evolution of game studies as an emerging discipline, framed ongoing discussions around games as unique kinds of media texts, and subsequently informed methodological approaches to the analysis of games, players and game cultures. The chapter then offers a short overview of qualitative and quantitative methods, before turning to the complex and often contradictory space of app-based media cultures and datafication, and their transformative effect on research methods and engaging with the field. As one of the more significant contexts of contemporary gameplay, we then turn to the way haptics and touchscreen devices demand the application of versatile methodological frameworks. Finally, we describe the fields of practice-led and design-based methodologies.

## The Emergence of Games Studies and the Ludology–Narratology Debate

In the inaugural issue of *Game Studies*, Espen Aarseth (2001) welcomed readers to 'Year One' of Computer Game Studies as a nascent disciplinary field, identifying games as 'perhaps the richest cultural genre we have yet seen' and as a medium distinct from other mass media forms, such as cinema and television. The key challenges posed by Aarseth concerned finding appropriate theoretical paradigms, conceptual frameworks and methodologies that could be applied to the study of games, or what came to be known as ludology. That is, because games are interactively *played* rather than watched – effectively simulated *doings* that are always in a dynamic and open-ended process of becoming – they cannot be analysed and understood as representational and closed narratives in the same way as other audiovisual media, such as film. Online multiplayer games, in particular, are comprised of communities of players, a radical departure from the notion of media audiences. Of course, as we discuss in Chapter 6, watching play has now become a popular mode of media engagement, with corresponding changes to how games are experienced and understood. But in these early stages, Aarseth and other game researchers, such as Jesper Juul, Marie-Laure Ryan and Gonzala Frasca, grappled with what seemed to be an impasse between narratology and ludology.

The resolution – or what might more accurately be called the dissolution – of this debate in the early-to-mid-2000s occurred amid a significant shift in media scholarship that saw game studies stabilize as a discipline in its own right. In his response to the narratology–ludology debate – 'Ludologists love stories, too: Notes from a debate that never took place' – Gonzala Frasca (2003) argued that game studies necessarily includes narrative concepts because games are playable stories, thus the methods of ludology include analyses of the formal mechanics of games, in addition to an appreciation of their narrative components. Similarly, Janet Murray (2005: n.p.) pointed out that '[t]hose interested in both games and stories see game elements in stories and story elements in games: interpenetrating sibling categories, neither of which completely subsumes the other'.

Importantly, Henry Jenkins (2004) developed several useful concepts that incorporated narrative into game theory: role-playing games, he argued, are modes of 'collaborative storytelling', and many games construct immersive worlds through spatial or 'environmental storytelling' that often relies on pre-existing associations within popular media culture, enabling gamers to enact emergent narratives. Thus, he claimed that 'it makes sense to think of game designers less as storytellers than as narrative architects' (Jenkins, 2004: 129). In the years that followed, media studies and game studies scholars openly collaborated at conferences, in research centres and through co-authored publications, and as participatory media practices became more playful and creative, the 'conceptual framework of play' has been increasingly adopted as a critical tool in studies of media practices and cultures (Raessens, 2014).

Nearly two decades on, the field has flourished with an array of different approaches that address the complexity, diversity and dynamism of games, players and game cultures today. Many examples can be found in Consalvo and Dutton's (2006) qualitative methodological toolkit, which guides researchers through the study of gameplay, in-game objects, game interfaces and in-game interaction mapping. Likewise, Lankoski and Björk's *Game Research Methods: An Overview* (2015) provides a survey of qualitative, quantitative and mixed methods approaches to games research as well as suggesting new directions for development. Given the interdisciplinary nature of game studies that draws on quantitative and qualitative methods, we will briefly outline these two approaches. Increasingly, we see mixed methods that coalesce these modes of analysis and interpretation, especially as various forms of data become commonplace in many people's everyday lives.

## Quantitative and qualitative methods

Quantitative research aims to generate numerical data that can be turned into statistical information. Quantitative methods are highly structured and most often involve the collection of big data sets. This can include surveys that rely on precise questions with a narrow range of answer options, or observations which may either involve counting the number of times that a particular phenomenon occurs or reframing secondary data, such as written or recorded information. Quantitative research obtains generalized averages from a large sample population.

Data visualization is another form of quantitative research, giving insight into the demographics of gaming. However, as Engebretsen and Kennedy (2020) have highlighted, the politics of visualization as a form of communication science involves a politics of vision and trust. Traditional, conventional visualizations are perceived to be 'truthful' and 'authentic' in contrast to creative ones that are viewed suspiciously (even when it's the same information!). The stories that data tells highlight the politics of who tells the stories and what content they want to address. In response to these concerns, with the rise of big data the importance of little data like ethnography has become heightened (boyd & Crawford, 2011).

Qualitative research seeks to gain an understanding of underlying reasons, opinions and motivations that form and maintain societies and cultures. Its methodologies often include: observation of participant activities; structured or unstructured interviews; focus groups with multiple participants discussing an issue; postcards or short written questionnaires; and secondary data, including diaries and written accounts of past events. Put simply, quantitative data generates and analyses numbers to interpret general trends and behaviours, while qualitative data seeks to uncover these practices in a more 'granular' form, to understand their reasons and full implications across a spectrum of users and demographics, including age, gender, race and culture.

One of the increasingly common qualitative methods is ethnography. Ethnography is a research methodology involving the in-depth study of social life and cultural practices. Primarily a method borrowed from social and cultural anthropology, ethnography involves hands-on fieldwork and on-the-scene learning or participant observation of the people it seeks to study. In games studies, ethnographic research focuses on games – the players, communities, platforms and interfaces – as an integral part of contemporary culture. For example, from 2006 to 2008 Tom Boellstorff and his co-researchers conducted two years of ethnographic fieldwork in the virtual world of *Second Life*, observing its residents in exactly the same way anthropologists traditionally have done to learn about cultures and social groups in the real world, exploring issues of gender, race, sex, economy, conflict and antisocial behaviour, the construction of place and time, and the interplay of self and group. In their book entitled *Ethnography and Virtual Worlds* (2012), Boellstorff et al. explore how ethnography can – especially through participant observation – inform insights into analysing online contexts. Taylor (2012), in her ethnographies of eSport, has highlighted the ways in which understanding the phenomenon requires detailing the often tacit and mundane aspects of everyday activities and invisible infrastructures.

In terms of quantified methods, the rise of datafication has given many researchers access to big data in ways previously unimagined. The term **big data** refers to the massive volumes of data that are vast in scale, fast-moving and highly complex, often so much so that they exceed processing capacity, or are difficult to process using traditional database and software techniques. Data, in this case, refers to computer-recorded material and digital information. Making sense of big data can offer unprecedented insights and opportunities, but it also raises concerns and issues around data privacy, security and discrimination.

Datafication refers to the technological trend that sees many aspects of our everyday life collected, interpreted and compiled into new forms of information and value. Put simply, datafication sees our actions and habits recorded both individually and collectively, with the information used by governments, corporations and other agencies to shape goods, services, governance and policy. With the expansion of ubiquitous technologies, the ongoing process of datafication can be understood as an attempt to tackle complexity and reduce uncertainty, while also representing a fundamental shift in the way we conceive citizenship and civic life. In the next section we explore some of the ways in which ludified and gamified data in everyday life is playing out in ways that challenge us to rethink and recalibrate our methods.

## Appified and Datafied: The Gamified Quantified Self

Data – and its locative possibilities and potentialities – can be found in almost all of our quotidian moments. It is transforming how we experience digital media, especially in terms of gamification. Mobile media devices such as smartphones, Apple Watches and fitbits – along with apps like *Strava* – weave multiple data trails of gamification. As we discuss further in Chapter 8, gamification is the application of game-like techniques to non-game contexts. Examples of gamification are endless. 'Reward' schemes can be found everywhere, such as shopping loyalty cards. *Strava*, as discussed in the introduction, converts running and bike riding activities into quantified segments (comparing different speeds) and users can gain kudos for 'winning' any particular quest. Employee leaderboards turn tasks and rewards in the workplace into games, and education software like *Mathletics* situates learning into game-like frameworks.

Much of the scholarship on datafication falls into one of two camps of belief – the dataveillance group who see empowerment narratives underscored by obligations often not understood by users (Ruppert, 2011; van Dijck, 2014; Lupton, 2016a), and those researchers more aligned with Quantified Self (QS) ideals that see the body as the laboratory for creative reflection and self-knowledge through numbers (Lupton, 2016b). QS is defined as a kind of 'self-knowledge' attained through digital tracking technologies such as fitness, health and productivity apps. Within the QS movement data gives us new insight into understanding ourselves and our bodies. Many of the sensing technologies and applications, especially around biometrics and exercise, have become a core part of everyday mobile media that contribute to quantified self-knowledge.

Since 2010, the significance of big data, and the response to it in the form of the QS movement, has been well-recognized (Kennedy et al., 2015). As danah boyd and Kate Crawford (2011) note, debates around big data need to acknowledge that no matter how 'big' the data, they are always *subjective* and specific to context. The questions that data seeks to answer are also riddled with the researchers' own perceptions and thus are inherently human in their scope. Moreover, they argue the need for transparency and access to the ways in which algorithms shape, and are shaped by, social norms and epistemological presumptions. As ethnographers Nafus and Neff note, big data, like little data, are about storytelling – they involve the narrativization of socio-cultural practices (Nafus, 2016; Nafus & Neff, 2016). Digital health experts, such as Lupton (2016b), have observed that datafication has created a double-edged sword for health practices – self-tracking offers insight and a space for reflection about one's own exercise, and yet, this same reflective data can be used by corporations in ways we are still only just understanding in the light of the Cambridge Analytica controversy.

Cambridge Analytica was a British political consulting company employed to help elect Donald Trump as US president in 2016. It was soon after revealed that the company had misappropriated large quantities of digital information and assets through data mining and had also purchased Facebook data on almost 100 million Americans without their knowledge. Since its exposure to the general public, attitudes towards Facebook shifted dramatically. Many people have become more mindful of what they share and disclose on Facebook as well as being critical of how algorithms can mirror certain realities and affects in different ways. Phenomena such as Cambridge Analytica, which unlawfully gamified the system, have led to issues of trust and ethics becoming increasingly central to questions around methods.

On mobile devices, apps are the embodiment of the ideal of gamification. Fitness apps in particular are indicative of how self-tracking through mobile media is playing a powerful role in people's lives, as one user's exercise becomes part of others' gamified movements, allowing the data overlays about place-making to be shared as a social act. For many game scholars, the gamifying of everyday data oversimplifies the powerful role of games, reducing their complexity and richness. But it also highlights the relevance of games in all facets of quotidian practice, tapping into the significance of games and play in the 'feel' of data. In the next section we explore the role of feeling data in game methods.

## *Feeling* Data

The rise of self-tracking QS measures on mobile media allows for reflection – what some scholars have called *feeling* the data (Lupton, 2017). Lupton has been working in the space of digital health for over a decade now. More recently her work has explored what digital health 'feels' like (Lupton, 2017). As Lupton notes, 'feeling the data' can be understood as a process in which movement, cartography, data and place-making coalesce into a heightened sense of networked proprioception – of the position and movement of the body in relation to online sociality and navigation. Data can help us to understand how we physically and affectively *feel* about our place in the world. The gamifying of data is often felt palpably across much of our everyday digital media practices. And yet the idea of 'feeling' data raises questions about the effect of media on our bodies – something that has been explored in some detail within game studies.

This discussion raises one of the key tropes in current game studies around what a game 'feels' like at both sensory and emotional levels. Game designers such as Swink (2008) have highlighted that unpacking the often-tacit notion of the game 'feel' that occurs in the feedback loop between game and player is crucial to understanding player engagement. In his book *Chris Crawford on Game Design*, Crawford likens this process of human–game responsiveness to a conversation, a 'cyclic process in which two active agents alternately (and metaphorically) listen, think and speak' (2003: 76). Likewise, Darshana Jayemanne frames videogame play as a kind of performance and outlines a comparative interdisciplinary methodology for analysing the performative aspects of gaming, art, digital storytelling and nonlinear narrative (2017). Game phenomenologists such as Brendan Keogh (2018) have also explored the role of game feel as part of the corporeal perception of the knowing, playing body. Yet, as important as 'feeling' might be to the affect of the game or medium, often it has been undertheorized. Understanding and articulating the feelings associated with media and data requires complex multisensorial methods to unpack these experiences.

As Lupton (2017) identifies, more work into understanding the multisensorial dimensions of spaces and places is needed – in sum, *affective atmospheres*. As a term developed in cultural geography by Gernot Böhme (especially within the field of mobility studies), it describes the affective and emotional attunements of humans and more-than-humans as they move through spaces and places. In areas like phenomenological psychopathology, it is being deployed to understand the importance of atmospheres in client consultation and treatment (Costa et al., 2014). Focusing on affective atmosphere puts lived experience at the centre. As Lupton (2017: 1) notes:

> Affective atmosphere is understood as an assemblage of affect, humans and nonhumans that is constantly changing as new actors enter and leave spaces and places. Affective atmospheres are shaped by their multisensory properties: how spaces and places are physically encountered via their visual, haptic, aural, olfactory and taste properties is central to the feelings they generate. Affective atmospheres can have profound effects on the ways in which people think and feel about and sense the spaces they inhabit and through which they move and the other actors in those spaces.

With the rise of haptic screens, the role of the digital as an embodied part of everyday life comes to the forefront. Games have long been a pioneering area in haptic interfaces – in effect, retraining people to 'touch the screen'. As David Parisi's work has highlighted, the now habitual practice of touching screens has been a learning process. In fact, for generations, screens and touching had been diametrically opposed (Parisi, 2015), but with the rise of game consoles like the Nintendo Wii and Switch, and the use of phones and tablets as game devices, users were taught to play tactilely, in and through the screen. Given the significant role of games in the evolution of haptic media studies as a field that coalesces key areas like sensory studies, new materialism and new qualitative non-media centric approaches, we will explore this area of study – and its methods – in the next section.

## Haptic Media Studies and Haptic Ethnography

Haptic media refers to the evocation of sensations of touch through a technological interface. Examples include touching a mobile phone, holding a vibrating game console or deploying a **virtual reality (VR)** glove that allows the user to experience complex textures of physical touch in an entirely virtual environment. The rise of haptics as part of contemporary quotidian media encounters has led to the emergence of a subfield of media studies – haptic media studies (Parisi et al., 2017). The study of haptic media has become an important area in games studies approaches as haptics increasingly becomes a key part of many gaming practices.

As Richardson and Hjorth (2017) note, haptic technologies, such as smartphone screens, are impacting our sensorial experience of being-in-the-world, being-with-others and being-with-media. Informed by and informing this approach, many researchers are increasingly focusing on the intimate, social and playful nature of mobile touchscreens. For some, the role of haptic technologies is especially important when it comes to vulnerable agencies, including the elderly, disabled and companion animals. Touchscreens allow for non-normalized bodies to engage differently with games, affording multisensorial approaches that encourage different lived experiences and skillsets, thus enabling the inclusion of diverse users. Haptic screens also refocus our attunement away from the primacy of the visual and aural towards other modes of knowing and perception. In this way, haptic screens require us to develop different techniques and methods in our ways of understanding the world and connect these understandings through the role of play and touch. Haptic media studies is one of these emerging disciplinary fields, as it seeks to capture the work, labour, affect and feelings associated with haptic screens. Within this field, haptic ethnography is a methodology that documents and analyses the ways in which bodies interact with screens.

Haptic touchscreens and consoles have revolutionized the types of games we can play and their effects on the body. Consoles such as Nintendo Wii engaged a whole new demographic through their mimetic and haptic interfaces, whereby whole-of-body movements in games like tennis were translated into the digital realm (Parisi, 2015). Similarly, the prolific rise of smartphones as haptic game devices has shifted how we understand, practise and conceptualize the embodiment of gameplay.

As we argue elsewhere, we need a theoretical interrogation of how we come to 'know through the hands', and a deeper understanding of sensorial experience via a tactile approach to digital ethnography (Richardson & Hjorth, 2017). That is, there is a growing need to develop a haptic ecology of media use that considers what researching *through* and *by* the hands might add to our methods and interpretative work as they relate to games. These haptic practices increasingly inform how we interact, experience and deploy games in our everyday lives.

Over the past decade, game studies has sought to examine the importance of touch in the play experience. As Keogh (2018) observes in his phenomenology of videogame play, there is a need to attend to the multisensorial dimensions of play through, in and around the screen interface and accompanying peripherals, such as controllers. Keogh argues that through 'an entanglement of eyes-at-screens, ears-at-speakers, and muscles-against interfaces players perceive videogames as worlds consisting of objects and actors with texture, significance, and weight' (2018: 1). Game consoles such as the Nintendo Wii have also been explored as providing multisensorial experiences of play, in terms of the 'gestural excess' (Giddings, 2017) and 'gestural economy' players employ as they learn to move with greater accuracy and speed. Simon (2009) argues that 'gestural excess', which describes the way players translate macro-bodily movement into the microworld of the game environment, is present in all videogame play.

As David Parisi (2009) suggests, it is important to document a media archaeology of touch in order to grasp the historical evolution of the relationship between touching and media interfaces. Through the example of the Nintendo DS, he notes that advertisements for the device had to teach people that 'touching is good' after decades of screen etiquette that impelled us *not* to handle screen surfaces. It is important to remember this history when considering the now normalized practice of screen-touching. Media practices, and the appropriate bodily repertoires that they involve, are generational and cultural; they are taught, untaught, retrained.

The rise of haptic media and trying to understand the phenomenon through practice has led to many sub-areas of ethnography, including multisensorial ethnography (Pink, 2009), tactile ethnography (Pink et al., 2016) and haptic ethnography (Richardson & Hjorth, 2017). In particular, haptic ethnography seeks to coalesce the work undertaken around mobile media in terms of the material, sensory and corporeal aspects of use (Richardson & Hjorth, 2017). This process requires deploying methods and techniques that give voice to experience through multisensorial elicitation. Richardson and Hjorth (2017) note in their ethnographic study of mobile games how questioning seemingly trivial gestures in and around mobile media practices actually embodies a wealth of 'deep' attitudes about privacy, boundaries between work and play, social etiquette and care for the device. A 'simple' gesture of having the phone screen face down when talking in face-to-face scenarios can reveal complex habits for negotiating engagement between online and offline worlds. As they note, 'it is clear that the bodily methods of interfacing with the materiality of the screen are of paramount importance to participants' engagement' (Richardson & Hjorth, 2017: 1653). The notion of haptic play seeks to engage with these new 'techniques of the body' that must be accounted for if we are to interpret the complexities and intentionalities of use.

In the context of mobile touchscreens, it is not that such devices demand a more embodied or sensory mode of interaction, but that they have 'alerted us to the sensoriality of our embodied and affective engagement with media in new ways' (Pink, 2015: 6). As we study the mutual imbrication of media interfaces and our embodied selves, the intimate connection between perception and meaning is always-already both individual and collective. Paterson (2007: 1) explores both the historical and contemporary theorizations and dimensions of touch. He argues that touch cannot simply be defined in physiological terms; it is also always 'a sense of communication', and more significantly, it is *manifold*. This turn to 'touch theory' is complexly inter-woven with the emergence of haptic technologies and, in media studies, is often applied to the analyses of computer and touchscreen interfaces. In Paterson, Dodge and MacKian's (2012) terms, haptic media engage the manifold facets of touch, a sense ensemble that incorporates cutaneous, kinaesthetic, proprioceptive, somatic, mimetic, metaphoric and affective modes of perception. Over the past decade such analyses of the haptic interface have enabled fertile connections between media the-ory and the disciplinary fields of sensory studies and new materialism.

Parisi (2015: 6), for example, traces an 'intensified focus' in game studies on the way digital games invoke and depend on the body's movement and perception, which has followed the success of gesture controls and haptics, such as vibrating or rumbling controllers, or mimetic devices and applications such as the Nintendo Wii and many mobile games. Gamers typically accumulate embodied memories of game controllers and touchscreens, which become imprinted on our sensoria through the repetition of particular actions (and effects), such that a 'haptic bond' is established with the inter-face (2015: 17–18). To capture these modes of engagement, researchers have devel-oped 'nuanced theoretical frameworks capable of accounting for the body's newfound centrality to the play experience' (2015: 6). Just as Parisi demonstrates the ways in which mobile gaming consoles advertisements sought to educate users about touch-screen interfaces after years of non-tactile screen cultures in the form of TV, so too can we see that the 'intuitive' nature of touch and play is actually culturally and histori-cally situated. This has a major impact not just on game studies but studying digital media more generally. We return to the significance of haptic interfaces throughout the book, with a particular focus on mobile touchscreen games in Chapter 10.

## Creative Practice, Practice-Led Research and Design-Based Methods

Within game studies and game design scholarship, practice-based research (PBR) and practice-led research (PLR) translate creative practice *as* research, and situate the game itself as a creative artefact central to the discovery of new knowledge, seeking to bridge the gap between practitioners and researchers (Candy & Edmonds, 2018). A PBR approach to games explores how the process of design and development can provide critical insight into human experience, knowledge-making and understand-ing more broadly. For example, designing player characters that challenge normative expectations relating to gender, and evaluating subsequent player experience, can enhance our understanding of attitudes relating to gender representation in con-temporary society. Many activist games, 'games for social change' interventions, and artists who use and modify games as an aesthetic medium (as discussed in Chapters 7 and 8) deploy games in this way. PLR is more narrowly concerned with investigating and critiquing the creative practice itself. For example, in the context of games, this might involve experimentation with a specific aspect of game design, such as a game mechanic or modality of play, and evaluating the player experience in terms of engagement and immersion.

Games research is also of key importance to designers and developers, who apply a range of methods to study players, game cultures and evaluate gameplay. Two seminal and innovative texts in this space have been Salen and Zimmerman's *Rules of Play: Game Design Fundamentals* (2003) and their co-edited text *The Game Design Reader: A Rules of Play Anthology* (2005). The first, a guide for what was at the time still regarded as the 'emerging discipline of game design', sought to develop new concepts and frameworks for thinking about games as systems, narrative mediums, sites of social play and cultural resistance. The second, a collection of essays by game designers, critics, fans and theorists, was published two years later as a companion work to *Rules of Play*, and aimed to situate games as significant cultural interfaces and game design as a critical practice. Since then, game design texts have proliferated, not least Swink's *Game Feel* (2008) and Schell's *The Art of Game Design* (2019), now in its third edition.

Play-testing is also an integral aspect of game design research, often occurring prior to the release of a game or as part of the beta-testing process, and involving an assessment of engagement, enjoyment and key problems with game mechanics. Early access and paid alpha schemes have become the norm for many games, especially independent games – many developers take this period of pre-release as an opportunity to collect and respond to player feedback before releasing the finished game to the market. Testing and evaluating can also involve surveys, interviews, observation (either present or remote), metrics, screen capture and 'think aloud' methods. The *Think Aloud Protocol* is one of the most commonly used testing methods in game development (Desurvire & El-Nasr, 2013); as the player progresses through the game, they are asked to explain aloud what they are doing, thinking and feeling, providing the game designer with useful qualitative data as-it-happens from the user's perspective.

In a broad sense, game design and development might be considered a fundamentally 'collaborative' process that occurs in partnership with players, as players enact and produce unique experiences through 'recreating' the game each time they play (Taylor, 2018b). Flanagan's (2009a) notion of *critical play* articulates this agency of the player who actively questions the social, cultural and political facets of the play experience, and recognizes the subversive potential of play more broadly. In a more practical sense, co-creative design as a methodological approach to game development explicitly encourages this blurring of the role between user and designer, as those who play the game become integral to the design process. As discussed in Chapters 4 and 7, game modding is often regarded as the creative culmination of this partnership between game makers and players, as the latter engage in practices of playbour and produsage, which in turn helps to sustain rich and vibrant game communities.

## Conclusion

In this chapter we have explored some of the ways in which methods in and through game play and game cultures can be understood. We began with more traditional models that became the subject of early debates in game studies between ludology and narratology, and then turned to contemporary frameworks for understanding the dynamic nature of games as cultural practice. As we discussed, the interdisciplinary nature of the field means that we are seeing both quantitative and qualitative methods being deployed in numerous ways. As we noted from the outset, methods shape – and are shaped by – the field, the technological interfaces and platforms, and player practices.

Exploring playful practices and the lusory attitude from the position of games gives us different ways to think through the role of data and algorithms in media cultures, from the QS movement and gamification to virtuoso play, creativity and playful resistance. Here, the playful can be seen as an orientation to action, a mode of inquiry and a set of practices that can help to expose some of the tacit power relations in and around the rhythms of data in everyday life. Play is fundamentally a creative, political and social activity. In an age of datafication and gamification, we need methods that attend to the messy ways the social entangles with both data and digital materialities (Lury & Wakeford, 2012).

As we have argued in this chapter, the field of game studies has come a long way from the early divisive debates around ludology versus narratology. As big data, livestreaming and mobile devices have complicated the ways games occupy our quotidian lives, so too do we need methods that acknowledge these complex modes of engagement. We have suggested that increasingly mixed methods are required to make sense of this complexity – for example, we need more ethnographic innovation to make sense of quantification, haptic interfaces and app-based media ecology. Moreover, as gamification moves into formal and informal usage within smart devices, we need more robust practice-centred models for understanding the perceptions and embodied affects of these practices in our lives.

### Further Reading

Egenfeldt-Nielsen, S., Smith, J. H., & Tosca, S. P. (2016). *Understanding Video Games: The Essential Introduction* (3rd ed.). London: Routledge.

Lankoski, P., & Björk, S. (Eds.) (2015). *Game Research Methods*. Pittsburgh, PA: ETC Press.

Lury, C., & Wakeford, N. (Eds.) (2012). *Inventive Methods*. London: Routledge.

*(Continued)*

Mäyrä, F. (2008). *An Introduction to Game Studies: Games in Culture.* Los Angeles, CA: SAGE.

Mortensen, T., Witkowski, E., & Toft-Nielsen, C. (2018). *MedieKultur Special Issue: Media-ludic Approaches: Critical Reflections on Games and Research Practice, 34*(64). Available at: https://tidsskrift.dk/mediekultur/issue/view/3656

Wolf, J. P., & Perron, B. (2014). *The Routledge Companion to Video Game Studies.* London: Routledge.

# 3

# Game Industries and Interfaces

Both game developers and game studies scholars problematize the term 'gamer'. Why do you think this is? Aside from 'casual' and 'hardcore' gamers, what other gamer types are there?

Why is the games industry sometimes described as 'toxic'? Do you agree?

Are inclusive practices necessary for the games industry to thrive? What are some of the ways diversity can be achieved?

Over the past decade, both the games industry and game interfaces have evolved, and now encompass new audiences and company models. Once characterized by distinctive proprietary platforms such as Sony PlayStation, Microsoft Xbox and Nintendo Wii and Switch consoles, the interface cultures of games have increasingly converged onto mobile devices and personal computers (PC). Mobile devices like smartphones and tablets have democratized the field, opening it to diversity in both player and industry contexts. The biggest revolution has been the rise in mobile gaming (see Figure 3.1) now estimated at US$68.2 billion. This is followed by the promise of cloud gaming, which will allow more accessibility to different PC games without requiring the purchase of expensive PC hardware, much like a game version of Netflix.

The rise of the mobile game market across mobile phone, tablet and smartphones (especially in terms of the haptic functionality of smartphone interfaces) has allowed new player demographics and independent (indie) game development to emerge.

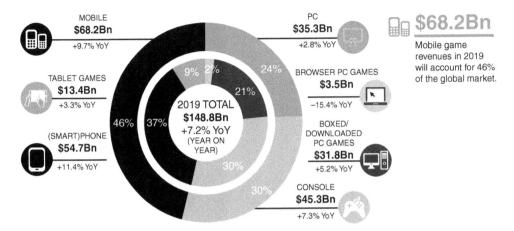

**Figure 3.1** Global games market (2019). Image: Newzoo.com.

Mobile devices encourage social and casual gaming to flourish (Willson & Leaver, 2016). This phenomenon has witnessed a de-stabilizing of traditional big AAA companies by smaller, more agile indie companies, while the social imaginaries of cloud gaming possibilities promises much in terms of videogame industry futures. In the growth of game industries and interfaces, the visibility of diversity and inclusion have become heightened, as we will explore in this chapter.

However, as we argue, there are still significant barriers in the implementation of a truly diverse workforce and industry that need to be addressed. This chapter begins by briefly summarizing the significant developments in the industry in terms of the evolution of platforms and interfaces, and the cultures that have emerged around them (see Chapter 4 for a more expansive discussion on game communities). We then focus on a key issue that permeates all aspects of the games industry and game development – diversity and inclusion – through a case study of a game company that sought to embed diversity and inclusion frameworks (Chee et al., 2020, forthcoming). This case study deployed ethnographic and codesign methods (see Chapter 2) through the deployment of an intervention into the practice and lived experience of the company's employees. As we suggest, by understanding motivations, we can gain insight into how a culture thrives and change can be implemented. Finally, we discuss how diversity and inclusion are becoming integral to the independent sector.

## Snapshot of the Industry Today

The global games market, comprising PC, console and mobile games, was valued at US$165 billion in 2020, doubling from nearly $78.61 billion in 2017. There are now more than 2.5 billion videogamers from all over the world, increasingly playing on mobile devices (Newzoo, 2020). Currently the Asia-Pacific region has the highest revenue gaming market at US$72 billion (Newzoo, 2020). Chinese technology companies such as Tencent have been key players in this revenue space (Figure 3.2).

Yet behind these figures of growth and expansion, the games industry is struggling to accommodate the many challenges that have followed its global success. Issues relating to inequitable and exploitative labour practices and work conditions, unsustainable workflows, economic uncertainty and toxic cultures both within the games industry and across many areas of the player base have come to light and intensified in recent years. Not only have there been numerous high-profile controversies exposing the games industry as propagating a toxic and hyper-masculine culture (Meunier, 2010; Locker, 2012; Matthew, 2012; Burrows, 2013; Robertson, 2014; Romano, 2014; Ramanan, 2017; D'Anastasio, 2019), but the industry has also become fractured – marked by a clash between traditional cultures of commercial

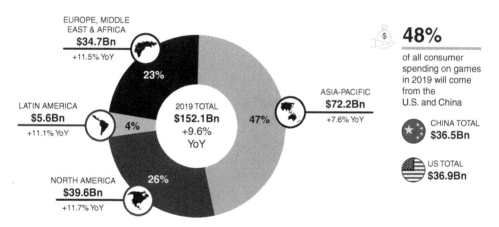

**Figure 3.2** Global games market by region (2019). Image: Newzoo.com.

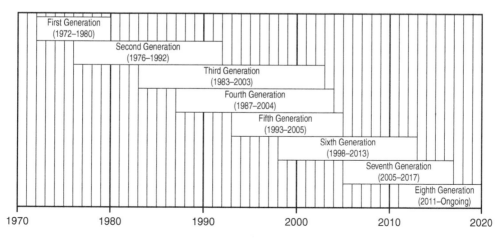

**Figure 3.3** Eight generations of video game consoles. Image: Hugh Davies.

studio models and the independent initiatives that seek more diversity and inclusion. Paradoxically, the industry and interface cultures are, on the one hand, diverse and inclusive (largely through mobile gaming development and consumption), yet on the other hand, still slow to embrace this new culture across the slow-moving and more exclusive big AAA companies. Moreover, with the rise of livestreaming, eSports and the potentiality of cloud gaming, the player base and industry diversity will no doubt become ever more complex.

## A Short History

Videogames cover a wide spectrum of technologies, economies and practices, including the games industry (from indie to AAA developers and producers), game interfaces, platforms and products, and a prolific network of gamer cultures and communities. Not surprisingly, there are many histories of the games industry that can be told, with each perspective marking out 'eras' or 'generations' according to different criteria. Some texts that have been important in telling these histories include Kent's *The Ultimate History of Video Games: From Pong to Pokémon and Beyond* (2001); Herman's *Phoenix: The Fall and Rise of Videogames* (first published in 1994, updated 2001), Donovan's (2010) *Replay: The History of Video Games* and Wolf's edited collection *The Video Game Explosion: A History from PONG to PlayStation and Beyond* (2007).

Games historian Mirko Ernkvist (2008) considers the evolution to have taken place over two periods: an unstable one (1970–1986) in which industry-wide crashes occurred in an immature industry, and a more stable one in which a relatively steady period of economic and technological growth has seen games evolve from niche popularity to a mainstream media entertainment form (1987–2005). Alternatively, games scholar Mark Wolf (2007) delineates three periods, the first two roughly corresponding to those of Ernkvist outlined above, with an additional third accounting for developments from 1995 to 2007. While there is some debate over the timeline, especially with regard to the console generations, within the games industry more broadly and associated marketing and journalism (e.g. *Gamasutra* and *Polygon*), the development of videogame interfaces and platforms tends to be divided into eight generations of technology progression. The representation of the generations in Figure 3.3 draws on the detailed comparative history assembled by Kemerer, Dunn and Janansefat (2017) and employs the format proposed by Christy and Kuncheva (2014) to allow for overlap between the generations.

The first generation emerged in the 1970s with dedicated computer games on massive computers connected to vector displays (Horowitz, 2018), and the design of consoles such as the Magnavox Odyssey and Atari'a PONG system (Baer, 2005). The second generation saw the arrival of cartridge-based systems, including the popular Atari 2600 together with arcade titles *Space Invaders* and *Donkey Kong*, and the rise of Nintendo, which began manufacturing videogames and consoles of its own (Yamazaki & Gorges, 2012). Interestingly, Lien (2013) has documented that during this time videogames in console and arcade contexts were popular among both men and women. Carol Shaw, who developed games for the Atari 2600 both within Atari and Activision, recalls: 'We never really discussed who our target demographic was ... We didn't discuss gender or age. We just did games we thought would be fun' (Shaw, quoted in Lien, 2013). In 1983, the videogame industry experienced a catastrophic economic crash, with revenues falling by 97%; by 1984, almost all consoles in North America were discontinued (Cohen, 1984). Historians debate the reasons for this downfall, attributing it to mismanagement, negative social perceptions of video-games and the introduction of the home computer, among other things (Cohen, 1984; Herman, 2001 [1994]; Campbell-Kelly, 2003; Williams, 2004). Subsequently, the videogame industry shifted to Japan, beginning the third generation. During the mid-to-late 1980s, Nintendo rebranded game consoles as more affordable toys, and developed the Nintendo Entertainment System (NES) and the first Game Boy (Ryan, 2011). During this time, Sega released the Mega Drive and the Commodore 64 and Amstrad CPC were repackaged as gaming units.

In the late 1980s and early 1990s the fourth generation brought in the 'golden age of gaming' with consoles that appeared much more futuristic, sleek and powerful (Kent, 2001). Harris's *Console Wars* (2014) provides an account of the fierce com-mercial competition between Sega and Nintendo in this period. One consequence of the rebranding of games as toys, an effect made explicit in the title of the increas-ingly popular Game Boy console, was that games now took on the gendering inher-ent to the toy industries. Following market surveys that showed videogames were slightly more popular among boys, game content developers increasingly focused on heroic and often violent narratives and action (Jantzen & Jensen, 1993) – the embry-onic beginning of an industry-enabled cultivation of hyper-masculine games, game advertising and gaming cultures. In their anthology *From Barbie to Mortal Kombat*, Cassell and Jenkins (1998) map debates during this era over whether 'games for girls' should reflect traditional stereotypes of femininity or appeal to the real-life interests and lived experiences of girls and women.

By the mid-1990s, a fifth generation saw home computers increasingly preferred as game platforms, with CD and CD-ROM-based games allowing game developers to integrate cinematic cut-scenes, pre-recorded soundtracks and serious storytell-ing into their games – a ground-breaking example is the now-famous first-person shooter *Half Life* (1998). Nevertheless, the Sony PlayStation and Nintendo 64 were also popular during this period. The sixth generation brought a shift in technology and domestic integration, most notably the adoption of DVDs for videogame media in Sony's PlayStation 2 (2000) and Nintendo's GameCube and Microsoft's Xbox, released in 2001. Sega's Dreamcast, released in 1998, was ahead of its time as the first console of the sixth generation with a built-in modem, pioneering the way for internet-enabled console gaming. Ultimately, however, Sega couldn't compete with Sony's market stronghold and bowed out of the console wars, with the Dreamcast being the last system released and Sega becoming a third-party software publisher (Horowitz, 2016, 2018). The sixth generation also saw a shift in industry vernacular with 'Triple A' or AAA games becoming the term to refer to big-budget games made by large studios (Consalvo, 2012a). For example, games such as *Halo 3* (2007) is estimated to have cost US$30 million to develop, with a marketing budget of $40 million (Zackariasson & Wilson, 2012), while *Grand Theft Auto V* (2013) was estimated at approximately $265 million to develop and market (Villapaz, 2013). The handheld game console market also expanded in the early 2000s with Nintendo's next generation Game Boy Advance (2001) and the first hybrid phone-game console, the Nokia N-Gage (2003). During this period, cultural anxieties over the violent trajectory of videogames and causal links to aggressive behaviour proliferated in popular media (Howard, 1998; Sefton-Green, 1998; Anderson & Bushman, 2001).

By the seventh generation, beginning around the mid-2000s, videogame consoles had become an important aspect of domestic and global IT infrastructure. All seventh-generation consoles, including the PlayStation 3, Xbox 360 and Nintendo Wii, supported wireless controllers, with the latter's inclusion of infrared (IR) tracking making it the best-selling device for domestic gaming. New billion-dollar **Massively Multiplayer Online** (MMO) gaming economies were also established during this period, with games like *World of Warcraft* and *League of Legends* accruing millions of players. Many of the people (predominantly male) who had grown up playing videogames were now becoming the makers, although AAA game companies were heavily criticized for cultivating high-pressure production conditions, long hours, unreasonable deadlines, poor pay and cultures of bullying (Schreier, 2017; McNeill, 2019). Development of dedicated handheld game devices, such as the Nintendo DS and PlayStation Portable (PSP), along with the iPhone and iPod touch, brought touchscreen gaming into the mainstream.

Between 2000 and 2010, the number of female players increased and the arrival of customizable massively multiplayer online role-playing games (MMORPGs) allowed both male and female players to experiment with gender identities (Trépanier-Jobin, 2017). Yet, the scarcity of women game designers, the marginalization of female players and the proliferation of passive or hypersexualized female characters persisted (Corneliussen, 2008; Consalvo & Harper, 2009; Huntemann, 2010; Sarkeesian, 2013). Nintendo's Game Boy DS and Wii each brought huge numbers of female players to the gaming public, while the rise of casual and social games did the same for desktop computer gaming. However, among some player bases, this also brought a perceived 'encroachment' of women and girls into what had been largely constructed as a male-gendered space (Consalvo, 2012a). Consalvo (2012a) notes that online sexist, racist, homophobic and ageist attacks were not isolated incidents but building in frequency and intensity.

Consoles of the eighth generation are mostly distinguished by their deep integration with other media, cross-platform functionality and improved online connectivity. Microsoft released the Xbox One (2013) with increased emphasis on cloud computing and social networking, Sony's PlayStation 4 (2013) featured a 'share' button to stream videogame content between devices, while the Wii U (2012) introduced a controller/tablet fusion with features that afforded the possibility of augmented reality in videogames. Meanwhile the popularity of casual and mobile gaming continued to surge, fundamentally altering the core demographic of game players (see Figure 3.4). Mobile devices and platforms such as Apple's iOS and Google's Android increased smartphone ownership to a quarter of the world's population by the end of 2014 (Emarketer, 2014). The proliferation of low-cost freemium games for these devices saw gaming cultures become larger and more diverse than ever before. A console market response to these factors was the Nintendo Switch, released in 2017, a device that combined the detached controllers of game consoles with the portability of a personal device in a single modular gaming unit. While the first seven generations were defined by competition between Sony, Nintendo and PC games, the rise of smartphones and indie mobile games and applications now challenged the dominance of consoles and desktop computer-based gaming in the field. Over this period, a gradual industry shift saw independently created games move into the mainstream.

As Martin and Deuze note, 'independent or "indie" game companies are best understood as individuals, small teams or companies creating usually self-funded, and often one-off game projects that are external to the mainstream process of creating, marketing, distributing, and playing digital games' (2009: 277). In the 2010s, independent game makers began creating and marketing successful games – independent titles such as *Minecraft* (2009), *The Stanley Parable* (2011), *Braid* (2009) and indie mobile games including *Angry Birds* (2009), *Fruit Ninja* (2010) and *Monument*

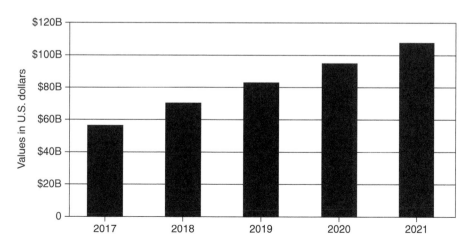

**Figure 3.4** Growth of mobile gaming (2017–2021). Image: GamingScan.com.

*Valley* (2014) – which made a substantial market impact. However, it was the emergence of new crowdfunding techniques through sites such as Kickstarter that saw a significant rise in diverse independent projects being implemented. Where a decade earlier the industry had been defined by AAA companies, following the 2008 global financial crisis (GFC) a number of factors saw indie game companies increasingly redefining the industry (Banks et al., 2013) – changing cloud-based distribution systems such as Steam, the rise of livestreaming, burgeoning game design and programming degrees, new platforms and business models, and mobile interfaces as portable game consoles in themselves. Independent games undoubtedly allow for small and inclusive designers to work together to design games that reflect their demographics, which in turn enables game representations and narratives to become more diverse, as we discuss in the sections below.

Within the games industry, identifying and targeting gamer types is important for the financial viability and success of game design and development, yet the ubiquity and prolific uptake of mobile games challenges traditional distinctions between casual and hardcore or 'real' gamers. As the games industry evolved, so too has its target demographic. As playfulness pervades the everyday practices of millions of people around the world – many who do not consider themselves 'gamers' – it is clear that distinctions between types of gamers (e.g. casual and hardcore) and their corresponding modes of gameplay are no longer accurate representations of the people who play games. As our ethnographic work has revealed, people who play supposedly 'hardcore' and immersive games such as *WoW* or *Subnautica* can also deliberatively choose to play in a 'casual' manner and sometimes primarily as an opportunity for socializing, using both the portability of a mobile device and network mobility to communicate with friends and fellow guild members in the 'third place' of an online game.

On the other hand, players can (and do) play casual mobile games intensively over many hours and become heavily invested in their progress. As Christensen and Prax (2012) have argued, the conventional divide between hardcore and mobile/casual games is based on 'older technological forms'; the move from the stationary interface of the desktop computer, to laptops and smartphones, has shifted how we understand and define both games and gamers. The reasons why people play, and their preferred modalities and contexts of play, are increasingly variable, suggesting that any attempt to define the 'gamer' or 'gamer types' is impossibly restrictive.

As Juul (2009) describes in his landmark text *A Casual Revolution*, the term 'casual', often equated with mobile games, becomes a misnomer for an increasingly broad spectrum of gameplay, and particularly the financial, creative and social investment of those who play mobile games (Taylor, 2012). Moreover, the spectrum of gaming has shifted to include playful social media and location-based apps, as gameplay traverses cultures, places and media interfaces and players engage in diverse modalities of play. Are we seeing the 'death of the gamer' as a specific cultural identity, as we all increasingly play games? This question about what constitutes a gamer continues to develop across a number of chapters throughout the book. Mobile gaming – across smartphones, iPads and tablets – has most certainly been largely responsible for a growth in the spectrum of who plays, shifting the demographic of the player as a young, white male to an older female. While 40% of players in the US are aged between 18 and 35, some 21% are 50 years and older (Statista, 2019). Yet throughout the 2000s and 2010s, as the community of game players widened, tensions around gender, class and race came to the forefront.

## A Toxic Industry?

A key feature of the eighth generation of the industry was that videogaming was becoming increasingly diverse, socially-embedded and digitally connected, but the corresponding values and communities of play were not universally inclusive or accepted. A defining cultural moment of the eighth generation was the Gamergate controversy, which involved a sustained period of harassment and online abuse against women in the games industry in 2014 (see Chapter 4 for a more detailed overview). While many were shocked at the sexist vitriol that was expressed at the time – not least game researchers who also came under attack (Mortensen, 2016) – others closer to the games industry recognized the incidents of sexist abuse as stemming from a long lineage of industrial nurturing of hyper-masculine game attitudes and behaviours. Game developer Anna Anthropy suggests that game publishers perpetuate a 'dangerous cycle' by repeatedly creating games for young men 'already entrenched in the existing culture of games' (2012: 7). For Anthropy, the games industry largely supported an 'insular and homogenous' group of developers, ultimately removing all diversity from the pool of developer talent as well as from player expectations of the real world.

For many people who have spent time in game spaces – both actual and virtual – Gamergate was an inevitable cultural expression of harassment that had been cultivated within games and the creative industries from the 1983 crash onwards. In the aftermath of Gamergate, this toxicity became clearly identifiable as a central problem within the industry, revealing that there were various competing cultures – in particular, the old school one in which men dominated, while the more contemporary indie developers and their players and supporters were leading the way in diversity and inclusion practices. Parallel movements, such as the #metoo movement in the film and TV industries, have since sought to expose male domination and abuse of women. Before long, the evidence was in – diversity and inclusion make good business sense (World Economic Forum, 2019). As Humphreys has argued, the games industry is diminished by misogyny, and:

as long as it remains risk averse, conservative, sexist, and complicit in cultures of racism and homophobia, it will remain marginal to other media cultures. It misses the opportunities to explore the complexities and nuances available – the rich possibilities of games to be so much more than they currently are. It puts a brake on innovation. (Humphreys, 2019: 837)

Shira Chess's (2017) *Ready Player Two* examines how videogames have achieved the dual position of entertainment revenue leader over film, television and music as well as being recognized for cultivating toxic cultures. Chess (2017) takes a feminist approach to videogame production, interviewing industry professionals, analysing game mechanics and scrutinizing game advertising to formulate the idea of a gamer's 'designed identity', which she diagnoses as 'a hybrid outcome of industry conventions, textual constructs, and audience placements in the design and structure of video games' (2017: 31). Chess focuses on two designed identities in the videogame industry that she titles Player One and Player Two. Player One is typically a male, white, affluent, able-bodied and heterosexual consumer of commercial releases on consoles and computers. Player Two is a woman who enjoys casual, mobile games. Chess points out that neither are factually rooted in actual demographics, but that the 'gamer' and 'casual' archetypes are nevertheless constructed and targeted by the videogame industry.

Books such as *Feminism in Play* (Gray-Denson et al., 2018) highlight the ongoing need for feminist and intersectional approaches to games that address the whole circuit of game cultures and development – consumption, production and industry. As the authors argue, a fundamental issue is that the male-oriented culture of the AAA games industry and the alpha consumers of its marketing machine have still not adjusted to the broader reality of games culture, or indeed to the world at large. Games are no longer primarily the domain of teenage boys and young men. Radical changes are needed in order for game makers to cater to new audiences as well as to evolve existing cultures into the present.

Games industry workers increasingly recognize these problems too. In a 2017 Developer Satisfaction Survey conducted by the International Game Developers Association (IGDA), 81% of respondents indicated that diversity in the workplace was 'very or somewhat important' to them (McNeill, 2019). The *2020 GDA Report* records that the games industry is still disproportionately male (75%); 21% of respondents identified as female, 2% said 'other' and 2% declined to answer (Favis & Park, 2020). With reports of 100-hour working weeks at AAA companies such as Epic and Rockstar, as well as a walkout and lawsuit implicating Riot Games in gender discrimination (Favis & Park, 2020), differing value systems around diversity and inclusion are playing out across game companies, publishers, designers and developers. According to the 2019 annual Game Developer Conference (GDC) *State of Games Industry Report*, the majority of game workers surveyed (54%) believed games industry workers should unionize; 9% were not sure, 21% said maybe, while only 16% were against it (Favis & Park, 2020).

In the next section we discuss diversity and inclusion initiatives within the industry as they seek to improve industry practices and attitudes. We then consider diversity more broadly within the independent gaming sector.

## Diversity and inclusion initiatives within the games industry

Diversity and inclusion remain serious issues in the global games industry (Harvey & Fisher, 2014; Busch et al., 2017; Harvey, 2019). Not only has the industry established a poor reputation in terms of hostility and exclusionary attitudes towards women, gender diversity and people of colour, but it has also been increasingly shown how workplaces that successfully promote and build diversity and inclusivity foster increased creativity and innovation, directly translating into the larger market share that the games industry seeks (Jain & Lobo, 2012; Page, 2017; de Aquino & Robertson, 2018). Moreover, diversity and inclusion have become integral to both employee retention and customer reputation of brands (Lowther, 2006; Gundling & Zanchettin, 2007; Branson, 2018; Hunt et al., 2018).

Beyond social equality and representation, championing workplace diversity in the games sector is an important business proposition. As already explored, areas of the games industry have begun to accept that change is required in order to maintain a successful and sustainable sector. Initiatives that bring about such changes in game content and development, as well as across the tech industries more broadly, have become the focus of many working in games, in management studies and in game studies.

For Weststar and Legault (2016), the 'pipeline' for women in game development careers occurs through alternative routes. As they state, the games industry reflects the underrepresentation of women in STEM (science, technology, engineering and mathematics) while 'pipeline' models for gendered career progression tend to encounter 'blocked' and 'leaky' practices (Weststar & Legault, 2016: 105; see also Vitores & Gil-Juárez, 2016). Weststar and Legault note that particular positions within the industry are highly gendered – men dominate in programming and management positions while women occupy predominantly design, art and user experience (UX) roles and are underrepresented in senior management. This lack of equal gender distribution in the games industry reflects that policies and procedures around diversity and inclusion are needed.

Westecott et al. (2019) point to the emerging area of studio studies within game studies, an area that examines the working culture of game development processes and practices. Related research in this field includes work by Whitson (2019), Consalvo (2012a, 2012b) and Kerr (2010, 2013, 2017) that investigates the conditions, cultures and contexts of game production. In an article titled 'Is game design for everybody? Women and innovation in video games', veteran game developer Brie Code (2017) highlights four barriers that affect the integration of women in this workplace: perceptions of computer science as a masculine domain; the rarity of non-stereotypical women avatars to inspire women players; unconscious bias during the staff recruitment process; and discrimination, marginalization and favouritism of women in game workplaces. Code recommends diversified production teams to foster innovation and improved working conditions.

More direct interventions are also occurring at ground level and directly engaging with employees within game companies. We offer two examples here. *IN SITU*, created and led by games scholar Emma Westecott (Westecott et al., 2019), is a feminist action research (FAR) project that was initiated to examine the opportunities, and impact of, creating diverse and inclusive work cultures for people identifying as women working in the games industry. This collaboration of industry and government aimed to study and inform diversity, inclusivity and belonging (DIB) task forces launched at a major game development studio in 2018. Undertaking interviews with leadership and DIB-identified employees, researchers within the *IN SITU* project undertook an ethnographic approach to document understandings and experiences of 'diversity', 'inclusion' and 'belonging' within the games industry. Participant responses and findings were clustered to identify attributes, opportunities, challenges and barriers that were then framed within a model (see Figure 3.5).

The research evidenced how diversity, inclusion and belonging are currently understood by leadership and employee participants at a studio firmly committed

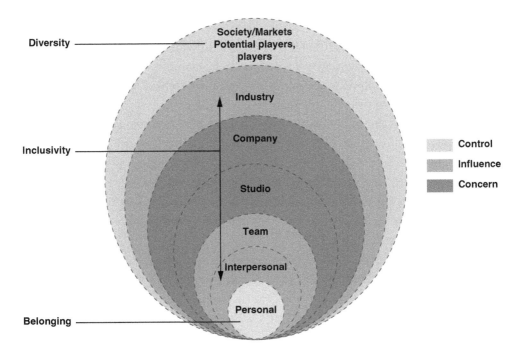

**Figure 3.5** The *IN SITU* Integrated DIB Model (2019). Reproduced with permission of Emma Westecott.

to diversity work, but also showed how these features are interconnected and can be understood through an ecological framework (Westecott et al., 2019).

Another example is found in fieldwork conducted by games researcher Florence Chee (Chee et al., 2020, forthcoming). Chee deployed a participatory ethnographic and codesign approach with a major AAA games company that recognized the problem of gender inequality in its workplace. It sought to address this issue through a series of codesign workshops that engaged staff in the process of 'co-futuring' towards best practices in diversity and inclusion. The workshops took place across the three company sites – two in the US and one in Asia. The workshops combined ethnographic and design techniques to frame the processes around participants-as-experts while allowing for iteration and understanding to be core to the workshop method. The ethnographic workshops involved several exercises that focused on developing empathy through understanding diversity. For example, one exercise involved participants deploying an '**avatar**', which was then positioned in a variety of circles depending on how the participant answered a series of questions, such as: 'Have you ever felt left out?', and 'Have you ever felt bullied?'. The aim was for participants to think about the way that culture breeds various types of inclusion and exclusion that might not be evidenced in explicit behaviours (see Figure 3.6).

In this way, participants were able to discuss and explore experiences of exclusion in the workplace while maintaining a safe emotional distance from the experience through the use of an avatar. The role of personas or avatars to develop empathy and understanding has become an important technique in codesigning. The persona can operate like a 'cultural probe' (Gaver et al., 1999), which allows participants

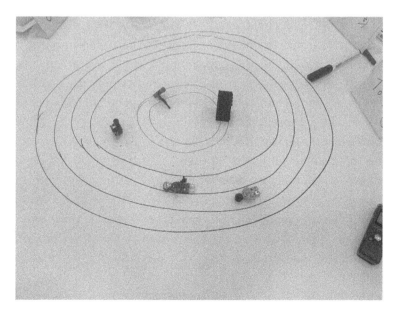

**Figure 3.6** Avatar empathy building exercise. Reproduced with permission of Florence Chee.

to develop empathy and reflexivity without feeling threatened or compromised by direct association with their personal identity. In addition, codesign exercises such as SWOT (identifying strengths, weaknesses, opportunities and threats) aimed to engage participants directly in decision-making processes, rather than experiencing such directives coming from upper management. Participants came to the conclusion that diversity and inclusion did make good business sense and needed to be integrated into their work culture. They then workshopped initiatives they thought would help change the culture, which were developed into an action plan and given to management for implementation.

Ethnography (as discussed in Chapter 2) is increasingly being deployed in contemporary work practice environments such as game studios as a way to understand practices and motivations and reflect critically on assumptions and biases within industry practices. According to Van Maanen (2006), ethnography offers distinct advantages within corporate environments. Specifically, it allows for a free flow of information and open rapport between researchers and participants, while offering opportunities for reflexivity and self-reflection through which participants may consider and reconsider thoughts and actions (Fayard & Van Maanen, 2015). Having outlined examples of deploying ethnography and codesign in workshops with big companies to change outdated cultures, we now turn to the independent sector.

## Lessons from the Independent Sector

Where the AAA commercial games sector has struggled in term of diversity and inclusion, the rising independent game sector from the late 2000s onwards has shown innovative exemplars of industry leadership. With the mainstream game development industry tending to favour male protagonists typically organized around competitive formats and technological expertise, independent models of game development have challenged these norms. This diversity of makers outside the norms of game production are pioneering models that are having a substantial and positive influence on the mainstream games industry. As Keogh (2018) has observed, AAA game firms have looked to independents not just for staffing and creative ideas, but also for innovation in terms of organizational structures, work culture and modes of distribution. Moore et al. (2020, forthcoming) note further borrowings from the independent sector with the use of the 'pay-what-you-want' model for bundles of games, and the adoption of crowdsourcing for projects not supported by mainstream producers and developers.

However, the fundamental shift most championed and implemented by the independent sector is cultural, behavioural and attitudinal. Through substantial community efforts – including festivals and awards that celebrate peer recognition, networks of gamers, modders and developers that openly and freely share resources, and actively supporting fairness and diversity – the independent game sector now offers an alternative culture of game production that challenges the dominance of the larger companies and their surrounding communities. These new configurations have not only nurtured more equitable dynamics of creation and production, but also support practices by which developers can regain creative control over their own labour (Guevara-Villalobos, 2011). Co-founders of New Zealand indie company Runaway Play, Zoe Hobson and Emma Johansson, for example, make games targeted at female players, such as *Flutter*, *Furistas Cat Café* and *Bird BnB*. Creative director Johansson comments that their team of 30 is intentionally 'close to evenly split between men and women, with employees hailing from 10 different countries' (App Store Preview, 2020: n.p.). Within their company, diversity is 'a constant conversation', and the studio promotes female developers through their #GirlsBehindThe-Games campaign, which shares 'positive, real examples where women are thriving in this industry' (App Store Preview, 2020: n.p.).

Such shifts towards gender parity and cultural diversity are documented in Anthropy's *Rise of the Videogame Zinesters* (2012), along with Golding and Van Deventer's *Game Changers* (2016); both note the misogynistic cultures within corporate systems of production, and call for fundamental change within the videogame industry that supports the diversity of gamers and represents a wider scope of human experience and identity. Golding and Van Deventer (2016) record how commercial videogames and the cultures they promote have been historically hostile to women and people of colour, and argue for a radical diversification of game cultures. Anthropy, whose own art game *Dys4ia* (2012) chronicles her experiences with hormone replacement therapy, suggests that games production needs to be taken up by those outside traditional industry contexts. More expressive, socially relevant and personal games can show how 'freaks, normals, amateurs, artists, dreamers, drop-outs, queers, housewives, and people like you' are reclaiming games as an art form (Anthropy, 2012: n.p.). Such critiques are part of an indie groundswell that seeks to shift the culture of game production and consumption towards diversity and inclusion.

Through an ethnographic study, Banks et al. (2013) identify how indie game companies are rewriting the industry in terms of work–life balance and workplace hierarchies. Banks and Cunningham (2016) also highlight that while new work practices are emerging, there are questions about sustainability in terms of the often-exploitative nature of the creative industries more generally. They argue that we need to shift focus from precarious existentialism (i.e. creatives being attracted to the field for its promised autonomy only to find themselves in increasingly casualized roles that tend to undermine work–life balance) to thinking about actionable reform (Banks & Cunningham, 2016: 137–138). This shift requires looking at ways in which the industry is transforming, especially in terms of alternative business models (that encourage diversity and inclusion) through new platforms such as mobile interfaces.

The success of these developments through the 2010s on the back of the ever-rising indie community have challenged the once dominant notion of a white, heteronormative games industry. In addition, games workers are increasingly enabled to fight for better rights and working conditions through unionizing the industry, while organizations such as Checkpoint have risen to champion mental health in the workplace. Meanwhile, feminist game researchers such as Bonnie Ruberg (2019, 2020) and designers such as Robert Yang (2020) who develops games about gay culture and intimacy (e.g. *The Tearoom* and *Ruck Me)* draw attention to the transgressive play inherent in videogames to illustrate that games have always been queer – that is, open to diversity and inclusion. Cultural change in the games sector is occurring; it is positive, gradual and independent-led.

## Conclusion

While the games industry is changing, reform needs to happen across all areas: practice, production, procedures and policy. As player demographics diversify, the only way for industries to remain in business is to engage seriously with diversity and inclusion as a crucial part of contemporary society. At present, games remain one of the least diverse sectors (Weststar & Legault, 2016; Harvey, 2019). Taking action to foster increased diversity and inclusiveness is more than just good in principle, the benefits have been proven to enhance business success (Atcheson, 2018). As the independent models show, it is especially important to weave diversity into the fabric of creative, knowledge-centric companies whose central currency is made up of ideas. Historically, evolutions in the games industry are commonly referred to as processes of 'creative destruction' (Ernkvist, 2008; Banks & Cunningham, 2016); the contemporary games industry could be understood as currently undergoing a process of destroying and reinventing itself.

As we have explored in this chapter, while diversity is a key issue in the industry and among players, it is uneven in its uptake. Devices such as mobiles and tablets have allowed the independent games industry to flourish, which, in turn, provides more diverse and inclusive models for industry practices. Through case studies that deployed ethnographic and codesign methods, we offered some practical examples of how we can better understand the underlying motivations that enforce particular work practice cultures. By understanding motivations, we can gain insight into how a culture can be changed. As we demonstrated, big AAA companies have been slow to embrace diversity and inclusion across all sectors of the business, whereas the agile and smaller models of the independent scene have been quick to adopt diversity and are reaping the rewards – more diverse industries engage more diverse player demographics, as we can see in the mobile gaming sector. In the next chapter we move from industries to game communities, especially reflecting on user-generated and productive practices such as modding and fandom.

## Further Reading

Bossom, A., & Dunning, B. (2017). *Video Games: An Introduction to the Industry.* London: Bloomsbury.

Harris, J. H. (2014). *Console Wars: Sega vs Nintendo – and the Battle that Defined a Generation.* London: Atlantic Books.

Hepler, J. B. (Ed.) (2017). *Women in Game Development.* Boca Raton: CRC Press.

Juul, J. (2019). *Handmade Pixels: Independent Video Games and the Quest for Authenticity.* Cambridge, MA: The MIT Press.

Ruberg, B. (2019). *Video Games Have Always Been Queer.* New York: NYU Press.

Smith, A. (2019). *They Create Worlds: The Story of the People and Companies that Shaped the Video Game Industry.* Boca Raton: CRC Press.

Zackariasson, P., & Wilson, T. L. (Eds.) (2012). *The Video Game Industry: Formation, Present State, and Future.* London: Routledge.

# Part II
## Communities of Practice

# 4

# Game Communities and Productive Fandom

A critical understanding of the relation between media and community requires some key concepts – imagined community, virtual community, participatory media culture, convergence culture. What do they mean?

What is meant by the term 'productive fandom', and why is it particularly apt as a descriptor of game communities?

The term 'produsage' is a portmanteau of 'production' and 'usage'. What does it tell us about contemporary media practices, and how does it relate to game communities? Give some examples of game produsage.

What was Gamergate? What did it reveal about game communities? Why is it important for us to acknowledge feminist perspectives on games and game cultures?

> Gamers do not just play videogames; they also make them. The boundaries between playing and producing and consuming are blurring. By collaborating and cooperating with each other and with professional developers, gamers design, produce, circulate and market compelling videogames. I call this process co-creative. (Banks, 2013: 2)

Game communities and fan practices are integral to the ongoing formation and structure of the games industry, the dynamic spectrum of game cultures more broadly, and fundamental to player identity, interaction and enjoyment. Videogame communities and fans not only prolifically share their common interest in particular games and related hardware, they also participate in a wide range of activities, as audiences and creators, archivists and curators, both online and offline. In this chapter we first consider the significance of online or virtual communities that coalesce around participatory media interfaces and content, and then situate their emergence in the wider context of fandom. Next, we focus more specifically on game communities, and provide a case study of modding as a particularly robust example of paratextual practice, produsage and 'productive fandom'.

## Imagined Communities, Virtual Communities and Fandom

Since the invention of the printing press in the 15th century, individuals' sense of community has gradually become increasingly embroiled in the processes of mediation. In his landmark text, *Imagined Communities*, Benedict Anderson (1983 [2006]) tracked the emergence of the newspaper and the way it gave rise to the 'imagined community' of the modern nation. He argued that the newspaper was directly nation-forming – it targeted a geographically defined audience and provided that audience with the stories or narratives necessary to inspire the collective imagining of national belonging. At the time of Benedict's writing, mass media such as newspapers and television operated as facilitators of social cohesion by enabling people to share experiences and knowledge, and to situate and recognize themselves as part of a nation, society or culture. The key point here is that the formation of communities is based not only on geographical or physical location, but also on the sharing of particular kinds of stories – on the circulation of 'communal narratives' (Anderson, 1983 [2006]). In highlighting the role of the media in the production of community, Anderson articulated how media are not only implicated in defining the boundaries of communities and nations, but are also important vehicles for the circulation of stories about community and belonging.

Today, this close relationship between media and community still persists, albeit in radically different forms. In contemporary everyday life, our experience of media is more often than not web-based and dispersed across multiple pathways and platforms; it is highly unlikely that any two people within a culture will consume identical media content in the course of a day. Additionally, much of our consumption is not in the form of broadcast or 'big' media, but rather 'small' media, or user-created content (UCC), and as consumers we also play a big part in sharing and circulating media narratives across online social networks. With the popularization of the World Wide Web in the 1990s, media and cultural theorists began turning their attention to the impact of networked communication on the formation of community. In 1993, Howard Rheingold published *The Virtual Community: Homesteading on the Electronic Frontier*, which challenged the idea that communities are of necessity grounded in geographical place. He wrote:

> People in virtual communities use words on screens to exchange pleasantries and argue, engage in intellectual discourse, conduct commerce, exchange knowledge,

share emotional support, make plans, brainstorm, gossip, feud, fall in love, find friends and lose them, play games, flirt, create a little high art and a lot of idle talk. People in virtual communities do just about everything people do in real life, but we leave our bodies behind. (Rheingold, 1993: 3)

A virtual community is not a place-based entity, but a social network of individuals who interact through online media interfaces and platforms, crossing geopolitical boundaries in order to connect with others who have mutual interests or goals. That is, they are *communities of interest*. Now recognized as normal practice, people's sense of belonging and connection to communal media narratives is achieved through participation on social media, blogs, wikis and other online networks, and communities are comprised of people who have more often than not never met face to face.

It is with the advent of participatory media in the 2000s, or what is sometimes termed Web 2.0, that online communities evolved into the complex amalgams they are today. While the first generation of the web provided access to information online, it was primarily and for most users a 'read-only' medium; with the second generation, the web became a *platform* for social software and networking services, enabling people to upload and share their own creative media content. This user-to-user interaction is integral to the formation and maintenance of web-based communities. More significantly, for the purposes of our discussion here, the evolution of the web-as-platform transformed the media landscape into a participatory domain. The rise of participatory media and what Henry Jenkins termed 'convergence culture' has reshaped the relation between media production and consumption, as we now co-create and communicate *with* media, *across* media and *through* media as part of everyday life.

In *Convergence Culture*, Jenkins (2006b) identifies three contemporary phenomena: media convergence, collective intelligence and participatory culture. 'Media convergence' denotes the increasingly interwoven relationships of digital media content, technologies and companies that have arisen through the evolution and mainstream uptake of the internet. In later work, Jenkins, Ford and Green (2013) coined the term 'spreadable media' in their book of the same name, to refer to the way media content now disperses through and across both formal and informal networks, both authorized and unauthorized. The term 'collective intelligence', theorized by philosopher Pierre Levy (1994), describes the potential of internet users *en masse* to form virtual communities that can substantially contribute to, regulate and orchestrate knowledge and expertise on topics of interest. 'Participatory culture' refers to the agency of contemporary audiences in taking a more active role in the creation, adaptation and consumption of media content.

A correlative important concept here is **produsage** (Bruns & Jacobs, 2006), a portmanteau word that captures the merger of two previously distinct practices – media production and usage. In contemporary media culture, we are all *produsers* – active agents in the collision of production and consumption. As media and game theorists have noted over the past decade, videogames represent an important site for the study of convergence culture as the 'creative barrier between consumers and producers' becomes increasingly porous (Postigo, 2008: 60).

Moreover, the ludification or 'playful turn' of contemporary culture (as discussed in Chapter 1) can be seen as the coalescence of participatory and social media with playful communicative practices, creative app-based ecologies and games. Indeed, games, game environments and the ever-expanding range of game-related peripheral or *paratextual* practices have been fertile ground for a new kind of relationship between media and community marked by produsage. Put simply, if we think of the core media text as the game itself, paratexts encompass the range of co-creative activities that surround the game.

Both convergence culture and spreadable media are evidenced by the many game-related paratexts, both original and remixed, that are created and shared by game communities and fans worldwide, including game walkthroughs, Let's Plays, mods, indie games, livestreams, websites, blogs, hacks, guides, reviews, wikis, cosplay, machinima, fan art, fanfiction, and more. In Chapter 6 we discuss two significant arenas of game paratextuality – Let's Play and Twitch. In the final section of this chapter we focus on another key paratextual practice – modding.

Within game cultures and in the wider media landscape, paratexts are also an integral aspect of **fandom**. Early research into fan cultures showed how the activities and outputs of fans become a form of cultural capital in which people invest (Fiske, 1992). For Jenkins (1992), fans are those who actively rework and supplement media texts, acting as 'textual poachers' – meaning that they deliberately appropriate, take inspiration from and manipulate content for their own creations. Over the past three decades, fandoms have grown from marginalized subcultures into mainstream online 'affinity spaces' (Gee, 2005) that directly impact upon the media industries (Hills, 2002; Jenkins, 2006a). Fans actively engage in 'interpretive and creative practices' or 'productive fandom' (Lamerichs, 2018: 14) around media products and narratives, and as such have long been the vanguards of participatory media culture. A key characteristic surrounding fandom in the digital environment is the speed at which users can communicate online. As Lamerichs (2018) observes, the internet has substantially increased both the visibility and quantity of fans and their creative practices.

Aiming to dismantle negative stereotypes of fans and to address their marginalized status as either maligned or entirely overlooked, in *Productive Fandom* Lamerichs (2018) argues that fandom is an area of productive, creative and subversive value. She explores a range of fandoms through ethnographic research, foregrounding the personal experiences and reflections of fans themselves, in order to provide a more nuanced understanding of communities of diverse individuals through their lived experiences. Lamerichs notes that relationships between producers and fans are both complex and specific. While fandom describes a communal cluster of shared interests, fans engage in highly individualized activities, from online fanfiction to offline 'material' practices of cosplay and festival attendance (see Figure 4.1). They should therefore, she argues, be considered on a case-by-case basis. Understanding fans is as much about understanding their processes of social connection and affective engagement as the end result of fandom itself.

Twenty-two years following Jenkins' seminal book *Textual Poachers* (1992), Bennett (2014) assesses the continuing trajectory of fandom as a field of research. Bennett surveys the contemporary terrain of fandom, accounting for the powerful new interactions and engagements within participatory culture that have emerged with social platforms such as Twitter, YouTube and Instagram, which have become central sites of fan practices. As Jenkins concedes in 'The future of fandom', fan cultures have radically expanded over the past two decades and fandom now infiltrates the full scope of the contemporary creative economy: 'fandom is everywhere and all the time, a central part of the everyday lives of consumers operating within a networked society' (Jenkins, 2007: 361). Within this expanded context, he asks: 'as fandom becomes such an elastic category, one starts to wonder, who isn't a fan? What doesn't constitute fan culture?' (2007: 364). That is, there is no longer a dominant culture against which fan subcultures define themselves (Bennett & Kahn-Harris, 2004), and therefore no cultural otherness within which 'the fan' can be located. Much like play, the concept of fandom has become ubiquitous, migrating across platforms and contexts, and integral to our quotidian engagement with media interfaces and content.

The edited anthology *Fans and Videogames* (Swalwell et al., 2017) constitutes the first sustained analysis of the phenomenon of videogame fandom and offers a series

**Figure 4.1** *Fortnite* cosplayers at E3 (2018). Photo: Sergey Galyonkin/Shutterstock. com.

of essays that, taken together, emphasize the fundamental value of videogame fans such as librarians, archivists, memory workers, preservationists and witnesses to games history. Game fans are revealed as a knowledge-rich community collectively compiling and sharing videogame records, game histories and technical expertise, in addition to resurrecting older games into playable forms on the internet. In the process, they also extend digital literacies through the imaging of cartridges and disks before these removable storage media deteriorate, and emulate obsolete hardware and software so that they can continue to be experienced as games. In this sense, game fans and their practices 'activate an expanded idea of the paratext' (Swalwell et al., 2017: 12), as they not only archive game history and produce derivative content in the form of walkthroughs, mash-ups, reviews and trailers, but also revive superseded retro-games such that they can be *played again*, effectively bringing together and sustaining niche communities of players around dynamic game artefacts.

In her analysis of game paratexts, Consalvo (2017) suggests that game modders can also create and engage a community of players in new experiences that challenge the notion of what constitutes a paratext within game studies scholarship. Citing the *Games of Thrones* mod for *Crusader Kings 2*, she describes how the mod substantially reshapes the storyworld and the gameplay, appropriating the original game text as raw material for an entirely different game. The creative and transformative productivity of game fans is undoubtedly prolific, and instrumental to the growth of game communities.

In his work on game communities, Mäyrä (2016) observes that although 'community' has remained a key concept in research for more than a century, there is little agreement on its defining characteristics. Noting the cultural history of gaming communities in areas as diverse as physical sports and board games, to ancient Greek Olympic and Roman gladiator games, Mäyrä observes the strong historical foundations of communities of games and play. In outlining that fans have evolved their own complex information behaviours around communities, Mäyrä draws attention to related work by Pearce (2009) and Turkle (1996). Pearce's *Communities of Play* (2009) examines how the nature of online gameplay can motivate players to develop deep commitments, forming communities and contributing to collective creativity and sharing, while Turkle's *Life on the Screen* (1996) is renowned for bringing to light the radical liberating potential of shared virtual gaming spaces such as multi-user dungeons (MUDs).

Not surprisingly, community emerges as a key theme in the context of online gaming cultures. With emphasis on cooperation, coordination and communication among players, many online games actively foster social experiences, player communities and bonds around shared interaction towards common goals. Mäyrä (2008) notes the special attention given to the social dimensions of online gaming, particularly in relation to massively multiplayer online role-playing games (MMORPGs). Yet while it might appear that online multiplayer games are manifestly 'social', for many gamers the motivations for playing vary significantly. For example, a study by Williams et al. (2006) of *World of Warcraft* in the mid-2000s revealed that a quarter of players interviewed considered in-game relationships as utilitarian and necessary primarily in terms of accomplishing set tasks. For a third of players from the Williams et al. (2006) study, the game strengthened and maintained existing offline friendships, while only a small percentage reported forming new friendships within the game, often extending those relationships outside the game and into their 'real lives'. Such research shows that participation in particular game communities is not uniformly motivated by a desire for social inclusion and a sense of belonging.

In much of the feminist literature on game cultures, game communities are often identified as sexist, abusive and intolerant of sexual and racial difference. The oft-cited example is the now infamous Gamergate incident (as mentioned in the previous chapter in relation to the games industry), which involved a harassment campaign against those – primarily women – who sought to expose sexism in both the games industry and within player communities. Following several years of aggressive attacks on women and feminists as both creators and players of games, in August and September of 2014 a large number of people assembled within the hashtag Gamergate to target journalists, designers, scholars and critics, most notably game developers Zoë Quinn (Stuart, 2014) and Brianna Wu (Gray et al., 2017), and media and game critic Anita Sarkeesian (Wingfield, 2014), who hosts the YouTube channel *Feminist Frequency*.[1]

While Quinn had already been subject to harassment as an overly 'political' game developer, Gamergate began when her former boyfriend, Eron Gjoni, wrote a blog post falsely accusing her of an unethical relationship with journalist Nathan Grayson. The online attacks that followed were initially directed at Quinn, but as the campaign gained momentum it expanded out to target other women in games, and included death threats, threats of rape, doxing and account hacks, predominantly via social media platforms 4chan, Twitter and Reddit. During this time, both Quinn and Wu fled their homes, and Sarkeesian cancelled a public appearance after threats of a massacre. At an International Women's Day event at the Sydney Opera House in 2015, Sarkessian said:

> To the thousands of men who turned their misogyny into a game, in which gendered slurs, death and rape threats are weapons used to take down the big bad villain (which in this case is me). My life is not a game. I've been harassed and threatened for going on three years with no end in sight. And all because I dared to question the obvious, self-evident sexism running rampant in the games industry. (Boluk & Lemieux, 2017: 275)

In her insightful analysis of sexism and homophobia in game studies, Humphreys (2019: 832) argues that such campaigns 'legitimize a culture of disrespect' that marginalizes and disempowers women, people of colour and those of non-normative sexualities. Throughout the Gamergate campaign, commenters and posters frequently suggested that the harassment was simply a harmless joke, further downplaying its very real damaging and marginalizing effects. For Humphreys, and the many girls, women and LGBTQI people who play games, it is clear that gamer identity is closely aligned with white, heterosexual, young male players and that 'older, queer, female, nonwestern gamers, are more marginal to this culture, at least discursively if not numerically' (2019: 833). The Gamergate controversy served to highlight the normalization of sexism and toxicity within game communities. Five years on, little has changed in many online multiplayer game spaces, which are still rife with player harassment (see Figure 4.2).

As Todd (2015) suggests, over time such practices have become culturally sedimented within game communities. Similarly, Paul's (2018) study of fandoms and the problems of toxicity analyses both the communities created around digital games and the content of the games themselves, to show how attitudes and ideologies adopted in the real world seep into, permeate and are sustained in virtual worlds. Paul critically examines how notions of meritocracy and neoliberalism are increasingly used to justify inequality in the real world and become actualized in games. While in many countries women now comprise approximately 46% of all players, the toxicity within game cultures and communities persists, mirroring and often magnifying the structural inequalities within society more broadly. For many game researchers, developers and players, it is imperative that we engage in *critical play* in Flanagan's (2009a) sense, and actively question the everyday politics that reside in the design of games, in player-character stereotypes and in gamer behaviour, including their paratextual practices.

Such critical reflection is evidenced in the experience of Matt, one of our research participants, who has been active in the game mod community for over ten years, as

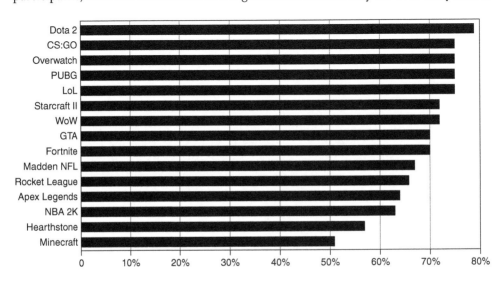

**Figure 4.2**  Player harassment in video games (2019). Image: GamingScan.com.

**Figure 4.3** Unaltered screenshot of the *Ultimate Simpsons Doom* mod shared on the Fandom Doom Wiki. Republished under a Creative Commons 2.0 License (https://creativecommons.org/licenses/by-sa/2.0/).

he described his personal and somewhat confronting experience of produsage. For much of that time he had focused on 'creating new textures, models and levels, but mostly for static or inorganic objects', and sought to challenge himself by modding 'a full-blown character'. Matt chose to tackle a rumour that one of the nine playable characters in *Team Fortress 2*, Pyro – a character shrouded from head to toe in a fire-proof suit and gas mask – was actually a woman. He noted that previous attempts at modding a female Pyro had 'ignored both the original proportions *and* the aesthetics of the game' by replicating a stereotypical, highly sexualized and scantily clad female form. He decided to retain the hunched, blocky build of the original character with armour that was more accurately representative of its strength and abilities. Naming the character mod *Femme Pyro*, he posted it up for download on a popular hub of user-created mod content called GameBanana. Almost immediately there ensued heated discussion about the mod, ranging from comments praising her 'assets', appreciative 'thanks' from purportedly female gamers, to requests that her proportions and posture be 'fixed' and outright demands that she be made skimpier, thinner, taller and more attractive. Mods and the commentary that surrounds them provide some insight into attitudes within gamer culture.

After a subsequent update and re-release of *Femme Pyro* (still retaining the original aesthetic of the game and character), Matt received over 1,000 comments and private messages, primarily pertaining to the 'non-normative' gendering of his mod. The experience has inspired him to initiate discussion and debate on game blogs and content hubs about 'hard-coded' constraints on the bodily limits of playable characters that work to reinforce stereotypes, and to develop other avatar mods that challenge these normative representations. As Matt's experience shows, while games may configure normative patterns of play, in an era of 'small media' innovation critical players can produce, enact and distribute subversively playful paratexts as they negotiate and modify those patterns (Roig et al., 2009: 93, citing Kücklich & Fellow, 2004). In the following section we continue to explore mod practices and their surrounding communities as a particularly salient example of productive fandom.

## Modding Communities

Game communities, and modders in particular, have been active 'produsers' since the 1980s when Silas Warner famously converted Muse Software's videogame hit *Castle Wolfenstein* into *Castle Smurfenstein* (Reseigh-Lincoln, 2017). In fact, modding actually predates Web 2.0 as a form of participatory and collaborative media engagement; an activity enacted by co-creative gamers as 'productive fans' enthusiastically sharing ideas, resources, skills and game content. Yet it is certainly the case that today online modding communities are now larger and more globally dispersed, and able to engage in the large-scale many-to-many interaction made possible by the internet. Modders appropriate, hack, alter and remix game assets, systems, maps and codes, creatively playing with and transforming game physics and environments for their own enjoyment. They also share their versions with other gamers and communities on platforms such as Steam, or through dedicated forums, blogs and wikis (see Figure 4.3). Using a pre-existing video game, a modder alters characters and environments or any number of other aspects to create a new or supplementary game experience. Sometimes these are minor or superficial enhancements to the game, such as the creation of higher resolution textures or skins, but mods can range from small changes through to an entirely new game (known as a 'total conversion').

Once considered a subversive practice akin to hacking, over the past three decades modding and mod communities have directly influenced the development of videogames and how we think about gameplay. Some mods have spawned entirely new sub-genres, such as MOBA (multiplayer online battle arena), a team-based real-time strategy (RTS) mode of play, typified by games such as *League of Legends* (*LoL*, Riot

Games, 2009) and *Defence of the Ancients 2* (*Dota 2*, Valve, 2013). Now one of the most popular game sub-genres, MOBA-style games are played at massive eSports tournaments around the world (see Chapter 5). *League of Legends* currently boasts up to 115 million players per month, with 8 million concurrent daily players.[2] The top three games by eSports prize pools, *Dota 2* (US$174 million), *Counter-Strike: Global Offensive* (US$69 million) and *League of Legends* (US$64 million), all began as game mods. Some games, such as *Doom* (id Software, 1993) and *Skyrim* (Bethesda, 2011), have welcomed modding into company business models, as developers are aware of how this integration significantly extends the shelf life of the game and expands the fan base.

Also, at times entire games, such as *Minecraft* and *Project Spark*, revolve around the processes of modding and distribution of user-generated content as an embedded part of the play (Moody, 2014). For many games, such as *Minecraft*, player-created mods are playfully intertextual and parodic, integrating characters from other games and transmedia narratives such as *Pokémon*. Other games, such as *The Sims*, hinge their commercial success on customization (Price, 2014). The participatory fan cultures that exist around *The Sims* engage in 'produsage' activities that range from reappropriating primary sources from cult media to building archives and databases of gaming mods and materials.

In their study of two amateur game design communities, Atherton and Karabinus (2019) show how the practices of amateur modders and designers often mirror professional game-making methods and workflows that include iterative design and extensive documentation processes. More recently, however, with the rise of microtransactions and DLCs (extra downloadable content available for purchase online), big game developers and producers have increasingly resisted freely available user-created content, and rarely release games with mod support. As noted in the previous chapter, the primary challenge to this exclusion now comes from the independent sector. With the growing pervasiveness of convergence culture, Planells (2017) notes that the co-creative affordances of digital technologies, and the rise of indie game models and trends towards crowdfunding architectures, have seen the emergence of prosumers, or consumers-as-experts participating in productive and decision-making structures at the highest level. In this system, the traditional top-down hierarchy of the games industry is challenged by bottom-up participatory models based on prosumer involvement in game development.

At the level of players, however, many mods are the non-profit creative outputs of game enthusiasts who seek to playfully augment their favourite games. Küchlich (2005) conceptualizes modding as 'precarious playbour', as it is a time-intensive activity that rarely receives monetary recompense, even in cases where the original game developer or producer profits from the mod. Others have employed similar terms, such as 'invisible labor' (Downey, 2001; Postigo, 2007) and 'free labor' (Terranova, 2000), to convey the absence of remuneration in return for the substantial 'work' that modders perform. Küchlich suggests that playbour typifies the changing relationship between work and play that can be seen across the creative industries and contemporary media culture more broadly; our prolific sharing on social media, for example, can also be understood as a 'playful' form of unpaid labour that translates into profit for media conglomerates like Facebook and Twitter. Sharing and open source models of distribution are also common practice for modders, who release their work as social and cultural capital for use and further modification to members within their game communities. Similarly, for Sotamaa (2010: 240), modding is one instance of the 'contemporary overlap between media consumption and production' that increasingly prevails in today's creative economy.

As Küchlich, Sotamaa and others have observed, the relationship between game companies on the one hand, and modders and their game communities on the other, is often fraught with moral questions around creative ownership and battles over the control of game assets. The history of modding provides numerous examples of such conflicts. Game companies can often benefit from the inclusion of modding and game communities into the creative process, as exemplified in the cases described above; on the flip side, actively excluding gamers as co-creators and not recognizing the interests and values of player communities can impact negatively on companies' profits and success. For example, Cova and White (2010) discuss the instance of *Warhammer* players, who felt twice exploited when the company producing the *Warhammer* game demanded that they pay a premium price after the fanbase had themselves participated in the improvement of the product. Ultimately, the *Warhammer* community abandoned the company and formed their own rival game and associated community called *Confrontation*.

Interestingly, and perhaps unique to the game medium, modding communities also coalesce around game engines; here, it is the game-making technology itself that shapes the relationship between developers and player co-creators. For example, the open architecture of the Quake engine, developed by id Software, not only supported but also actively encouraged game fans to develop add-ons and modifications. In 1996, the game *Duke Nukem 3D* was released, an alien invasion first-person shooter (FPS) game with a dark but ironically humorous world that was much appreciated by its players. Avid fans of the game, frustrated with the long wait for the promised sequel, *Duke Nukem Forever*, made their own game mod entitled *Duke It Out in Quake* using the Quake engine in 2001 (Nieborg & van der Graaf, 2008). The original developer of the *Duke Nukem* brand, Apogee Software, viewed the mod as a serious breach of copyright and requested that it immediately cease development and distribution.

Following the confrontation, through online forums many players and modders expressed deep frustration with outdated copyright law and its disregard for the creative labour of modders seeking only to extend enjoyment of the *Duke Nukem* storyworld for loyal and supportive fans (Nieborg & van der Graaf, 2008). While many within the game community recognized the legitimacy of the copyright owners and their control over creative works, they argued that it also pointlessly worked against the production of quality content. That is, as Postigo (2008) argues, copyright owner-ship in a participatory media environment not only interferes with the enjoyment of those products but can impose unnecessary limits on the ways the creative industries can benefit from convergence.

In discussing the tensions between modders and the copyright holders of the games they remix and augment, Postigo (2008) suggests that modders adopt a ration-ale rooted in Jenkins's (2008) concept of a 'moral economy' to justify their appro-priations. For Jenkins, the term moral economy 'refers to the social expectations, emotional investments and cultural transactions which create a shared understand-ing between all participants within an economic exchange' (Jenkins, 2008: n.p.). This understanding is undergoing fundamental change and renegotiation as a result of participatory media and the *cultural* process of convergence that has (sometimes contentiously) brought together the roles of consumption and production.

Productive fans, including modders, hold complex attitudes towards the creators and owners of media content, balancing a mix of respect and frustration that often fluctuates according to culturally-inflected beliefs about creative rights and economic interests. The *Duke Nukem* narrative is one often repeated in contemporary participa-tory media culture, and is characteristic of deep conflicts over produsage practices more generally. Indeed, media critics and researchers alike have argued for over a decade that in an age of remix culture, where much of our media content is recom-binant, current copyright law is fundamentally 'broken' (Lessig, 2008; Kawashima, 2010). This issue speaks to the heart of what constitutes creativity and creative prac-tice in today's society, and is one of the core debates played out daily within game communities.

Another more complex tale of conflict between modders and game developers concerns the free software development tool Creation Kit released by Bethesda, that allows players to modify content for the popular title *Skyrim* (Moody, 2014). Utiliz-ing the kit, modders create and publicly release their authorized mods through the Steam platform. However, while this model of co-creation seems unproblematically fair and open, as Moody (2014) observes, existing modders had already established effective third-party platforms for distribution and experienced the Steam Workshop Channel as a disruptive intervention into the community's practices, a move that forcibly took control of how the creative outputs could be shared among players. In this instance, it is not ownership of the game content itself that is an issue, but rather the dynamics and processes of distribution. In his exploration of a digital media pro-ducer's attempt to control the transmission of fan-made production, Moody shows the tension between innovation and control within the community, and empha-sizes modders as diverse innovators with their own hierarchies, histories, values and motivations.

These examples point to how modders and player communities – and co-creative 'produsers' more broadly – are vulnerable to the hegemonic and sometimes exploitative practices enacted by those who legally own the 'original' media content. Yet while thus far our mod stories have focused on the negative aspects, research also shows that modders and players derive significant social, educational and wellbeing benefits from their practices and contributions (Au, 2002; Kücklich, 2005; Postigo, 2007). Mäyrä (2016) notes that social capital within modding and player communities has been associated with both physical health and subjective wellbeing. Although many modders remain disempowered despite the creative and community-based impact of their work, player-creators nonetheless take enormous pleasure in their labour (Prax, 2019). This is echoed by many game design students, who quite strenuously resist being situated in a position of exploitation; they enter knowingly into the relationship and point to the mutual benefit that arises from the collaborative act. More significantly, they explicitly recognize the social, cultural and symbolic capital that is acquired in the act of sharing their work with their communities.

In this context, as Poor (2014) suggests, game modding involves a composite of factors, including the enhancement and display of digital skills, the benefits of play and playing together, the self-efficacy gained through making and remixing, and not least, the sense of belonging to a community. Research undertaken by Wirman (2014), for example, drawing on email interviews conducted with Finnish players, explores modding practices among players of *The Sims 2*, and considers the importance and construction of gendered and national identities that emerge within the game. Indeed, the motivations of modders have occupied scholarship for over ten years, revealing the complexities of gamer identities and the ways they are intrinsically tied to specific communities. Overwhelmingly, modders are inspired to improve and add to games for themselves *and* other players; their creative outputs are designed to be played.

This is not to say, however, that modders have little interest in recognition from the games industry. Hong and Chen (2014) acknowledge that while modders may primarily seek approval and social capital in game and modding communities, they can also be highly motivated by the possibility of securing a job in the games industry, using modding as a means of practising their skills. Hong and Chen insightfully focus on the concept of co-creative labour, arguing that a more complex and nuanced understanding of labour practices needs to be developed in order to account for levels of *intensity*, in terms of the different degrees of involvement, commitment, time, effort and affectivity or emotional attachment.

Similarly, Olsson's (2019) study of the *Fortnite* community also identifies numerous motivations behind gamers' co-creative practices, or what he terms 'prosumption' (a combination of consumption and production). These include community feedback, but also the possibility of recognition and credit by Epic that can be leveraged for future job opportunities. Through analysis of a *Fortnite* forum on Reddit, Olssen identifies positive attitudes among modders in regard to the empowerment and engagement they gain from the community of *Fortnite* players, but also reveals their disappointment in regard to the lack of authentic and supportive communication from the game's developers.

Beyond actual or perceived recompense, community still emerges as a central motivation for game modders. A strong sense of community takes form among game modders in terms of the value they attribute to both social interaction and collaboration (Poor, 2014). Modding communities are often described by the gamers that inhabit them as safe spaces for socializing and interaction, where like-minded people can share their passion for games in ways that would not always be possible with offline friends (Poor, 2014; Marone, 2015). Highlighting the importance of interaction and collaboration in production, Marone (2015) argues that modding communities serve as 'discursive studios' where members share and build on each other's skills, co-creating mods that add to their own play experience and the enjoyment of others. In this way, modding communities are exemplary of affinity spaces (Gee, 2005), comprised of participants who share expertise.

In significant ways the communities that gather around and support mod practices can be described as sites of both *productive* and *transformative* fandom (Dym, 2020), as exemplified in Consalvo's (2017) analysis of mods that exceed their status as paratexts to become new game experiences. In this way, as Dym (2020) suggests, modding is somewhat comparable to **fanfiction**, as both are constitutive of participatory media culture in Jenkins's (2006a) terms. Both creatively appropriate, remix and augment existing media content, and in many instances go beyond simply adding value to an original core text; when they offer a new context, narrative or playable experience, they shift from the periphery to become central texts around which communities of fans congregate.

## Conclusion

In this chapter, we have aimed to show the significance of game communities, not only as groups of people who play and share a common interest in games, but also as integral to both the games industry and the ongoing formation of participatory media culture. We first considered the way media more generally are complexly interwoven with our collective imaginary – how they effectively 'call communities into being' in Anderson's sense (1983 [2006]). As the advent of the internet and Web 2.0 ushered in participatory media and convergence culture, the relationship between media and community has quite radically shifted to accommodate our own contributions as produsers. Simultaneously, as Jenkins so astutely observed, fandom has become normalized; our participation as consumers, users and creators of media now means we all engage in fan practices. Within the specific context of games, as Jenkins claimed over ten years ago, 'fan practices are shaping the games industry' (2007: 359–360).

Throughout this chapter we have shown how this claim still accurately represents the transformative impact of game communities as productive fandoms and provided a detailed exploration of modding as a particularly salient example. While modding has increasingly become superseded by independent game making, or otherwise controlled and absorbed into many game companies' production models, it is nevertheless the case that mod activities still retain destabilizing dimensions. The subversive and experimental aspects of modding still play an important role in game development and remain integral to many game communities and gamer identities. In many ways, modding and mod communities offer a window into the future of games, providing a space for innovation and provocation. In the following chapter we turn to another important facet of game cultures – the exponential rise of videogames as a form of sport and spectatorship in their own right.

## Further Reading

Chess, S. (2017). *Ready Player Two: Women Gamers and Designed Identity*. Minneapolis, MN: University of Minnesota Press.

Gray-Denson, K., Voorhees, G., & Vossen, E. (Eds.) (2018). *Feminism in Play*. Basingstoke: Palgrave Macmillan.

Jenkins, H. (2006). *Fans, Bloggers and Gamers: Exploring Participatory Culture*. New York: NYU Press.

Lamerichs, N. (2018). *Productive Fandom: Intermediality and Affective Reception in Fan Cultures*. Amsterdam: Amsterdam University Press. doi: 10.2307/j.ctv65svxz

Swalwell, M., Ndalianis, A., & Stuckey, H. (Eds.) (2017). *Fans and Videogames: Histories, Fandom, Archives*. New York: Routledge.

## Notes

1  https://www.youtube.com/user/feministfrequency
2  https://www.pcgamesn.com/league-of-legends/player-count

# 5

# eSports and Fantasy Sport

Can eSports be considered a form of 'sport'? Why or why not?

Explore some of the regional specificities around eSports. Why do you think different cultures engage with eSports in different ways?

Why are eSports and fantasy sport described as 'hybrid' forms of entertainment?

What are some of the motivations of fantasy sport players?

In this chapter we focus on what are often described as 'hybrid' game practices that bring together digital gameplay, sport and large-scale broadcast media entertainment, and traverse both virtual and actual domains of engagement. We first explore the increasingly popular phenomenon of eSports, which has emerged from early forms of watching play in arcades and players' homes to feature on livestreaming platforms, with some of the larger tournaments staged at massive arenas around the world. Perhaps more than other videogame practices, a diversity of disciplinary perspectives and concepts have been applied to the analysis of **eSports**, as it both replicates and diverges from traditional sports practices. Our discussion also considers how eSports players enact a particular mode of 'performativity', investigates some of the key motivations of players, livestreamers and spectators, and examines how sexist attitudes found within game communities more generally (as discussed in previous chapters) are also present in eSports. We then turn to the equally prolific medium of **fantasy sport** as a unique blend of online and offline worlds, the way it modifies the viewing and consumption practices of traditional sports fandoms, and is integral to the datafication processes that increasingly permeate our everyday lives, our work and leisure activities, and contemporary media cultures.

**Figure 5.1**  *Counter-Strike*: Global Offensive eSports event in 2019 (Moscow, Russia). Photo: Roman Kosolapov/Shutterstock.com.

## eSports

eSports, also known as 'cybersports', 'competitive gaming', 'virtual sports' and 'electronic sports' (Seth et al., 2017) is a rapidly growing form of entertainment, combining videogame play with the competitive and media broadcast elements of professional sports (Lin & Zhao, 2020). Against a field of contested taxonomies and debates over the distinction between eSports and traditional sport, Hamari and Sjöblom offer a technical definition, suggesting that eSports is 'a form of sports where the primary aspects of the sport are facilitated by electronic systems; the input of players and teams as well as the output of the eSports system are mediated by human–computer interfaces' (2017: 221). Yet this perfunctory explanation does not capture the way eSports is fundamentally a competitive mode of videogame play (as not all games are competitive) that is recorded or livestreamed *for an audience*. Within this framework, Boluk and Lemieux identify two modalities of gameplay specific to communities of gamers: 'the player-versus-player competitions of strategy, fighting, and first-person shooter communities and the player-versus-records of the speedrunning, high-scoring, and some MMO communities' (2017: 243). Contemporary eSports events have become increasingly popular globally, often attracting tens of thousands of attendees at real-world tournament locations (see Figure 5.1), while simultaneously being viewed by hundreds of thousands of people online (Taylor, 2012).

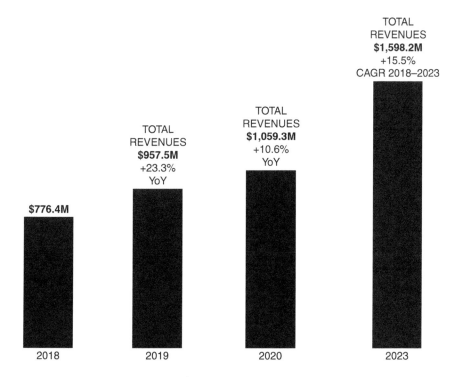

**Figure 5.2** eSport revenue growth. Image: Newzoo.com.

Global eSports revenue is expected to reach US$1.6 billion in 2023, a compound annual growth rate (CAGR) of 15.5% from $957.5 million in 2019 (see Figure 5.2). Global eSports spectatorship is predicted to surpass 495 million in 2020, a year-on-year growth of 11.7%, with emerging markets such as Southeast Asia, India and Brazil at the forefront of this rise in online and offline audience engagement (see Figure 5.3). Of that total audience, almost half tune in multiple times during the week and see themselves as enthusiasts (Newzoo, 2020 [see Figure 5.4]; Steinkuehler, 2020).

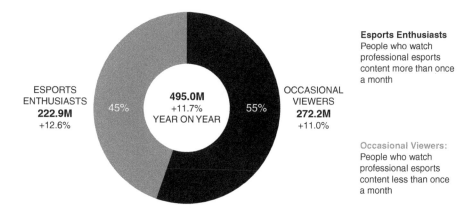

**Figure 5.3** Global eSports audiences. Image: Newzoo.com.

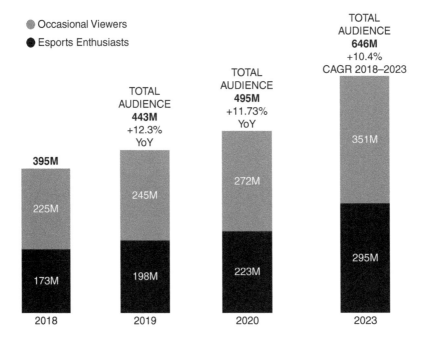

**Figure 5.4** Global eSports audience growth. Image: Newzoo.com.

Three-quarters of the total eSports market earnings come from revenue streams such as media rights, merchandising and publishing fees, with sponsorship taking by far the largest portion (see Figure 5.5).

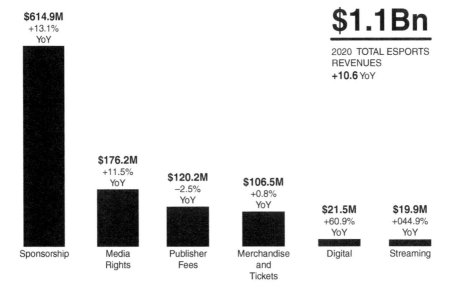

**Figure 5.5** eSports revenue streams. Image: Newzoo.com.

The meteoric rise of eSports has also attracted a subsequent increase in eSports scholarship across game studies, media studies and sports studies, although there is some debate around its origins, history and success. Wagner (2006), for example, dates eSports back to the late 1990s, when first-person shooter (FPS) games such as *Doom* (1993) and *Quake* (1996) were networked in the US and Europe, and 'clans' formed and began to compete in online tournaments. Edwards (2013) locates the origins in the Atari *Space Invaders* tournament in 1980 that drew more than 10,000 participants. In contrast, Taylor (2018b) loosely identifies three 'waves' of eSports development and uptake, the first emerging in the 1970s and 1980s as a form of local play in arcades and domestic spaces following the distribution of home consoles. In her analysis, the practice of watching others play games has always been intrinsic to game cultures, although multiplayer online gaming and the rise of an eSports industry into 'a more global formulation of the competitive space' (Taylor, 2018b: 4) didn't occur until the 1990s (the second wave).

Towards the end of this period, throughout the early-to-mid-2000s, Taylor notes the close link between the rise of eSports, livestreaming and 'cam cultures' – i.e. the emergence of Facebook in 2004, YouTube in 2005, and Tumblr and the iPhone in 2007 saw 'an intense period where everyday life was being interwoven with network culture, where people were producing content for each other' (Taylor, 2018b: 54). Much of this user-generated and shared content comprised gamers recording their private play and uploading it for online audiences (see Chapter 6 on Twitch and Let's Play practices). The current and third wave, as theorized by Taylor (2018b) and generally agreed upon by scholars in the field, began around 2010 with the advent of livestreaming, monetization and the massive upscaling of eSports as a form of 'networked broadcasting' (Taylor, 2018b). The livestreaming platform Twitch figures prominently in this new media ecology and has generated a significant shift in the role of viewing audiences, as the interface affords users a mode of *interactive media entertainment* through the real-time chat window that sits synchronously adjacent to the livestreamed play. In this way, as Taylor (2018b) suggests, eSports as networked broadcasting coalesces network and participatory media cultures, digital play and the well-established medium of live televised sports events.

The large-scale emergence of eSports communities throughout the 1990s is also often traced to South Korea, attributed to the rapid growth of broadband infrastructure in the region and the launch of dedicated television channels and eSports leagues supported by the government's Ministry of Culture, Sports and Tourism (Bruton, 2019). While South Korea began establishing team houses and support facilities for players and formed corporate-sponsored teams in the late 1990s, substantial investment in eSports infrastructure in the West didn't begin in earnest until the mid-2010s (Bruton, 2019). Today, while amateur leagues continue to flourish worldwide through the participatory playbour of gamers and fans, the largest and most established eSports competitions that attract millions of viewers are hosted by organizations such as the Electronic Sports League (ESL) and Major League Gaming (MLG), and AAA game developers such as Riot, Blizzard Entertainment and Valve (Taylor, 2018b; Steinkuehler, 2020).

The geographic differentials intertwined with the emergence of eSports have seen the activity evolve with regional nuance. For example, in contrast to the United States and Europe where FPS games such as *Counter-Strike* dominate, South Koreans prefer MMORPGs such as *Lineage* (1998) and real-time strategy games (RTSG) such as *StarCraft: BroodWar* (1998) (Wagner, 2006). Several scholars and commentators have also noted how eSports has played into much larger domains of competitive nationalism, especially between the US, China and South Korea (Yu, 2018; Lin & Zhao, 2020). In recent years, China has overtaken South Korea as the mecca of eSports (see Figure 5.6) and now surpasses North America and Europe as the world's largest eSports market, with its own stable of preferred games, such as *PlayerUnknown's Battlegrounds* (PUBG) (2016), *League of Legends* (LoL) (2009) and *Overwatch* (Yu, 2018). In 2017, dedicated eSports viewers in China exceeded those in the US more than threefold, at a ratio of 70 million to 20 million (Wong, 2017). Media analysts such as Lin and Zhao (2020) and Yu (2018) outline how the contemporary staging of eSports events in China is intertwined with neoliberal politics, capitalism, meritocracy and nationalism – part of a deliberate strategy to expand and consolidate its digital economy through digital empires such as Tencent and Alibaba, and to visibly transition away from manufacturing and agriculture towards the services sector.

The analysis of eSports as a contemporary phenomenon takes place in and across contested transdisciplinary terrain; questions persist around whether it can be defined as entertainment, videogame or competitive sport, with ongoing debates over the status of professional videogaming as a form of work or recreational play (Wagner 2006; Witkowski, 2009; Brock, 2017; Freeman & Wohn, 2017; Hallmann & Giel, 2017). In their review of the extensive corpus of literature on eSports up to

**Figure 5.6**    Hong Kong eSports & Music Festival, Hong Kong Convention and Exhibition Centre, 2019. Photo: Yiucheung/Shutterstock.com.

2018, Reitman et al. (2020) found it is the subject of multiple disciplines, including game studies, media studies, play studies, informatics, business, sports, science, sociology, law and cognitive science, each with their different foci. Across scholarship, they identify eSports as an unfolding and rapidly growing research area.

Many analyses of the topic concern the situatedness or place of eSports within society – i.e. where it properly fits within contemporary leisure and work practices – and consequently apply (or discard) frameworks that have been similarly applied to traditional sports, in terms of consumption, marketing and the celebrated identities of individual players and teams (Adamus, 2012; Witkowski, 2012; Seo, 2016; Sjöblom & Hamari, 2017). In their study of eSports players in China, Lin and Zhao (2020) document the arduous training regime (12 hours a day) and strict living conditions imposed on those striving to reach the 'extremely narrow apex' of success, and discuss the 'precarity' of a profession that is solely dependent on embodied skills, much like that which is experienced in traditional sports. Others have examined the similarities between successful eSports players and international sports athletes in terms of the financial rewards. For example, Newell (2018) has shown how alongside eSports viewership, professional player salaries are comparable to professional sports – Faker, a world-famous player, earns US\$2.5 million annually in addition to \$1.1 million from prize pools and revenue from Twitch livestreaming (Newell, 2018). In terms of broadcasting practices, Taylor (2018b: 170) observes that eSports broadcasts now simulate those of traditional sports – games are narrated by seasoned sports commentators and in between games full-scale media teams produce and curate additional contextual content, such as personal stories, player rivalries, interviews and interstitials.

The topic of eSports has also regularly featured in key sports journals for over a decade, such as Jonasson and Thiborg's (2010) analysis in *Sport in Society*, which boldly posited that eSports may comprise a 'new phase in the evolution of sports' (p. 287), and Llorens's (2017) comparative study entitled 'eSport gaming: The rise of a new sports practice' in *Sport, Ethics and Philosophy*. While the proper disciplinary place for eSports may not seem of particular importance in terms of how we understand its mediatic, institutional and economic evolution, for Taylor (2012), the issue of whether eSports is considered a 'real' sport is of key significance. As she notes, professional sport and eSports have a similar 'competitive architecture' that emphasizes athleticism, player embodiment, formal rules and the valorization of gambling and betting. This similitude is also embedded in the deep association between our commonly-held views about professional sport and conventional notions of masculinity, which directly impact on the ongoing exclusion of women within eSports.

The marginalization of women within eSports is doubly reinforced by the misogynistic attitudes that exist within many game communities, as discussed in previous chapters in relation to the Gamergate controversy. In their narrative study of the internal discourse of eSports communities on the social media platform Reddit,

Xue et al. (2019) explore the 'stories' that eSports fans and players tell about themselves to each other. They found that Reddit is frequently used as a medium to actively promote a discriminatory gender politics against women and correlative strategies of inclusion and exclusion. They note that although games industry reports indicate that women represent almost half of all gamers, the underrepresentation of, and discrimination against, female participants, along with other marginalized groups, is increasingly propagated – and called into question – within eSports communities.

Similarly, through online questionnaires and interpretative analysis of discussion on game forums, Ruotsalainen and Friman (2018) examined women's participation in eSports and competitive gaming and found that these domains are largely dominated by toxic meritocracy and hegemonic 'geek' masculinity. They describe the experience of a competitive *Overwatch* player, Glisa, who is verbally abused by team members during the entirety of a 16-minute match. This included calling her 'ugly', informing her that as a woman she should not be voicing her opinions, and alluding to rape. Ironically, the abuse Glisa receives stands in stark contrast to the intent of *Overwatch*'s game developer, Blizzard, and highlights the persistence of misogyny regardless of the game environment or narrative. *Overwatch* has been lauded as a game that affords players the exploration of alternative sexual orientations and ethnicities, as the game lore found in associated comics and animations includes a diversity of characters. The game's developer, Blizzard, has quite deliberately integrated inclusivity into the transmedial storyworld.

Far from being an isolated occurrence, Ruotsalainen and Friman show that such behaviours are 'distressingly common' for women gamers who play competitively online. Such stories are repeated in numerous studies. In her work on eSports, Witkowski (2018a: 191) reveals that women 'are persistently derailed as authentic participants' at the personal, community and institutional level, and Taylor (2018b) argues that such marginalizing and disempowering practices within the eSports industry are experienced by people of non-normative gender, race, class, sexuality and disability, where normative is defined as white, young and male. Moreover, the exclusion of women from eSports overflows into the ongoing construction of eSports audiences. Taylor writes:

> The people esports sales teams are selling to – be they advertisers, sponsors, or game developers/publishers – often have audience models that tend toward a fairly conservative and outdated view of games as the domain of young men. Pitching alternate productions and audience formulations simply doesn't get traction. The upshot is the continued same old story in which the imagined audience member is a young single man. This only helps reify the dominance of this demographic in everyone's minds. If you keep surrounding yourself with that model of participation, it's not surprising that you start thinking it *is* reality, which in turn limits how you might formulate more up-to-date possibilities. The cost of this decidedly unvirtuous circle has been several decades of inequitable access and participation opportunities for women and girls to digital playing fields, and that is now flowing over into audience construction. (2018b: 188)

Such attitudes and behaviours run somewhat counter to the notion that eSports challenges the boundaries of institutions and media cultures in other ways. That is, for many theorists within game studies and media studies – arguably the most popular conceptual domain for eSports research – it is recognized that eSports is fundamentally *transformative* in terms of the way it significantly alters how we think about and experience sport, videogames and media entertainment. As Hutchins suggests, eSports is a 'cyber-athletic competition' that has emerged as a new hybrid form of entertainment that implodes the 'institutional and material boundaries' of media, sport and computer gaming (2008: 865). Similarly, as noted above, Taylor (2018b) argues that eSports represents a complex convergence of television, games, the internet and online communication networks. For Burroughs and Rama (2015), eSports as a form of livestreaming effectively traverses both 'real' and 'virtual' domains, as the boundaries between game environments, online sociality and face-to-face communication (i.e. at live events) are no longer clearly demarcated. The transformative effects of eSports are further discussed by Boluk and Lemieux, who trace Valve's adaptation of *Dota 2* into an eSports platform, changing how it was 'distributed, spectated, networked and monetized in relation to the larger Steam marketplace' (2017: 245). Significant here is the way spectatorship was from the outset built into the game-as-platform as a *mode of play*, such that it 'is no longer a superfluous byproduct of gaming, but a productive part of a much broader ecology in which all player activities are measured and funnelled back into the development of the game' (Boluk & Lemieux, 2017: 245).

Indeed, as Seo and Jung (2016) suggest, the consumption of eSports merges a complex assemblage of knowledges, skills and competencies, requiring that we think in broader terms about the practice of watching games as an active and participatory mode of engagement, as distinct from watching other forms of screen media, such as cinema and television. Taylor (2018b: 39–40) identifies a number of reasons why people watch eSports and livestreams of professional gamers that reflect the complex diversity of audience motivation in the specific context of games and eSports. These include: aspiration (wanting to be a better gamer); education (to learn more about a particular game); inspiration (as a mode of fandom, to enjoy a visceral and aesthetic experience of a favourite game); entertainment (simply for the pleasure of watching); community (for social engagement and connection through 'gestures of reciprocity, familiarity, or intimacy' from the streamer and co-watchers (Taylor, 2018b: 91)); and ambience (background noise, similar to having the television on while doing other things, as a form of mediated companionship). In the following chapter we explore the motivations of watching gameplay further through the perspective of some of our research participants, and how it offers gratification through an increased sense of community and what is termed *parasociality*, which describes the unique and mediated relationship that exists between fans and celebrities (Blight, 2016).

The motivations of eSports players, and game streamers more generally, also include the element of social connection to a community of players and game spectators, but are also more closely linked to professional aspirations and expectations, and to their capacity to creatively transform the 'play experience' (Taylor, 2018b: 70–71). In this way, the game provides a dynamic space or environment within which the 'performative nature of gameplay' unfolds (Taylor, 2018b: 244); each play sequence is an individual performance of expertise, and it is this uniqueness that is integral to the networked ecology of sharing and broadcasting. Indeed, through content-sharing and livestreaming platforms such as Twitch and YouTube, over the past decade certain modes of gameplay, such as Let's Play, speedrunning and eSports, have evolved to become explicitly performative, thus shifting from a personal in-the-moment experience to something that is shared and curated for an engaged community of watchers. eSports, as 'big' media events that are broadcast to hundreds of thousands of people globally, might be regarded as a particularly high-stakes 'platform-based' performance.

Acknowledging that each platform has its own affordances that shape, and are shaped by, communities of practice, Lamarre's (2017) concept of *platformativity* allows for a more nuanced notion of performance that recognizes the technical, social, political and material affects of each digital platform on both users and 'produsers' of content. Across networks and modalities of produsage and sharing, each have their own platformativity, determined both by the interface and cultural practice, as a combined effect of technology and society. In the context of eSports, this may involve the regional specificities that distinguish South Korean eSports production and consumption from that which dominates in the US and Europe, for example, or it might describe the unique affordance of Twitch's fast-scrolling chat window as a chaotic yet oddly coherent form of 'crowdspeak' that is legible only to more seasoned watchers (Taylor, 2018b). Examining the rich complexity of eSports activities, Witkowski and Manning (2019) have documented how the staging of live play takes place through a complex assemblage of actions that include individuals (players, spectators and the diverse experts involved in the process of networked broadcasting), institutions (owner franchises and international and local leagues), infrastructures (platforms and modes of distribution) and the game communities that collectively comprise eSports fandoms.

In the following section, we turn to another assemblage of gameplay that also involves a hybrid of network media, sport and computer-based gaming – fantasy sport.

## Fantasy Sport

The industry of fantasy sport is a combinatory product of broadcast content, sporting leagues and franchises, official and unofficial web content (the latter an aspect of participatory media), fandom, social media and social networking. In short, it involves fans acting as virtual managers or coaches and forming teams comprised of actual players across a sporting league, such as football, basketball, cricket or baseball. Fans then compete with other fans to accumulate the most points according to the actual statistics of each team player week by week, which are transposed into the fantasy league as the actual games are played (Schirato, 2012, 2016). Jutel and Schirato (2008) observe that avid fantasy sport players strive to process all available information and statistics about particular sports, and function as virtual managers who draft actual players, bid for them in auctions and form virtual teams that mirror real numbers and positions. In North America, fantasy sport comprises a $7.2 billion industry with well over 60 million people or 16% of the population now actively playing in the US and Canada (Forbes, 2019; Statista, 2019). Major fantasy sports companies, such as DraftKings and FanDuel, distribute over $1 billion in prizes each year (Farquhar, 2018). Today, the fantasy sport industry has expanded to encompass an ever-increasing array of competitive activity, including hockey, auto racing, cycling, college athletics and even bass fishing. Over the past decade, it has evolved into a significant modality of play within contemporary media cultures (Ruihley, 2010; Billings et al., 2017).

In the scholarship surrounding fantasy sport, studies have found that the motivations of players are frequently associated with traditional sports fandom, such as an appreciation of and commitment to the game and affective attachment to specific athletes. However, there is some evidence to suggest that participants' engagement increases in terms of watching more live sport (outside their favourite teams' games) and following additional kinds of sport as a consequence (Farquhar, 2018). Comparing tendencies and motivations between a survey group of 1,261 traditional sport and fantasy sport fans, for example, Billings and Ruihley's (2013) study revealed users experienced elevated levels of enjoyment, entertainment and social interaction when compared to traditional fans. Not surprisingly, fantasy sport players are also drawn to the interactive components that bring the audience 'into the activity' beyond traditional forms of spectatorship (Jutel & Schirato, 2008), although there is some variation depending on demographic, age and gender (Brown et al., 2012; Billings & Ruihley, 2013). In their survey of the theoretical frameworks that inform the literature on fantasy sports, Tacon and Vainker (2017) critique the fact that quantitative methodologies and analysis of consumer behaviour predominate, and that there is a lack of ethnographic and qualitative approaches that explore the experiential dimensions and social significance of fantasy sport participation.

As Hutchins and Rowe (2009: 357) suggest, fantasy sport is an example of how online and offline worlds coalesce, an effect of the convergence of social, location-based and mobile networked media, such that 'grounded' and 'mediated' experience and content intermesh in the social worlds of fans. In Halverson and Halverson's (2008) analysis, fantasy sport is also an instance of competitive fandom and a significant trajectory of the current shift towards fan-related produsage, in which fans have moved from the margins to a key position in 'current thinking about media production and consumption' (Jenkins, 2006b, cited in Halverson & Halverson, 2008: 291).

The practices of fantasy sport participants or 'coaches' engender participatory media spaces that stretch across both cable and free-to-air television, dedicated websites, livestreams, blogs and YouTube, and blend seamlessly with the networked social interaction around the game. Fantasy sport practices are complexly enacted through what Halverson and Halverson (2008) call 'triple planes of activity'. These can be described as: first, fans' primary engagement with the actual game; second, as activities derived from the primary plane (the refashioning of primary content into new narratives and stories and published through blogs, forums and content-sharing sites); and third, the fantasy game, which allows players to create an 'autonomous plane of game play' and compete with each other in a shared gamespace in terms of the 'primary plane characters, themes, rules, and narratives' (Halverson & Halverson, 2008: 295, 302).

Activities on the latter two planes also include 'mash-up production' (e.g. the construction of fantasy teams, a practice consonant with other fan practices, where the original content is remixed and used as material for the generation of user-created content) and the 'transmedia complex', an intertextual network of media content – both formal and fan-generated – that obfuscates and challenges the relation between corporate media and participatory media. Although fantasy sport has defined rules and quantifiable outcomes, so would in formal terms be defined as a game, the merger of real-world events (the actual game and points accrued by real players) and online fantasy teams that have no equivalent in the real sport means that it crosses the boundary of the 'magic circle'. That is, it is more like an 'augmented reality game' that creates a 'hybrid world that is part real, part virtual' (Halverson & Halverson, 2008: 294).

Fantasy sport is also a fundamentally social game, as fans form leagues often with friends and through friend networks, and communication between and across fantasy leagues is prolific, as evidenced by the liveliness of forums, blogs and activity feeds on official and unofficial fan sites. In Australian Football League (AFL) fantasy sport, for example, a league is comprised of 18 teams, each drafted and managed by a coach, and membership often involves an array of social activities – both online and offline – that are intrinsic to gameplay and the fostering of cohesive groups. Coaches contribute to activity feeds via the official AFL website, which provides an online 'Coaches Box' enabling fantasy coaches to post messages to others within their league, who often refer to their teams as if they were 'real' teams. As coaches, they experience the same issues with injury, penalties and poor performance as actual coaches might.

The playing of fantasy sport not only becomes inflected in networked and face-to-face interaction between fans. As Shirato argues, the digital mediation and commodification of sport effectively modifies the 'visual regime' of spectatorship (Schirato, 2012, 2016) as the focus of fantasy league coaches shifts to the performance and statistics of individual players in a coach's fantasy team, and away from the performance of an actual team they support. Indeed, much of the focus in fantasy sport research has been concerned with identifying how fantasy sport fandom differs from traditional sport fandom (Brown et al., 2012; Billings & Ruihley, 2013; Billings et al., 2017). As McDonald has observed:

> We see fans watching more games that don't involve the team they support. We see fans using multiple screens to watch two games at once. We see fans watching games that would typically be considered one sided and boring, because they are watching a player [on their fantasy team].... Perhaps most importantly, we also see fans preferring to watch at home because they have better access to statistics and other games. (2013: n.p.)

Fantasy sport coaches thus negotiate an ongoing conflict between supporting their actual teams and allegiance to their fantasy team, a contradiction that impacts upon viewing practices and, some might argue, transgresses the boundary of 'proper' sports spectatorship and fan behaviour. In addition, fantasy sport coaches will often devote time that extends well beyond when actual games were played. As Schirato has also noted, fantasy sport players are often expert fans (or prosumers) and follow the minutia of the game on a daily basis: '[f]antasy sport never rests: there are always texts, sites, information, news, trends, rumours, rankings, statistics, discussions, lists, trades and other activities, resources and developments to consider' (2012: 82). The kind of dedication involved in fantasy football fandom is also facilitated by the apps that allow players to 'check in' on their team or receive updates relating to injuries, substitutes and late withdrawals, sometimes many times a day throughout the week during the lead-up to the next round.

In some ways, fantasy sport may be understood to operate as a kind of fanfiction of actual sports, in that the range of activities balance official textual information with the narrative desires of fans. To achieve this, fantasy sport relies on a combination of ancillary foreground information, such as commentary, opinions and predictions, as well as a hyper-detailed backdrop of accumulated big data sets. Stauff (2018) details the intertwining of sports and datafication since the 1990s, noting how combined they have informed the success of fantasy sport. He notes that since 2006 'the speed, position, and break of every pitch in Major League baseball have been measured in real time. In basketball, the NBA introduced a system that automatically tracks players, refs and the ball, capturing 72,000 coordinates per game for each tracked item' (Stauff, 2018: 42). For Stauff, media sports, fantasy sports and big data are deeply integral to the formation of the sports industries today. A number of theorists and commentators have also observed the close relation between the exponential growth of sports websites, which afford the tracking and exchange of statistics and live information, and the ascent of fantasy sport (Isidore, 2003: 1; Billings et al., 2017). More broadly, Hutchins (2016) has documented how datafication now influences all aspects of contemporary sports, from scouting and coaching to fan consumption and content distribution. In contradistinction to the more global ecology of eSports, however, fantasy sport is more often location-based, and the specificity of place and geography is infused in the play practices and player-generated content surrounding the game. It is a form of engagement that coalesces place with broadcast, participatory, mobile and web media.

## Conclusion

Both eSports and fantasy sport are now multi-million-dollar media industries that reside at the nexus of videogames, online social networks, media broadcasting and traditional competitive sport. The practices of eSports and fantasy sport communities are another significant iteration of participatory media ecology, as players and spectators engage in various modes of produsage, co-creation and remixing of existing content to enhance and extend their experience of both fandom and the game. In the next chapter, we pivot our attention more closely to the act of watching play, revisiting the platform Twitch as a significant interface for game spectatorship, in addition to exploring the rise of Let's Play on YouTube. As we suggest, the activity of watching others play fundamentally challenges the *raison d'être* of videogames as something to be *played*.

### Further Reading

Taylor, T. L. (2012). *Raising the Stakes: E-Sports and the Professionalization of Computer Gaming*. Cambridge, MA: The MIT Press.

Taylor, T. L. (2018). *Watch Me Play: Twitch and the Rise of Game Live Streaming*. Princeton, NJ: Princeton University Press.

Witkowski, E. (2018). Doing/undoing gender with the girl gamer in high-performance Play. In K. Gray-Denson, G. Voorhees, & E. Vossen (Eds.), *Feminism in Play*. Basingstoke: Palgrave Macmillan.

Witkowski, E., & Manning, J. (2019). Player power: Networked careers in esports and high-performance game livestreaming practices. *Convergence, 25*(5–6), 953–969. https://doi.org/10.1177/1354856518809667

# 6

# Livestreaming and Let's Play

Videogames are meant to be played. How do game livestreams and Let's Plays challenge this statement? How does the practice of 'watching play' transform the media modality of games?

What is meant by paratextuality and parasociality, and why are they important concepts in the study of livestreaming and Let's Play?

Research suggests that gamers spend more time watching videogame play than actually playing games. List some of the reasons why people watch rather than play, paying particular attention to the formation and experience of community.

What are some of the innovative research methods we can use to study game livestreaming?

How do game livestreams and Let's Plays challenge traditional notions of copyright and creative ownership?

Today, everyday media users create, share, collaborate and play *with* and *through* media. In this process, we simultaneously consume and (re)make culture by remixing our own and others' media texts. As noted in previous chapters, in Bruns and Jacobs's (2006) terms, we have become *produsers*, conflating the practices of producers and users. These new communicative practices are integral to our online and offline identities, changing the relationship between makers and consumers of media, transforming the way we interact and form communities and social worlds, and affording new pathways of participation.

In the broader historical and cultural context, as we have discussed throughout the book, Raessens (2012) argues in his seminal work *Homo Ludens 2.0* that playfulness has become central to our cultural practices and the way we engage with media texts.

Not surprisingly, games and gaming cultures are the predominant arena for this ludification process. Games and the practices surrounding gameplay are also a lens through which to understand the largely playful turn in culture. Yet while the migration of the *playful attitude* (Sicart, 2014) across many aspects of our daily lives is in part due to the rise of games, it is also evident in playful communication such as snapchatting and tweeting, and the growing array of gamified activities in our social and cultural practices. In the words of Celia Pearce:

> If we telescope out to the larger picture, we find that networked play is not simply confined to the game worlds ... In fact, network play has insinuated itself into many other aspects of life. It could be argued that YouTube is a networked playground of sorts, even more so when we take note of the numerous machinima films created in games by players. ... These trends move far beyond traditional gamer fan culture. They point to a growing 'play turn' in which, far from being a marginalized fringe activity, play is beginning to pervade every aspect of our lives. We see games and play increasingly embedded in social networks, in mobile phones, on web sites, and in domains as diverse as education, military and corporate training, activism, even politics. (Pearce, 2009: 278)

As we observe these dynamic and transformative media effects and practices in our ethnographies of gamers and players, we would concur with Thomas Malaby's claim, that *play* does not describe a distinct human activity – and it is perhaps doubtful if this has ever been the case. Rather, as we have suggested, play can be used in an ambient sense to designate a *'mode of experience*, a way of engaging with the world' (Malaby, 2007: 102). Ambient playfulness – as a way of engaging with the world – resides in the merger of social media, games, playful mobile apps and the very ordinariness of that integrated use in our everyday lives. The focus of this chapter is how we are increasingly using social, mobile and network media as a means of *performing* and *watching* play, and how these nascent, vicarious and performative media practices can be described as conduits of ambient play. We first explore the concepts paratextuality and parasociality, key terms for understanding participatory media culture, before turning to Twitch and livestreaming as a living archive. We then describe Let's Play practices as a significant form of community, connection and sharing, and consider how uploading and sharing videos of gameplay constitutes a mode of transformative media textuality.

## Paratexts, Parasociality and Performance

The playful attitude is central to what Jenkins, Ford and Green (2013) term 'spreadable media' practices, which blur the boundaries between production and consumption, and big and small media. In this new mediascape, we have moved past mutually exclusive categories of user and producer, gamer and creator, towards a more flexible, open – and often irreverent and playful – dynamic. Today, we participate in everyday media *produsage* that is cooperative, shared and clustered around online communities of interest, often involving the repurposing, remixing and (re)circulation of existing media content. The effects are and continue to be transformative. They modify and reshape the way we engage with media, and how media content is circulated and part of our experience as social beings. It is here, at the core of spreadable media and produsage, that we locate the now prolific practice of performing, uploading, sharing, livestreaming and watching gameplay. Over the past decade we have seen both the *performance* and *watching* of gameplay as a burgeoning mode of entertainment in its own right. The act of watching people play videogames online is both *paratextual* and *parasocial* – both characteristics that can be described as ambient.

**Paratexts** refer to media content and practices that circulate around a central media text. We might say that *Harry Potter* pyjamas or a *Sons of Anarchy* belt buckle are paratexts, but more often they comprise user-created content, such as fanfiction, a blog about *The Walking Dead*, or funny *Game of Thrones* lip sync videos. In this chapter our focus is on the paratextual media practices surrounding games. Media and game theorists have written at length about the paratextuality particular to games, which includes discussion and commentary in game and fan blogs, taking part in cosplay events (for example, going to *Supanova*[1] dressed up as your favourite game, comic or superhero character), game modding and the creative sharing of gameplay. These activities all exemplify a kind of cultural playfulness that is vernacular and informal, and sometimes this evolves into significant money-making ventures, as is the case with the more popular Let's Play channels and Twitch livestreamers. Regardless of whether it is monetized or not, playful paratextuality is intrinsically spreadable and ambient – terms that also capture the viral nature of social and participatory media.

**Parasociality** refers to the way we feel emotional attachment or connection towards public figures, celebrities or icons of popular media culture (Wulf et al., 2020). Traditionally, in the broadcast era, this has typically been a one-sided relationship, although in an age of participatory and social media, there can often be moments of authentic interaction that take place between fans and their luminaries. Instagram influencers might acknowledge specific followers, politicians often reply to members of their constituency and Twitch game streamers will thank individual viewers for donations as they play. The way in which we embrace popular figures, and the network communities that surround them, as integral to our social worlds, reflects a form of mediated and ambient sociality, or is an aspect of what Farman (2012) calls *social proprioception* – the ambient awareness of others in the network.

## Twitch and Let's Play (LP)

Livestreaming refers to simultaneously recording and broadcasting video in real time. Via Facebook Live, YouTube Live, Instagram Live, Twitch and other streaming

platforms, it is becoming an increasingly normalized way of sharing everyday hap-
penings in-the-moment, sometimes banal, sometimes involving criminal or pranking
behaviour, sometimes more innovative and creative activities. Much livestreaming –
especially when it is prescheduled and intentional – involves a kind of performativity or loosely scripted performance.

Twitch – owned by Twitch Interactive, which was acquired by Amazon for US$970
million in 2014 (Wikipedia, 2019) – contains both non-game and game content,
although it is predominantly known for and used as a platform for livestreaming
gameplay, eSports tournaments, and game-related talk shows. It attracts over 2 million daily broadcasters and 15 million unique viewers daily, with concurrent viewership at around 1 million, frequently outstripping major television networks such as
CNN and FoxNews (Mansoor, 2019). The Twitch platform enables gamers to create
their own channel, livestream their gameplay – with or without a screen-in-screen
inset of themselves as they play – and interact with their viewers via synchronous
chat that runs alongside the video. Popular games include *Fortnite*, *Minecraft*, *Overwatch*, *League of Legends* and *Dota 2*, and streamers can monetize their playbour
through subscriptions, ads, sponsorship and donations.

As Burroughs and Rama (2015) note, the streaming space of Twitch effectively
blurs the boundaries between games, social networks and face-to-face or real-time
communication. The *liveness* of the medium gives a sense of immediacy to the experience, and viewers often describe the play as unpredictable, thrilling and suspense-
ful (Wulf et al., 2020) – much like watching live sport on television. As one of our
research participants, Jonno, a 16-year-old *Overwatch* gamer from Perth, said:

> It's one of my favourite things to do. When we're not playing *Overwatch*, me and my
> mates will hang on Discord [a free voice and text chat service for gamers] and watch
> streams together. It's exciting and funny, and sometimes if there's not too many on
> at the same time you can chat to other people. It makes you feel like you're part of
> something. And you can learn stuff too.

Annie, a 24-year-old fan of *League of Legends*, enjoyed watching Twitch streamers for
several reasons:

> Sometimes if I'm a bit anxious and feel like some company, I'll watch imaqtpie or
> sneaky on my laptop at night and drift off to sleep, they're so chill and relaxed. I
> watch pokimane if I want to get some girl vibes, or Shiphtur for tips on how to
> improve. Sometimes between queues [when players have to wait to join teams in
> live multiplayer games] Shiphtur'll watch YouTube cooking videos about street food
> in Japan, so we all watch along with him... he's just a good guy. I don't really like
> loud streamers like Dom [IWillDominate] and Yassuo, they can be a bit toxic for me
> [laughs].

For Annie, the parasocial aspect of watching play affords a sense of connection and
companionship, achieved through the ambient presence of her favourite streamers

and the watching community. Other participants liked the way players could see and reply to viewer donations and comments, and even modify their gameplay in response to viewer requests. In many cases, this personal friend-like interaction between players and viewers is further extended – paratextually and parasocially – through social media on Facebook, Twitter and YouTube.

A Let's Play (LP), in contrast, is not live, but rather a video recording of gameplay uploaded post-production to the web. Videos are accompanied by the gamer's humorous or entertaining voiceover and an inset of their face and/or upper body and reactions as they play. The term Let's Play originated in the mid-2000s, emerging from the online discussion threads of somethingawful.com, a comedic website containing a blog, feature articles and forums devoted to internet media and game reviews. Since then, we have seen the exponential rise of subscriber channels that feature LPs on YouTube.

The video-sharing website YouTube is deeply connected to the game community – every day more than 200 million people view gaming content on YouTube, and in 2018 that amounted to 50 billion hours (Takahashi, 2018a). YouTube subscriber channel functionality is also the exemplar of networked media distribution; it is through the subscriber system that we've witnessed the rise of 'professional fan' practices and the evolution of LP into 'one of the most disruptive entertainment forces of the last decade' (Wadeson, 2013: n.p.). The prolific sharing of game content and gameplay on both YouTube and Twitch has escalated the hierarchy of games within contemporary media culture, and further challenged the way games function as entertainment. No longer are games exclusively interactive media to be *played*, they also generate content that is *watched*. Nearly half of YouTube gamers say they spend more time watching gaming videos than playing games (Petrova & Gross, 2018).

The most popular LP channel is PewDiePie (aka Felix Kjellberg), who boasts over 96 million subscribers and since late 2013 has been the most subscribed user on YouTube, with over 24 billion video views as of January 2020 (Statista, 2020). Kjellberg's current earnings, primarily generated through the monetization of his channel, and other associated products, are estimated to exceed US$15 million per annum. Other popular LP subscriber channels include Dude Perfect (43 million subscribers), Badavun (40 million), El Rubius (35 million) and Fernanfloo (33 million), to name a few. Typically, each Let's Player, like the Twitch streamer, has their own game genre specialty and signature style or commentary, and their own unique way of interpreting and narrating their gameplay.

Popular livestreamers and Let's Players are engaging and informative, giving viewers 'an entertaining performance of play' that often includes an expert evaluation of the game as the player reflects on 'mechanics, design, game play, "feel", and other aspects of the game' (Taylor, 2018b: 75). At first glance, Twitch livestreams and LP videos may appear similar to game walkthroughs, which provide gamers with tips and guides for their own gameplay. This instructional aspect has led some game theorists to call them 'affinity spaces', a term coined by literacy expert James Paul Gee (2005) to refer to online communities of interest that share knowledge and facilitate informal learning. Yet, as many of our research participants described, watching and commenting on LP content or Twitch livestreams is often not driven by a desire to play the game, but is about aesthetic or critical appreciation of a new media form and gaining a sense of belonging to online communities.

In the remainder of this chapter we provide an analysis of livestreaming in China followed by an exploration of Let's Play as both a connective space and as a transformative media practice. Through the eyes of players who identify as habitual watchers of games, we show that not only is watching gameplay fundamentally about dispersed or ambient social connection and the sharing of gameplay as-it-is-experienced, but that such practices are changing the way we think about videogames as media that are necessarily – or even primarily – something to be played.

## Livestreaming: Living Archives

Every day thousands of people globally livestream. Every day millions of people watch. As a rich new field of player and audience activity, one that is largely recorded and found online, livestreaming presents a huge resource of research opportunity. These practices also require and invite new research methods to interpret them.

Phenomena such as livestreaming and LPs have rewritten the boundaries between games, fans and performativity. As Lamarre (2017) notes, each platform creates and curates its own form of performativity – what he calls platformativity. For example, Twitch is predominantly used by Western audiences and reflects those values (Taylor, 2018a). Douyu, on the other hand, is shaped for and by Chinese audiences – in turn, mirroring those practices and understandings (Zhang & Hjorth, 2017).

In their article 'Methods for analyzing Let's Plays', Radde-Antweiler and Zeiler (2015) propose a matrix for the content analysis and archiving of LPs that involves undertaking an investigation of the LP as an object, the Let's Player as a personality, and the comments and commenters of the videogame itself. For Taylor (2018b), the livestreaming phenomenon coalesces private play with public entertainment. Understanding this phenomenon requires deploying qualitative methods like interviews and participant observation to map the ways in which it moves from branding to business practices.

In *Watch Me Play* (2018b), Taylor explores the emergence of livestreaming in the form of eSports. Giving close attention to the livestreaming platform Twitch, Taylor examines its management, governance, branding business practices as well as the creativity, social and emotional labour of the game streamers and hosting communities that use the platform. Exploring the issues and challenges faced by streamers,

Taylor also discusses the shifting meaning of ownership and intellectual property as these new forms of creativity take hold. She writes:

> They [the livestreamers] are frequently insightful theorists of their own experiences, identifying the ways that they dance between their own desires and legal or economic structures. … They knowingly, and often with great pleasure, engage in forms of affective and performative labour on platforms that they recognize to be never fully in their control. The challenge for us as researchers and scholars is to honor their experience as active meaning-making agents who undertake complex navigations in everyday life, but not lose sight of serious forms of structural inequality and precariousness. (Taylor, 2018b: 259–260)

While Taylor's study focuses mainly on Western livestreaming like Twitch, Ge Zhang explores the phenomenon in China through the platform Douyu. In '*Zhibo*: An ethnography of ordinary, boring, and vulgar livestreams', Zhang (2019) investigates the rise of Douyu and the practices of *Zhibo* ('direct cast') in contemporary quotidian Chinese life. In his research process, Zhang deployed innovative ethnographic methods to document, capture, analyse and archive the complex media of livestreaming, interviewing players and audiences in online and offline contexts. He provided an interdisciplinary context for the medium by situating the phenomenon at the intersection of media, TV, internet, games and celebrity studies.

Zhang's fieldwork documented key livestreamers over a period of one year. This required him to archive gigabytes of material and reflect upon the politics of archiving a medium that is meant to be 'live'. Understanding this politics required that he contextualize the media in terms of other 'live' media, such as radio and TV, both of which were initially live until the development of recording infrastructures. Zhang develops a 'Livestreaming Theory' to consider how livestreaming performs across three segments: liveness, streaming and video. Building on various critiques of liveness, Zhang argues for the technological specificity of livestreaming video; that is, its experiential aspects of watching and its distinct forms of performative expression.

For Zhang, framing the event is crucial to understanding livestreaming conceptually, theoretically and methodologically. He argues that 'event forms the basic unit of memories of the full stretch of a livestream' (Zhang, 2019: 67). His digital ethnography of Douyu involved fieldwork such as long-term online participant observation to offline interactions with various participants and informants. Zhang developed a specific notion of event-based ethnography in response to the methodological challenges posed by liveness and real-time media. Arguing for the practice of *chafang* (inspecting livestreams while livestreaming), Zhang creates a form of attention management during the observation of ordinary livestream events, alongside various aspects of building a digital archive of livestreams utilizing screen-recordings, screenshots, chatlogs and transcriptions. As Zhang's study shows, the methodological challenge presented by livestreaming – eloquently depicted in Taylor's (2018b) words above – in terms of archiving 'liveness' and understanding the complex often-invisible infrastructures requires us to renegotiate the limits of what methods can capture.

## Let's Play: Community, Connection and Sharing

The performative modality of Let's Play – its unique 'platformativity' – is closely linked to the affordances of YouTube as its primary site. The way in which platforms such as YouTube empower amateur media creators to foster new publics and online communities has been described as 'one of the most transformative dimensions of contemporary new media' (Lange & Ito, 2010: 284). YouTube gathers active communities of interest and practice around subscriber-based channels, and much of its content is accompanied by abundant commentary about both user-generated videos and big media. As Burgess and Green (2009) point out, it is a *communicative space*, not simply a platform for media distribution. One of our participants, a male gamer in his first year of university and a prolific commenter on the Let's Play channel Rooster Teeth, spoke about his recent shift away from Facebook as his preferred social media platform: 'I used to check Facebook ten times a day on my phone, now I'm mainly [watching and commenting] on YouTube. Lots of my friends are doing the same.'

In his incisive presentation to the Library of Congress, Michael Wesch (2008) tells a story about the beginnings of YouTube by tracing the global community of produsers that came together around Gary Brolsma's web-cam dance to *Numa Numa* (recorded in his 'dismal-looking suburban bedroom'). The video inspired tens of thousands of people from all over the world to 'share the joy' and upload their own versions of the song and dance. For Wesch, the *Numa Numa* phenomenon marked an important moment in the emergence of 'seriously playful participatory media culture' mediated by YouTube and other services that have empowered us to upload and share our own content online. In Wesch's words, it was 'a celebration of … new forms of community, and types of community that we've never really seen before, global connections transcending space and time, a celebration of new and unimaginable possibility' (Wesch, 2008: n.p.).

These new forms of community have also been described as *network publics*, a term that rethinks media consumption and mediated communication. That is, we are no longer 'audiences' but complex collectives of media users and produsers 'that are bottom-up, top-down, as well as side-to-side' (Ito & Okabe, 2005: n.p.). Although this seemingly inclusive community-building has been enthusiastically embraced by some, other media theorists, such as Jenny Kennedy, are wary of such an uncritical 'rhetoric of sharing' (Kennedy, 2013). That is, the connectivity that infuses social and network media is often celebrated as unproblematically open, collaborative and communal, whitewashing the underlying politics of data handling, ownership and monetization.

Focusing on LPs from the perspective of those who watch and subscribe to You-Tube channels provides us with an opportunity to more deeply explore the complexity and diversity of online communities, and the playful and ambient dimensions of contemporary media practices. Through Let's Play, we can better understand the dynamics of network publics, produsage and participatory media consumption. As conveyed by our research participants and Let's Players themselves, there are many motivations to seek out and watch LPs, and there is significant debate within game communities about the purpose of LPs.

To better understand LP practices, it is useful to think through the different layers of play that surround games. Ang, Zaphiris and Wilson (2010) distinguish between *intrinsic* play – or play that takes place inside the game – and *extrinsic* play – play that extends beyond the game into paratextual activities that effectively change the intrinsic game experience. Within the domain of extrinsic play, which we are focusing on here, they identify two categories of engagement: reflective play and expansive play.

Reflective play involves the communication, sharing and discussion that surrounds intrinsic play, such as that which takes place in game blogs, live chat and conventional walkthroughs. Expansive play refers to playful practices, activities and modes of produsage that 'transgress the original game boundary', often working to modify players' perceptions and experiences of the game (Ang et al., 2010: 364). In reflective play, content is created to enable reflection and tactical or strategic learning about the game; that is, it is largely motivated by a desire to talk about the game itself. In expansive play, on the other hand, the aim is to generate media texts that 'test the game boundary' and create 'new types of enjoyment' (2010: 368, 372). Both modes of extrinsic play bring together and strengthen game communities, possibly more so than intrinsic play (2010: 373). LP and livestreaming are instances of both reflective and expansive play, as they inform gameplay and add a dimension of vicarious engagement that quite radically transforms the way games are experienced.

The more fervent purists of LP videos argue that they should be more about reflective play – 'closed' texts that are complete linear progressions of a game from beginning to end, focusing exclusively on technique and expertise. For 27-year-old Aaron, the purpose of watching LPs is primarily instrumental, instructional and metatextual, a way to learn difficult game strategies by observing expert gamers and engage in critical reflection about the medium: 'I prefer LPs that stick to talking about the game and have worthwhile opinions about game design and mechanics.'

Others appreciate the entertaining personalities and antics of their favourite Let's Players. Jake, a 16-year-old high school student, spoke enthusiastically about the LP channel Cow Chop:

> I used to watch PewDiePie but it's gone all political, so now I go on Cow Chop. They're just normal guys who mess around pranking and doing stupid stuff, they're

not great gamers but they're funny. If I want to find out about good games or how to play them, I'll go on the PS [PlayStation] website.

Here, Jake reveals how LP videos have emerged as a distinct form of entertainment, with Let's Players becoming media celebrities with dedicated fan bases, often irrespective of the actual games featured on their channels.

Frequently, the authenticity and immediacy of the LP as a 'live performance' of play is important, with the associated perception that the commentary and reactions are spontaneous, unscripted and in-the-moment (Nguyen, 2016: 12). Yet somewhat at odds with the demand for authenticity, accomplished video-editing skills are also highly valued – zooming in on expressions, jump-cutting to humorous images, animations or in-house jokes, subtle use of filters and other effects. Rob, a 19-year-old who works in IT support, commented:

A lot of LPers are really fake, their reactions are just silly and over the top. I prefer watching LPs that are more real, or ones that are put together well. You can tell when they're professionals, they've put some thought into making a quality video.

The sense of liveness and immediacy conveyed by LP videos is enabled by the use of both audio commentary and facecams, where the gameplay is experienced *as it unfolds*. Aside from providing authentic sound and vision of the player, this also evokes a personal, emotional and parasocial connection between LPers and their fans. Sara, a 22-year-old studying vet nursing, stated: 'I love GameGrumps, they're cool guys who talk about their life experiences, like with drugs and relationships and stuff like that. It's like watching and listening to real people, people I'd like if I met them … I feel like they're part of my life.' Another female teenage participant, Jen, was particularly keen on LPs of horror games. Linking it to her enjoyment of the horror genre in film and books more generally, she also suggested it offered something extra, a closeness or intimacy as she experienced the fear and surprise of someone 'actually in the game … You can hear their screams like when a zombie appears out of nowhere, it's like being in their lounge room.'

For these LP viewers, watching their favourite LPers is clearly an emotional, vicarious and sometimes visceral experience. For Zariko, this intimate attachment follows from the uniqueness of LP as a medium, as it enables 'the transferring of textures of feelings and emotions' from the player's body to the body of viewer (2016: 20). She evocatively relates her own engagement with LPs:

A *Let's Play* video allows the experience of playing the game with another…. [It is] not the same as watching a video – I empathise with the player, with every jolt and start. I am able to experience the game without the pressure of being in control. … ChristopherOdd takes me with him. Even though I am not the one playing the game, I accompany him in his play experience. He plays the game for me. (Zariko, 2016: 14)

For a number of our participants, it was clear that LPs provided a means of *parasocial* and ambient connection, whether they identified as active posters or preferred to remain watchers and lurkers. They returned to watch their favourite players because they experienced a sense of like-mindedness and companionship, simulating the experience of 'playing together' with friends. As previously mentioned, media theorists have discussed this sense of parasociality at some length. Online fandoms and followings are largely sustained by this phenomenon and the ambient **co-presence** afforded by mobile and online connectivity and playful interaction (Hjorth & Richardson, 2016). In the case of LP (and other forms of watching others' antics online), this parasociality takes on an embodied and even visceral quality, as evidenced by Jen's experience of watching horror games. As another participant said: 'You can literally *feel* their frustration when they're not playing well, or the game's lagging or super tricky … sometimes I have to stop watching.'

Our participants often reflected ironically that watching someone else's gameplay had little to do with a desire to play the game, but was more about the pleasures of vicarious experience and being part of global and net-local game communities. John, a 20-year-old accountancy student, commented: 'I watch *League of Legends* ex-pros so I can improve my game. But sometimes I watch stuff just because I'm curious about a game, like *Deadly Premonition*, I want to see how it's played, even though I'm never going to play it.' Nicola, a young 14-year-old female gamer, relayed her avid enthusiasm for *Minecraft* LPs, even though she had never played nor intended to play the game. She watched them mainly on her iPad in her bedroom at night, for the most part because they were 'funny and interesting' and because she derived pleasure and satisfaction in following another's progression through the game: 'It's like you can keep tapping into a never-ending story or journey.' For Nicola, as for many of our participants, the paratextual practice of LP is fundamentally social: while those who upload their gameplay seek to share their creative outputs, those who watch LPs often feel a sense of ambient co-presence, affinity and intimacy.

While in Western contexts LPs are largely experienced in domestic settings, in the slums of the Philippines, the physical and social architectures collapse public and private spaces together giving rise to distinct practices of play. Drawing on ethnographic research conducted in Metropolitan Manila, Soriano et al. (2019) show how unique forms of performative intergenerational and public forms of play, spectatorship and surveillance entangle around the arcade-style vending machines known as *pisonets* (a conflation between the Filipino *piso* [currency] + inter[net]).

The *pisonet* operates like an arcade cabinet machine and provides cheap internet connection or gaming time by inserting a one-peso coin. Unlike computer game use within enclosed or semi-enclosed computer shops and cybercafés with strict rules of use, the *pisonets*, which are often located along slum alleys, offer comfortable and organic forms of access to locals in low-income communities. Functioning as an extension of domestic space, it is common for youths to use the *pisonet* while dressed in household clothing or for male users to use them while shirtless due to heat and humidity. Children will watch LPs on *pisonets* together, while parents and others in the broader neighbourhood monitor their children from afar in a manner that constitutes a familial or 'friendly' surveillance of care (Soriano et al., 2019).

The publicness of *pisonet* units in Manila resonates with the broader reality and communal nature of slum life that sees relatives, neighbours, local children and pets commonly flocking together along street alleys and variety stores in impromptu but natural gatherings. As a result of being located in these extended domestic environments, the activities of playing videogames and watching LPs become easily and closely monitored by family members, neighbours, friends and the broader community. These practices thus result in a playful socialization of neighbourhoods in which videogame play becomes entangled with community values and locally relevant socialities. As Soriano et al. (2019) show, such entanglements mean that the whole neighbourhood participates indirectly in crafting the play environment and its opportunities and meanings as well as forming broader communities of game

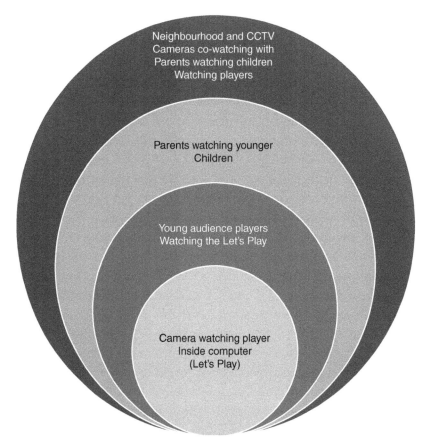

**Figure 6.1**  Filipino model of sociality and surveillance in the collective watching of Let's Play. Reproduced with permission of Cheryll Ruth Soriano.

spectatorship and care (see Figure 6.1). These broader communities extend to include both the local community of *pisonet* owners, who share experiences of running gaming hubs, including local perspectives on the economic and moral dimensions of gaming, as well as the broader global community of LP users and spectators.

Through these unique social and spatial architectures, the *pisonet* provides a space for distinctly Filipino understandings of the multiple dimensions of 'watching play' across public online and offline spaces.

Across diverse cultural contexts, the engagement with LP as an indirect experience of another's media activity clearly challenges the common argument within ludology that games are by definition an interactive, player-centred, simulative *doing*. In this way, as we will explore in the next section, as media texts LPs call into question our assumptions about what games are for, and the underlying ontology of games as interactive media.

## Changing the Game: Let's Play as Transformative Media Text

As play and playfulness become deeply embedded in our contemporary media sensibilities, across multiple screen interfaces and contexts, in some sense we all become players, an identity that reflects the expanding range of participatory and creative activities, and a *paidic* dimension to ourselves as media users. *Paidia* describes the ambient sense of playfulness typical of the dispersed practices of extrinsic play (Caillois, 2001 [1961]). It is often ambiguous and spontaneous, and interwoven with everyday media use. Not only do the paratextual and parasocial practices surrounding LP and livestreaming typify the *paidic* dimension of gameplay, they reveal a different relationship with audiovisual media and an alternative playful experience of sociality altogether.

As discussed in the introductory chapter, historically within game studies the 'magic circle' has been used to distinguish between game and non-game elements, playing from not playing, the unserious from the serious, and fantasy from real life. Over the past decade, however, game theorists have questioned what they see as the artificiality of the magic circle. They argue that we need a broader, messier and more flexible description of game boundaries and practices. For Roig et al., the LP experiences of our participants show us that games and their surrounding game cultures have spawned, quite literally, *new* media practices – they are markers of significant change 'not only regarding how media are produced and consumed, but also in the way leisure is organized and the role of play in our everyday life' (2009: 89). Games and playful media infuse everyday life and erode the boundary between play and not play, as exemplified by the *supra-lusory* practices of LP.

In the broader context of creativity and playfulness around media content production, our participants also had informed opinions about authorship, copyright and ownership, and the rigid boundaries demarcating original work from repurposed and remixed content. Those respondents that considered themselves part of Let's Play culture held strong views supporting the validity of LP as a creative, innovative, original and artistic mode of digital content production. As Taylor (2007) has argued, players and game developers should rightly be regarded as the 'collective authors' of the play experience, as it is through the *act of play* that meaning is given to the game characters, backstory and emergent narrative.

Games are fundamentally *lived experiences*. That is, they are things *to be played*, or at least not narrative experiences in the same way as a film or novel. Yet LPs are also quite literally stories of gameplay that provide 'narrative commentary on an experience as it is being experienced' (Smith et al., 2013: 133) and this clearly blurs the distinction between *active* and *passive* as it applies to interactive and non-interactive media. There is an added layer where LP commentary transforms the gameplay into 'a new form of entertainment' (Burwell & Miller, 2016: 113). The LP creator becomes more than a player, but also a narrator, critic and entertainer. In this way, LPs function as story-based meta-media situated outside the ludic frame-work of the original game content. Many LP channels feature serialized episodes of the player's progression through a single game, and a number of research par-ticipants conveyed their pleasure in this narrative experience, as they vicariously enjoyed the game journey *enacted through play* as each episode was uploaded, from beginning to end.

In this sense – an argument that could be applied to *all* gameplay – the video-game itself is only ever an experience *in potential* until the player actualizes a par-ticular trajectory as it unfolds in the moment of play. As Zariko has so insightfully explained, in recording and simultaneously reflecting upon their own performance of play on the fly, the Let's Player creates a unique and unrepeatable videotext nar-rative, one single execution of the game's multiple possibilities. The significance of narrative to this mode of playful media production is blatantly obvious, as the LP turns gameplay into a story, capturing and changing it into a permanent text avail-able for replay, repeated consumption and on-sharing. It is this process, in tandem with the ambient and networked sociality that accompanies the watching of game-play, that represents an important shift in playful media practices and participatory media consumption.

## Conclusion

In this chapter we have explored the curated performance of videogame play as a robust example of participatory media produsage, playful culture, paratextuality and parasociality, focusing on livestreaming in China and Let's Play in the Philippines and Australia. We explored research methods that can be applied to the study of livestreaming cultures and practices, and considered the diverse ways LP content is experienced, from assisting gamers to better strategize their gameplay, to facilitating an ambient sense of connection, belonging and sharing. Finally, the chapter turned to LP as a unique kind of media text that challenges how we think about gameplay, fostering new forms of creativity, collaboration and storytelling. In the dynamic and ever-evolving space of the web, the huge popularity and transformative effects of both Let's Play and game livestreaming render them particularly noteworthy as modes of ambient play.

This chapter ends Part II of the book on communities of practice. In the next part, Artful Interventions, we turn to the way games are deployed as aesthetic and creative conduits for art practice, social innovation and urban play.

## Further Reading

Consalvo, M. (2017). When paratexts become texts: De-centering the game-as-text. *Critical Studies in Media Communication*, *34*(2), 177–183. https://doi.org/10.1080/15295036.2017.1304648

Soriano, C. R. R., Davies, H., & Hjorth, L. (2019). Social surveillance and Let's Play: A regional case study of gaming in Manila slum communities. *New Media & Society*, *21*(10), 2119–2139. https://doi.org/10.1177/1461444819838497

Taylor, T. L. (2018). *Watch Me Play: Twitch and the Rise of Game Live Streaming*. Princeton, NJ: Princeton University Press.

## Note

1  See https://www.supanova.com.au

# Part III
## Artful Interventions

# 7

# Between Art Games and Game Art

---

What has motivated the transformation of games – materially and conceptually – into art? Why do artists incorporate games and game elements into their work?

How has game art evolved since its emergence in the late 1990s?

How do art games and game art challenge traditional attitudes and perceptions about what constitutes art?

How does game art modding differ from game modding as a form of produsage? Are there different copyright issues associated with each practice?

---

This chapter focuses on the intersection of art and games – i.e. the 'artful interventions' in, and around, games and gaming cultures – to explore the possibilities of videogames as an artistic form. In particular, it seeks to examine how games have been deployed by artists as a new cultural interface for political and social intervention. While **art games** can encompass digital art for games and game art by fans, in this chapter we focus on artists deploying games as a barometer for political, social and environmental issues. Specifically, as the internet and game cultures become mundane, new types of creative practice emerge. These practices, entitled 'post-internet art', refer to the use of both online and offline formats to engage with and reflect on contemporary digital culture (Vierkant, 2010). We investigate the potential of games to transform our perceptions and assumptions through their relationship to art, providing both a historical perspective on the use of games as a mode of artistic intervention and an analysis of the various ways contemporary artists deploy games as critical commentary on contemporary life.

We begin by discussing some of the contested ways 'art games' have been defined – especially as an indicator for how popular culture is understood. We then examine how game developers and arts practitioners are modifying existing games into new configurations, such as modding, machinima, performance, installation and place-based interventions. This discussion is then followed by an outline of two contemporary artists, Shanghai-based artist Lu Yang and American multimedia artist Cory Arcangel, whose practices deploy game elements and popular culture to remix definitions of game art.

## Game Design as Art

Within the games industry, education and training, the term 'game art' is used to denote the design and production of games. While recognizing the art of game making within the creative industry, this chapter focuses on how artists have taken up the concepts, concerns, tools and techniques of videogame making in their creative practice. Many game design, game production and game studies books, while touching on game aesthetics, neglect the important and varied notions of games-as-art in public debates around the playful and creative use of urban spaces and environments, and the place-based experience of cultural identity. Specifically, we adopt the contemporary position that games are an artform, as illustrated by the increasing number of artists deploying games as a medium.

In the introduction to *Gamescenes: Art in the Age of Videogames*, Matteo Bittanti defines game art as works 'in which digital games played a significant role in the creation, production, and/or display of the artwork' (2009: 9). Bittanti admits his definition is broader than most, as it encompasses traditional artefacts, such as painting, sculpture and photography, as well as sound, animation, video, performance or gallery installation (Bittanti, 2009). For arts writer Lana Polansky (2016), game art constitutes conceptual works that approach games not as a form, but as raw material in the creation of art works. Polansky makes a distinction between 'game art' and 'art games', with art games referring to videogames intended to provoke artistic ideas, but still understood contextually *as games*, which is to say playable experiences of entertainment value. However, as Polansky admits, the distinctions between art games and game art have blurred and converged over time. We can surmise that neither art nor games are easily defined but can be identified through a number of characteristics, yet as Bittanti (2009) highlights, defining game art often involves boundary crossing in areas that have been closely guarded. Moreover, individual games can be made as works of art, often termed 'art games' or 'artgames'.

The term 'artgame' was first pioneered by new media artist Tiffany Holmes (2003) to describe interactive works by a visual artist that challenge cultural stereotypes or offer social or historical critique. In her paper, 'Arcade classics spawn art? Current trends in the art game genre', Holmes specifies art games as works that contain 'at least two of the following: a defined way to win or experience success in a mental challenge, passage through a series of levels (that may or may not be hierarchical), or a central character or icon that represents the player' (2003: 46). For Holmes, art games are non-commercial experiences designed for a single play through. In a 2005 article titled 'Art games as genre', digital arts writer Kristine Ploug concurs with Holmes, noting that: 'art games are neither addictive nor meant to be played over and over, but merely shorter comments.... They are made by artists as pieces of art' (Ploug, 2005: n.p.). Certainly, game art and art games are closely aligned in their contextualization within the world of art and outside the industrial domain of commercial games.

According to Celia Pearce, art games may be viewed as 'a collision between the worlds of art and video games' (2010: 130). At the 2010 *Art History of Games* conference, Pearce noted that art games drew from process-based avant-garde movements like Fluxus (i.e. Nam June Paik) and evoked the spirit of artists like Marcel Duchamp, father of the 'readymade', or art made from manufactured objects. In her art game examples, Pearce discussed hybrid mixed reality projects such as Frank Lantz's *Pac-Manhattan* – a transposition of the 1980 game of *PacMan* onto the grid of Manhattan, New York (a project further explored in Chapter 9).

Along with Pearce, game designer John Sharp (2015) and game designer and historian Mary Flanagan (2009a, 2016) also acknowledge the important role of the 20th-century avant-garde work of the Dadaists, Surrealists, Situationists International (SI) and Fluxus in informing the contested definitions of contemporary game art. Flanagan (2016: 152) attempts to define contested game art taxonomies in terms of five different and self-descriptive definitions: the art in a game; games as a creative form; games made by artists; games with artistic intentions; and exemplary instances of a game. As Flanagan (2016: 152) notes, these shifting, merging, and contested definitions are part of the excitement of working in an emerging form such as games.

## Game Art

Exploring the origins of game art, Sofia Romualdo (2015) suggests the form emerged in the 1990s, taking various manifestations. The first artworks to appear, she notes, were mainly traditional artefacts, such as paintings, photographs and videos, which either referenced videogames or directly appropriated game content through photography. As the videogame medium matured and became more centralized in popular culture, artists began to explore the physicality of videogames through mod-ding, hacking and performance, ultimately blurring the boundaries between virtual and physical space in the process. In the final stage, and as technologies became more accessible, artists began to create entire videogames from scratch. Romualdo (2015) argues that the first examples can be found in the work of Chinese artist Feng Mengbo, who incorporates videogame aesthetics into his art practice. Mengbo's *Video Endgame Series* (1993) mixed images from the Cultural Revolution (1966–1976) with his childhood memories of playing 8-bit videogames.

Soon after, Greek painter and multimedia artist Miltos Manetas began produc-ing several paintings based on videogame culture and was among the first artists to depict the act of gaming. Painted in 1997, the piece *Christine with PlayStation* cap-tures the eponymous girl or woman kneeling on the floor in front of the television, leaning forward and resting her elbows on a large floor cushion, and holding what is clearly a game controller (Apperley, 2013). Through the late 1990s and early 2000s, videogame objects such as controllers and consoles appeared in the sculptures and installation practices of several artists, including Ricky Swallow's *The Architecture of Video Games* (1998) and Patricia Piccinini's *Game Boys Advanced* (2002) (see Figure 7.1). Videogames as objects and cultural artefacts had moved into mainstream dis-course and, as such, surfaced as pressing concerns for artists to address.

At the turn of the millennium, artists moved from simply depicting videogames to taking them up as materials in their work. This period of game art is characterized by the 'appropriation' (Stockburger, 2007: 29) and 'modification' (Cannon, 2007b: 45;

**Figure 7.1** Patricia Piccinini, *Game Boys Advanced* (2002). Reproduced with permission of Patricia Piccinini.

Stockburger, 2007: 25–37) of existing game software. Quaranta (2014) suggests that the introduction of such categorizations or sub-genres within game art at this time established critical appreciation and comprehension of the category. As game art grows in acceptance and reputation, new understandings of the form continue to arise. Apperley (2013) identifies several prevailing modes in relation to game art appropriation and modding, notably modding practices such as game patches and game hacks, machinima, and performance and in-game interventions. In the following sections we explore these categories with attention to artists and their work.

## Modding

As we discussed in Chapter 4 in the context of game communities, the process of modding gained momentum in 2000 with players developing pathways for dialogue, critique and parody. Modding has arguably become one of the key remixing Do it Yourself (DIY) skills of internet culture. It was through the practice of modding existing videogames at the turn of the millennium that saw an explosion of videogames as a creative medium. Crucially, modding was used by game developers and artists alike to create new works from existing game materials.

Game art modding, Rebecca Cannon recalls, 'was initiated in the nineteen-nineties when artists began to appreciate the aesthetic and technical qualities of computer games and decided to make use of these resources in their own artistic practice' (2007a: n.p.). In her paper 'Introduction to game modification', Cannon (2007a) notes that art modding came into full swing in the late 1990s when innovative (and sometimes mainstream) game developers released free software allowing game makers, players, fans and artists to customize the levels and characters in their games. Practices of modding by both artists and game developers alike led to a proliferation of game art throughout the 2000s.

Among the first artists to create mods based in videogames was Orhan Kipcak, who with Reini Urban in 1995 used the *Doom II* engine and Autodesk's AutoCAD software to create *ArsDoom*, a virtual replica of the Brucknerhaus exhibition hall (the venue for *Ars Electronica Festival* in Linz). Kipcak and Urban also invited artists to create or submit virtual artworks that could be displayed in the virtual territory. Armed with a shooting cross, a chainsaw or a brush, the player could 'kill' the artists and destroy all the artworks on display (Jansson, 2009).

A similar approach was taken up by Swedish artists Tobias Bernstrup and Palle Torsson, who began modifying existing videogames, such as *Duke Nukem 3D* (1996) and *Half-Life* (1998), to reconstruct art museums including the Arken Museum of Art in Copenhagen and Moderna Museet in Stockholm. The result, *Museum Meltdown* (1996–1999), allowed players to 'run around the museum, shoot monsters, and destroy art' (Jansson, 2012). The artist-duo Joan Heemskerk and Dirk Paesmans, under the name JODI, began modding old videogames, such as *Wolfenstein 3D*, *Doom*, *Quake* and *Jet Set Willy*, stripping the games down to basic elements while leaving them technically fully playable. This deconstructivist approach allowed the game mechanics to be interpreted in new and abstract ways. In something of a reverse tactic, Joan Leandre, under the name Retroyou, produced glitch hacks of popular PC games, radically altering the interactive experience while maintaining the same graphics assets and game engine.

Within gaming cultures, modding has also provided a space for play, critique and reflection within and about game cultures and society more broadly. Given these tactics, it is no accident that early examples of modding often playfully critiqued contemporary politics – a form of political in-game intervention. In-game interventions involve, as the term suggests, interference in online game spaces in order to upset game norms. The political game *Escape from Woomera* (2004) – a 3D first-person point-and-click action-adventure game developed by a team of Australian game developers and artists – was created as a patch on the popular commercial first-person shooter *Half-Life*. The game explicitly tackled the issues and implications of Australian detention centres (Figure 7.2). Other key examples of the online intervention genre are *Velvet-Strike* (2002) by Anne-Marie Schleiner, Brody Condon and Joan Leandre, which is an intervention within the game *Counter-Strike* (2003), and Eddo Stern's *RUNNERS: EverQuest* (1999–2000). Stern's political commentary is strongly voiced in his real-time performances, most notably *Tekken Torture Tournament* (2001), which sensorially immerses the player by delivering electronic shocks every time onscreen damage occurs, a powerful commentary on psychological warfare tactics.

**Figure 7.2**   *Escape from Woomera* (2004). Image: *Escape from Woomera* development team.

In his collaborative work with C-Level (particularly with Peter Brinson, Condon, Michael Wilson, Mark Allen and Jessica Hutchins), Stern commented on the 1993 Waco massacre in his work *Waco Resurrection* (2004), by rendering the tragedy into a game. In this game space, every player becomes cult leader and antagonist David Koresh for the duration; the aim of the game is to die and become a martyr like Koresh, forcing *Waco Resurrection* players to experience the inescapable tragedy of the event. With his background serving in the Israeli army giving him firsthand experience of violence and bloodshed, Stern's works are highly critical of the relationship between media depictions (in game spaces and in popular media) and the real world. This is highlighted in Stern's first machinima in 1999, *Sheik Attack*, a palpable depiction of Israel's bloody history.

In the 2010s, as technologies to create videogames became more available and user-friendly and artists became more literate in the medium, they moved from solely modding practices, to designing and developing their own games from scratch. This occurred against a broader games industry shift that saw more independent game makers with interests in the domain of visual and media art, creating their own playable experiences (see Chapter 3 for an extended discussion of indie game development).

Several artists and games that simultaneously straddled the indie game world and art world have risen to prominence over the past decade, such as Jenova Chen's (That Game Company) *Journey* (2012), Lucas Pope's *Papers, Please* (2012) and *Return of the Obra Dinn* (2018), and Bennett Foddy's *Getting Over It with Bennett Foddy* (2017). A key development of this era were generative videogame artworks such as US artist Ian Cheng's *Emissary* trilogy (2015–2017). Featuring a series of virtual landscapes and ancient tribal figures whose actions and interactions are randomly generated

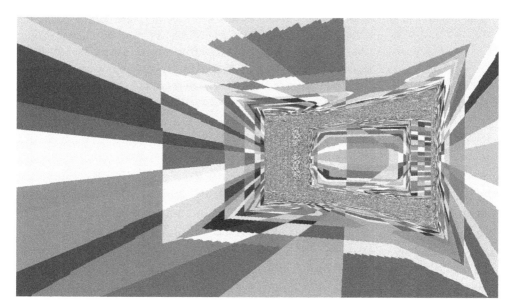

**Figure 7.3** Ian MacLarty, *Catacombs of Solaris* (2016). Reproduced with permission of Ian MacLarty.

by artificial intelligence (AI), Cheng describes the work as 'a video game that plays itself' (MOMA, 2017). Meanwhile, Australian artist Ian MacLarty's *Catacombs of Solaris* (2016) presents a dazzlingly colourful virtual space, whereby physical Euclidian dimensions radically and unexpectedly abstract and distort through player movement, giving rise to new patterns and experiences of space (Figure 7.3, see previous page).

These works challenge expectations of game spaces, the role of players and notions of interactivity, and increasingly, distinctions between 'art games', 'game art' and 'games-as-art' begin to dissolve. At the same time, opportunities for presentation and recognition for artists working with games have arisen with festivals and exhibitions acknowledging their practice. We return to the arena of game-related art exhibitions, installations and events below, but first we provide a brief overview of machinima and game art performance.

## Machinima

Within the modding genre emerged practices of **machinima** (machine cinema) – a drawing together of cinema and games. As a genre initially evolving from gaming cultures, machinima has grown to become an artform in its own right. Fusing art, cinema, new media and games, machinima's genealogy echoes that of other misunderstood genres, such as net.art (Arvers, 2010). According to French games critic Isabelle Arvers:

> Machinima can be seen as following in the footsteps of Dadaism and Surrealism, which saw play and entertainment as the most subversive and also as the ultimate forms of art. Even outside of an art context, it is important to remember that as soon as the first personal computer was created, MIT computer scientists hacked the computer code to conceive the first digital creation: Spacewar! And Spacewar! was a computer game. So, if computer game history is related to the roots of digital creation and to digital code hacking, machinima can be understood to follow this tradition. (Arvers, 2010: 236)

For Arvers (2010) and aforementioned Flanagan (2009a), machinima may also be paralleled with critical play techniques evoked by avant-garde movements such as the Situationist International (SI), with its creative synthesis of politics and art, utilizing urban movement, the cut-up process, and the 'modding' or daubing of amateur flea market paintings. Machinima demonstrates that play can be a way to explore and innovate, signposting the notion that playful intervention can be a form of social and cultural practice (Sutton-Smith, 1997). In *Critical Play*, Flanagan (2009a) highlights the important role artists/activists have played in shaping game culture. Through alternative games, Flanagan provides new ways of thinking about game design and play, specifically from an avant-garde context. Drawing on an art history canon, *Critical Play* 'outlines how play has influenced the history of creative exploration of the social and the political' (Flanagan, 2009a: 2) (see Chapter 8 for further discussion of Flanagan's design methodology).

Machinima not only provides a medium to explore the transitions between the analogue and the digital through playing with voice and image combinations, but also creates a critical space to consider politics, often implicitly rather than explicitly. Machinima frequently deploys intertextual references across different genres and media as a way to reflect upon games. One key example of early machinima made for and by gamers is the *Red vs Blue* series (2003–present) adapted from the *Halo* (2001) game engine. Its creators deconstruct the genre of first-person shooter (FPS) games by deploying postmodern techniques such as irony, intertextuality, pastiche and parody.

Rather than performing the typical FPS features of *Halo*, some *Red vs Blue* characters are sensitive, reflective, 'new-age' personas – the antithesis of *Halo*'s typical hyper-masculine avatars. This intertextual deconstruction of FPS is most prevalent in the 2006 series of *Red vs Blue*, in which the characters challenge stereotypes around violence and videogames, and are deployed to expose fictions around identity politics in the US. In playing up this antithesis, *Red vs Blue* utilizes, again, the classic machinima tension between analogue and digital through the use of human voice and humorous dialogue, evoking analogue affects that works against 'cold digital spaces' (Arvers, 2010). In this way, machinima proffers a space to critique and challenge notions such as violence in games.

These concerns are taken up in Baden Pailthorpe's 2013 work *Cadence III*, which combines methods of modding and machinima to arrive at an ambient dance of war rendered through videogame imagery (see Figure 7.4). Pailthorpe's work is achieved by hacking a popular videogame engine to produce a motion-staggering effect

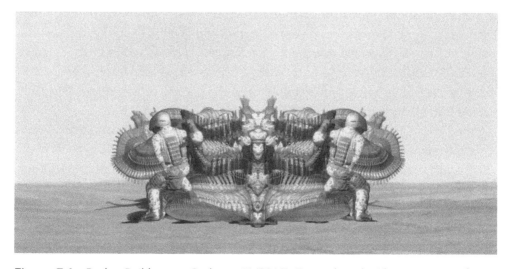

**Figure 7.4**   Baden Pailthorpe, *Cadence III* (2013). Reproduced with permission of Baden Pailthorpe and Sullivan+Strumpf.

whereby each frame of movement remains on the screen. These effects are then mirrored and recorded into a machinima clip to create a mesmerising Rorschach-like image in which multiple interpretations are embedded.

Other artists have fused machinima and in-game intervention to experiment on more abstract levels. For instance, artists like Julian Oliver create generative and hardware mods with the real-time capacities of games to produce works that continuously evolve. Oliver's *ioq3aPaint* (2003–2010) is a generative painting system modded from the game *Quake III* (1999), a poignant example of formal abstraction within the game modding genre.

In contrast, Chinese artist Cao Fei's *RMB City* (2008) delivers a more representative approach, manifesting as a *Second Life* installation featuring utopian skyscrapers accompanied by sinking Mao statues in a collision of Chinese popular culture references. For Cao Fei, *RMB City* represents a laboratory for past, present and future interdisciplinary collaborations across design, art, politics and cinema. The artist highlights that the open world of *Second Life* is much more than just corporate, educational or experimental; it can be activated as socio-cultural critique. Works such as *Red vs Blue* and *RMB City*, and other machinima art more generally, are also modalities of virtual performance.

## Performance, Installation and Place-based Intervention

The political implications of videogame art became particularly salient in relation to the War in Iraq that took place at the beginning of the millennium, especially through artistic interventions known as 'performance art' developed in and through gameworlds. For example, during the 2004 Republican National Convention in New York, in a work titled *Operation Urban Terrain (OUT): A Live Action Wireless Gaming Urban Intervention*, Anne-Marie Schleiner 'armed herself with a mobile Internet connection, a bicycle, a battery-powered video projector, a team of players and technicians, and a laptop' (Flanagan, 2009a: 179), entered the US army recruiting videogame *America's Army* (2002) and discussed anti-war ideas with the players, projecting the live game session into urban space.

Other in-game performances at this time include the aforementioned *Counter-Strike* intervention named *Velvet-Strike* (2002) and Eddo Stern's *RUNNERS: Wolfenstein* (2002). Likewise, through his in-game performance *Dead-in-iraq* (2006–2011), Joseph DeLappe typed the names of American soldiers who died in the Iraq War in the in-game text speak for five years between 2006 and 2011. Questions have arisen about the activist nature of these performance works – that is, whether they can be considered legitimate interventions in the performance art tradition or simply instances of 'greifing', a type of bad faith play whereby videogame players deliberately irritate and harass other players within the game (Kuchera, 2006). More recent videogame performative works, including the 2019 invasion of mainland Chinese *Grand Theft Auto V* servers by pro-Hong Kong independence activists, have further amplified questions around the distinctions that separate performance art, activism and trolling.

With game artists often taking on activist interests, the increasing accessibility of videogame production has resulted in games being created in rapid response to issues of protest in the real world. Making sense of this phenomenon, there have been a variety of analyses of in-game activism, from Chan's (2009) discussion of Chinese in-game protests, Koenitz's (2014) and Sezen and Sezen's (2016) exploration of videogames produced during Turkey's Taksim Gezi Park Protests, to Davies's (2020) examination of videogames in response to the 2019 protests in Hong Kong. For Koenitz, games such as *Occupy Istanbul* (2013) offer a form of civic participation in virtual urban space, enabling players to test strategies of engagement, from passive bystander to violent activist. Chan has remarked that the medium of videogames has emerged as a new field of performative struggle, while Davies has suggested that increased restrictions upon physical spaces for activism sees videogames such as *Revolution in our Times* (2019) and *Liberate Hong Kong* (2019) emerge as key sites of protest. Such games redeploy the space of play as a site of political critique, inviting the player to explore and enact an activist mode of performativity.

Game art, in its performative modes, often took the form of installations and place-based interventions. Early exhibitions of art games include Anne-Marie Schleiner's online exhibition *Cracking the Maze* (1999), *Synreal* (1999) in Vienna, and *SHIFT-CTRL* (2000). In 2001, Ars Electronica awarded the Golden Nica prize to an online interactive computer game, *Banja*, developed by TEAMcHMAn in France. In the same year, the Massachusetts Museum of Contemporary Art (MASS MoCA) presented *Game Show*, an exhibition that explored how artists were using game content, structures and mechanics in their work, and The Whitney Museum of American Art presented *Bitstreams and Play's the Thing: Critical and Transgressive Practices in Contemporary Art*. Also, in 2001, San Francisco Museum of Modern Art (SF MOMA) hosted *ArtCade: Exploring the Relationship between Video Games and Art* (Fuchs, 2005).

Through the 2000s and early 2010s, other exhibitions around the world similarly showcased game art, including Rebecca Cannon's *Trigger* (2002) in Melbourne, Australia; *re:Play* (2003) at the Institute for Contemporary Art (Cape Town); *Game On* at the Barbican, London, UK (2002); *Arcadia: Video Games Subvert Art* at the Govett-Brewster Art Gallery in New Zealand (2003); and *Space Invaders* (2011) produced collaboratively by FACT (Foundation for Art and Creative Technology), the Nikolaj Copenhagen Contemporary Art Centre, and the Netherlands Media Art Institute (Amsterdam) (Stuckey, 2012). Events such as *Now Play This* in the UK, the *Freeplay Independent Games Festival* in Australia, *Game On* in Brazil, and *A MAZE* in Germany have explicitly sought to include game art in their exhibition repertoire.

Many of the games that appeared in these exhibitions were also featured on the now defunct SelectParks.net, a website devoted to the exploration of art games and art game modding. Maintained by Rebecca Cannon, Julian Oliver and Chris Dodds (Ryan et al., 2014: 274), the site offered links to categories such as 'Art Mods', 'Art Games' and 'Political Games', serving to illustrate both the emerging definitions and categorizations of game art and the different manifestations that it could take.

A number of artists have developed artworks that allow game spaces to intervene in the physical world. Antoinette J. Citizen created *Landscape* (2008), an installation that transformed a gallery room into a *Super Mario* level, complete with interactive boxes with questions marks and bricks that produced sounds. Berlin-based artist Aram Bartholl has created several works that bring videogame elements out into the real world, such as *WoW* (2006–2009), a performance work in which participants' names are cut out of green cardboard and made to hover above their heads as they walk around akin to avatars in *World of Warcraft* (2004) (Figure 7.5). Bartholl is one of a growing cadre of artists whose work seeks to blur online and offline cultures, imagery and practices.

As Bartholl and Citizen's creations suggest, contemporary art games are not always digital but deploy installation practices, some of which take place in gallery settings. For example, Brenda Brathwaite's *Train* (2009) – an art board game about the holocaust – has generated worldwide acclaim, and the fortune-telling games of Hugh Davies, *I-Ouija* (2015) and *Omikuji* (2016), recall the ancient and religious past of game practices as a means of premonition.

While game art has increasingly fashioned its own exhibition contexts, these practices have also become more integrated into museum and gallery settings. Institutions once resistant to game art have begun to recognize the significance of game-like playfulness across a broad range of art practices. Writing in 2014, artist Katarzyna Zimna notes '[t]erms like "play," "playground," and "playful" have become part of

**Figure 7.5**  Aram Bartholl, *WoW* (2006–2009). Reproduced with permission of Aram Bartholl.

the modern art vocabulary' (2014: 2). These terms became deployed to demarcate works that are 'process-oriented, participatory or interactive, based on performance', often using 'art objects as props or environments' (Zimna, 2014: 2–3).

Further cementing this shift, art world heavyweights, such as Hito Steyerl and Harun Farocki, acknowledged the conceptual gravity of videogames in their work, largely through video essays that involved significant elements of machinima, such as Steyerl's *Factory of the Sun* installation (2015) and Farocki's *Serious Games I–IV* (2009–2010). Also working within the context of conventional art and gallery spaces, Japanese net artist Akihiko Taniguchi's racing game *ARTSPEED* (2020) is a remix rendering of conceptual artworks from Marcel Duchamp's *Fountain* to Umberto Boccioni's *L'homme en mouvement* as racing cars competing on a track (Figure 7.6). Mikhail Maksimov's *Moscow Modern Art Massacre* (2020) allows players to visit a fine art gallery and earn points by destroying the artworks. Both works allude to the competitive and often-ferocious atmosphere at the highest echelons of the art world elite.

As these examples illustrate, contemporary practitioners working at the intersection of art and videogames are challenging the norms, boundaries and cultures of both the art world and the games world alike. Robert Yang's games highlight the homoerotic tropes present in ostensibly hetero-normative games underscoring the queerness permeating game cultures. His shower simulator *Rinse and Repeat* (2015) and *Radiator 2* triptych (2016) destabilize videogame establishment norms and assumptions of masculine identity. Meanwhile, GameGirl Power, who has been making machinima of intensely muscular women on virtual steroids since 2013 – initially to demonstrate alternatives to mainstream portrayals of female characters – has discovered that her femdom muscle fetish figures have found an unexpected cult appeal online (see Figure 7.7).

Increasingly, artists working with games no longer identify as game artists or think of their output as 'game art' or 'art games'. Games have been absorbed as media that

**Figure 7.6**  Akihiko Taniguchi, *ARTSPEED* (2020). Reproduced with permission of Akihiko Taniguchi.

**Figure 7.7**   GameGirl Power, *Luna* (2017). Reproduced with permission of GameGirl Power.

artists deploy as they address concerns about both contemporary politics and the cultural effects of games. To make sense of this distinction, in the final section, we provide a more detailed analysis of the practices of two significant artists in the field.

## Cory Arcangel and Lu Yang

Cory Arcangel and Lu Yang are among a contemporary milieu of visual artists using the currency of games as part of collective global memory and cultural practice. Both artists tap into the nostalgia held by a growing demography of curators and buyers, but do so in different ways, appealing to different generations of game players. Cory Arcangel created touchstone game art works in the early 2000s reflecting that era of practice, while Lu Yang has become recognized for her work throughout the mid-to-late 2010s.

Cory Arcangel is best known for his interventions that remove all interactive elements from early Nintendo cartridge-games, including *Super Mario Clouds* (2002) (Figure 7.8 and 7.9) and *Tetris Screwed* (2004), a *Tetris*-styled game modified to prolong the movement of falling blocks over many hours. Arcangel admits to favouring older games as the software and hardware is easier to hack and modify than their contemporary counterparts.

Studying composition and electronic music at the Oberlin College Conservatory of Music, Arcangel's passion for everyday popular media and sound is clear. From *Super Mario Clouds* to his *Self-Playing* series (including *Self Playing Sony Playstation 1 Bowling* [2008] and *Various Self Playing Bowling Games* [2011]), Arcangel transforms iconic game moments into mundane signs that comment on the meditative, abstract

**Figure 7.8** Cory Arcangel, *Super Mario Clouds*, game cartridge (2002). Reproduced with permission of Arcangel Studios.

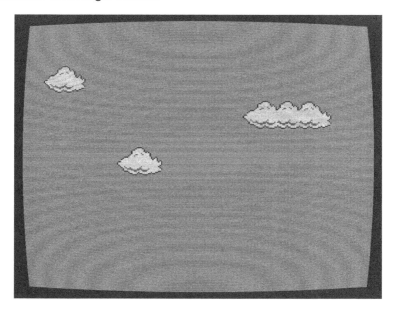

**Figure 7.9** Cory Arcangel, *Super Mario Clouds*, screen image (2002). Reproduced with permission of Arcangel Studios.

and prosaic elements of games. For associate curator at MoCA Ruba Katrib, Arcangel's work references avant-garde practices which have often sought to problematize technology (Katrib, 2011). Specifically, Arcangel's *Structural Film* (2007) draws heavily from Nam June Paik's *Zen for Film* (1962–1964). Beyond the explicit attempt to locate his art within an avant-garde tradition of critical play, however, the 'revolutionary' aspects of Arcangel's practice are questionable, especially when taken out of the rarefied context of the visual arts and placed into the realm of machinima.

Arcangel's interest in game art goes beyond game engine textures; it also involves the way in which games are packaged. Interlaced between videos that deploy machinima and YouTube techniques, one can find various 'tributes' to games and older media, such as cassette tapes. Here we see that the growing acceleration of technological obsolescence driving much of today's lifestyle cultures leaves in its wake a history of cultural artefacts (Wilson & Jacobs, 2009). In Arcangel's *Masters* (2011), the audience could not only touch the game but also 'participate' in its play. After a few attempts at hitting the virtual ball, however, one realizes that the game is continuing on its own path regardless of player actions. As Paul describes:

> In Arcangel's *Masters* (2011) … viewers can play an interactive golf game in its regular setup by putting a golf ball but their actions will not lead to a corresponding result in the virtual world. No matter how players hit the ball, it will never end up in the hole. As in *Various Self Playing Bowling Games*, Arcangel humorously employs the failure of game play to highlight a subtle point about the technology of the game. In this case, Arcangel's intervention questions the relationship between the actions of a human body in sports and their extension into a virtual environment, playfully commenting on the nature of 'simulating' a physical activity in the virtual world of a game. Golf itself is a simulation of a simulation, a highly stylized reproduction in which people engage in the imitation of a chase (after a ball) in an artificial landscape. For Arcangel, simulation is a key element of our world and our obsession with highly manufactured renditions of reality. (Paul, 2011: 6–7)

*Masters* may be viewed as an analogy of Arcangel's practice in terms of what it contributes to art games, as it simulates interactivity as part of a fake performance. *Masters* also fuses machinima with game genres, confusing and infusing the limits of where games end and machinima begins; what appears like an interactive golf game is actually machinima. While the work is a form of interactive art, inviting the viewer to physically engage with the game, the art-as-game is itself ironically non-responsive; the magic circle of the game becomes an audience watching other people as they 'fail' to interact. Here we see an example of machinima as live performance, in which the work is less about 'watching' the screen but, rather, about watching others engaging with a game that is simultaneously not a game in the physical space of the gallery.

Bodily engagement and perception also occupy the work of Shanghai-based artist Lu Yang, but in an altogether different register. Lu Yang creates sculptures, installations, videogames and digital art to forge new intersections between biotechnology, spirituality and contemporary digital cultures. Embracing a range of new technologies, spanning 3D-animated films, holograms, neon, VR installations and bio art, Lu Yang explores the fluidity of gender representation through 3D animated works inspired by Japanese *manga* (comics) and gaming subcultures. With a fascination of the human body and neurology, and keen interest in science, religion and popular culture, Lu's work explores profound questions of consciousness and being through vibrant and chaotic games, music, animations and other popular media forms.

Lu graduated from the China Academy of Art in Hangzhou, in the new media department led by Zhang Peili, a renowned pioneering Chinese video artist. While often associated with a lineage of Chinese game artists such as Cao Fei and Feng Mengbo, Lu's work is deeply influenced by the Japanese videogame and *manga* fandom subcultures of Otaku. Her aesthetic inspirations and explorations of spirituality evidence pan-Asian elements drawing from religious traditions across India, Japan, Tibet, Indonesia, Malaysia and China. The work draws together many conceptual and material threads defying easy categorization.

Lu Yang embraces technologies and practices through frequent collaborations with performers, designers, experimental composers, robot companies and pop idols, who bring their own areas of expertise. In her scale of production, and as with the videogame franchises, *manga* and anime universes upon which she draws, there is a world-building aspect to Lu's work, which offers rich universes of protagonists, religious deities, complex architectures, soundscapes and dance routines.

A key example is Lu's *The Great Adventure of Material World* (2018; Figure 7.10), a videogame artwork combining all the protagonists from past works into a playable universe explorable by players. Once a player enters the videogame, they transform into knights in the Material World and explore the Universe, absorb energy, are destroyed and achieve rebirth, fighting emotions, desires and, eventually, themselves. The multidisciplinary nature of Lu's practice reflects broader movements in

**Figure 7.10** Lu Yang, *The Great Adventure of Material World* (2018). Reproduced with permission of Lu Yang.

contemporary culture, not least games, away from siloed and binary modes of thinking and operating, and towards more fluid practices and identities.

Both Arcangel and Lu have been described and classified as practitioners of 'post-internet art'. The field of post-internet art overlaps with the 'New Aesthetic', a term used to describe practices in which the visual language of digital technology and the internet are expressed in the physical world (Bridle, 2011). Yet both artists resist being pigeonholed into ostensible movements. For his part, Arcangel eschews the term post-internet, describing his practice as 'Internet aware' (Quaranta, 2014). Lu states 'I am not a new media artist, nor a post-internet one, I don't even understand what "post-internet" means. I am many things' (Lu, quoted in Cerini, 2018). While often labelled as a female or Chinese artist, Lu rejects such categorizations. In interviews she has claimed that she doesn't identify as Chinese, and feels more affinity with her online identity than her national one. As Lu notes:

> I like to say I live on the Internet … because it's the only place I feel unburdened from social expectations. When I chat to people on [Chinese micro-blogging site] Weibo or other platforms, I don't have to specify whether I am a man or a woman, or what country I am from. I can be anyone I want. (Lu, quoted in Cerini, 2018: n.p.)

There is more than the medium of games that connects the work of Lu and Arcangel, as both artists embrace a variety of techniques and practices. While both reflect the growing appeal of games in their work, they each also recognize that games comprise one of the many facets intertwined within the complex assemblage of contemporary popular culture, which as artists they acknowledge and embrace.

## Conclusion

This chapter has presented and explored the possibilities of videogames as an art medium, investigating how they have been deployed by a range of artists and their status as a new cultural form. Through an exploration of game art practices with a focus on art modding, machinima, performance, installation and place-based interventions, we have noted how game art more broadly began to manifest in museum and gallery exhibitions, in addition to becoming established in games industry settings and post-internet art.

Concluding the chapter, we reviewed work by two well-known artists who utilize game material, content and media – Lu Yang and Cory Arcangel – illustrating how both seek to avoid prescribed definitions of their creative practice. At the heart of these deliberations is a question that is touched on in this chapter and crystallizes in the next: *what are the purposes of games and how are they manifested across a range of cultural settings?* As cultural forms and creative tools, the medium of games offer potent conceptual, formal and experiential affordances – but to what end?

## Further Reading

Bittanti, M., & Quaranta, D. (Eds.) (2009). *Gamescenes: Art in the Age of Videogames.* Monza: Johan & Levi Editore.

Flanagan, M. (2016). Game Art. In G. Raiford & H. Lowood (Eds.), *Debugging Game History: A Critical Lexicon* (pp. 151–158). Cambridge, MA: The MIT Press.

Sharp, J. (2015). *Works of Game: On the Aesthetics of Games and Art.* Cambridge, MA: The MIT Press.

Tavinor, G. (2009). *The Art of Videogames.* Oxford: Wiley-Blackwell.

Zimna, K. (2014). *Time to Play: Action and Interaction in Contemporary Art.* New York: I. B. Tauris.

# 8

# Serious Games and Games for Change

To what extent are serious games 'playful'? Do they qualify as 'games' if their primary purpose is functional or instructional? Or do games always involve an element of learning?

What is meant by 'critical play'? How does one 'play critically'?

What is the potential for games to activate change and social transformation? Can you think of any instances where games have changed your attitude or your perspective on the world?

How is the process of game design integral to creating games for change?

Can games help make a better world?

Games allow people to take risks they can't take in the real world. They provide playful, safe spaces for collaboration and creative problem solving. They involve constant iteration and negotiation. They are social, creative and innovative. It is for this reason and more that there has been a rise in **serious game** movements such as *games for change*, which deploy game design for social causes, and **game jams**, which utilize large interdisciplinary non-gamer groups to come together and create games to solve a health or social problem.

Serious games encompass many areas, including education, health care, art, politics, cultural heritage, military and emergency management. They focus on games as more than just entertainment; instead, they become a tool for alternative learning, collaboration and storytelling. There are many sub-genres of serious games, such as games for change (G4C) and urban games. In this chapter we focus on outlining serious games and then discuss examples of G4C which could easily be adapted into a classroom context.

Many fields, such as health care, are attracted to serious games because they allow alternative methods and pathways for knowledge exchange and implementation. As Simon Egenfeldt-Nielsen (2005) argues, serious games keep people 'engaged' and 'motivated' and embed learning through experience and action. He argues that serious games link training to fun and learning – i.e. edutainment (entertaining education). Advocates of serious games argue that they provide deep learnings that can be transferred into real-world contexts (Ritterfeld et al., 2009).

The games for social change movement, spearheaded by the likes of Colleen Macklin and Frank Lantz, often takes the forms of public, urban games (or 'big' games) that bring people's attention to key problems that they seek to address. Macklin's *Budgetball* (2009), for example, sought to use big games in university contexts to focus on issues relating to finance and power by pairing up students (who pay hundreds of thousands of dollars for a university degree) with staff working in university finance. Through play and collaboration, they were able to explore ideas and engage in conversations they couldn't have in real life.

In this chapter we reflect on the role of play and games for learning and engagement. We then explore some of the literature around serious games across game jams and G4C. Underscored by the movement towards design for social innovation and fields of critical and transformative design, we explore how G4C techniques such as game jams are being used for social good and wellbeing. We then run through several examples of serious games sub-genres, including a serious game for ecological concerns in a primary school context, and a socially-engaged art exhibition that deployed play and games for social innovation workshops.

## Serious Games

> Using games to explore complex ideas is a relatively new phenomenon, but this is not because games are not necessarily the right medium, or because play cannot be complex. There is simply not a great mass of games used in this way yet. One of the things that is attractive about games and play is the sense they offer for encountering something special – games may provide a framework for a new system of thinking, or offer glimpses of divergent logic. Play, both in an open sense and within the structure of a game, can serve as a lens for creating something beautiful. In other words, games are systems for imagining what is possible. Games and play environments are particularly useful frameworks for structuring systemic and conceptual concerns due to their multifaceted and dynamic, rule-based nature. (Flanagan, 2009a: 52)

Djaouti, Alvarez, Jessel and Rampnoux (2011) argue that while serious games might sound like an oxymoron (i.e. games are meant to be *fun* and thus the opposite of *serious*), they allow for different forms of learning, engagement and training that are often far more meaningful and compelling than conventional literacy formats. This type of thinking is reflected in the work of many literacy scholars, such as James Paul Gee (2005), who argues that videogames can help us to innovate in literacy and learning contexts and methods.

According to David Crookall (2010), the debates around serious games have plagued the history of videogames and can be traced back to Clark Abt's *Serious Games* (1970), in which he argued for the power of games to improve educational practices. It was Ben Sawyer (2007) who popularized the term with The Serious Games Initiative. Crookall prefers the term 'computerized simulation/game for training or learning ... and also because a learning game is indeed serious, almost by definition, and so does not in itself really need the epithet' (2010: 905). He argues that:

> Some say that *serious* is not serious and gives an unserious connotation to the very serious work of simulation/gaming. Others, often doing the hard (serious) spade-work, put forward the argument that *serious* makes games seem less frivolous to funding agencies and to conservative (or even forward-looking) educational bodies that want to be seen as experts in the serious, and increasingly competitive, business of teaching and research. The more enlightened bodies now see serious games as a means of leveraging greater competitiveness. (Crookall, 2010: 905)

Crookall's point is clear: games have always involved learning and literacy and so the 'serious' addition seems to suggest otherwise. This is in part because of the way competitiveness can be seen to counter diverse forms of literacy – only some people learn through competition and others see it as distracting. It does highlight the unevenness of education around the digital, much of which has been explored and addressed by Digital Media Learning (DML) scholars Mizuko Ito, Katie Salen Tekinbaş and Henry Jenkins.

Often there can be confusion between serious games and gamification as both are deployed for learning strategies in industry and real-world contexts. Serious games are designed not for entertainment (although they can be entertaining, as in edutainment), while gamification deploys game-like mechanics to incentivize players through leaderboards, badges and point systems to increase engagement. In this respect, serious games can deploy gamification strategies, as they coalesce education content and e-learning, serious purpose and serious fun, game techniques and storytelling.

One of the main areas of discontinuity is that serious games aim to focus on education and learning rather than entertainment as their primary objective. Moreover, while serious games focus on education (informal and formal), gamification is often used as part of commodification, i.e. the application of 'game-like' techniques for marketing or to attract consumers. Gamification seeks to leverage competition and achievement through point scores and badges, activities that are not necessarily for the enhancement of learning. Serious games, on the other hand, can be seen to reside at the intersection of learning, games and simulation through the deployment of techniques such as training exercises, edutainment and the simulation of real-world tasks and activities.

Serious games are considered actual games (rather than 'game-like' as in gamification). Some examples of serious games include flight simulators such as the *Microsoft Flight Simulator* (1982), and various works of the serious games research centre, Tiltfactor,[1] which has designed a series of games to tackle social change in society, including games such as Mary Flanagan's *LAYOFF* (2009b; Figure 8.1). *LAYOFF* sought to create empathy and understanding around human values through an examination of the 2009 financial crisis. As the *LAYOFF* press release notes:

> In the game, players play from the side of management needing to cut jobs, and match types of workers in groups in order to lay the workers off and increase workforce efficiency. During the game play, players eliminating many workers in a row find financiers and bankers taking the place of working class jobs. The financiers in this game cannot face layoffs. (Flanagan, 2009b: n.p.)

For Flanagan (2009a), games – both digital and material – have the power to transform social ideas, attitudes and behaviours. Deploying both digital and non-digital game design, Flanagan sees games as a way to create stories and pathways of discovery that can impact people and communities in powerful ways. In her article, 'Creating critical play', Flanagan (2010) describes the large-scale collaborative urban game, massively multiplayer *SOBA*. Initially played in the Queens area of New York City (and then adapted to other contexts, such as Shanghai), the team-based game

**Figure 8.1** *LAYOFF* (2009b). Reproduced with permission of Mary Flanagan.

sought to link players as collaborators in terms of the way that neighbourhoods are traversed. Through food sharing and making, it brought people together in playful ways that modified their habitudes and routines. For Flanagan, both the game play and design focused on social dimensions and sedimented values to elicit change. As she notes:

> The design allowed for a variety of play strategies: collaboration for those who may not be competitive, or specialization for those who excel at particular kinds of challenges. Play was combined with the opportunities for engagement to allow for game players to mix and interact with residents in meaningful ways, while challenging preconceptions of race and language. Rather than simply using these neighborhoods as host sites in which the game takes place, we have made these communities central to the focus of SOBA, with longer interactions and storytelling exchanges with community members as the central goal of the project. (Flanagan, 2010: 51)

As Flanagan argues, games play a powerful role in helping us think through complex issues in empathic and creative ways. She identifies serious games sub-genres such as the 'activist game', in which game scholars or researchers use the creative dimensions of games to change and intervene in our conversations about society and culture.

Within game design, some developers and designers clearly define their games as 'activist' rather than 'serious'. This is partly due to the ways serious games have been deployed by the military and big business, which might be considered politically problematic. Activist games tackle social issues within and around poverty (*Ayiti*, Global Kids and Game Lab), the fast food industry (*McDonald's game*, Molleindustria) and terrorism (*September 12th*, Gonzalo Frasca), to name a few. For instance, Frasca's *September 12th* conveyed the pointlessness of the 'war on terror' in a cartoonish game set in a Middle-Eastern village; through violent actions, bombing and shooting players are unable to win the game. The game's intention is to promote debate, and although initially controversial, is now used in educational contexts as a tool to discuss terrorism. The emergence of activist games has seen a burgeoning in games for social change, which converge education with political issues to provide new insights into social problems. Flanagan claims that in this way, serious games demonstrate the power of games and play when they effectively integrate design strategies and frameworks with a view to implementing social innovation.

## Play for Social Innovation

Social innovation is 'a novel solution to a social problem that is more effective, efficient, sustainable ... and for which the value created accrues primarily to society as a whole rather than private individuals' (Hill and Vaughan, 2017: 9; see also Preskill & Beer, 2012: 2). Social innovation is about iteration, adaptation and testing, with the understanding that the social is inherently messy and uncertain. As a field, it has become increasingly deployed within games to find alternative ways for problem-solving social issues.

Play, too, can be understood as its own form of social innovation. As design practice takes on more sophistication around social innovation techniques, we see new forms of game and play methods for social change. With digital games becoming more quotidian, the role of game and play literacy comes to the forefront (Giddings, 2014). Starting with play can often be provocative, an invitation to reconfigure techniques and develop alternative ways of achieving knowledge translation. Play can be a powerful tool for probing personal, cultural and social attitudes and practices. As an interdisciplinary practice that has multiple histories in various disciplines, play can provide great insight into how to do translatable research differently. And yet, understanding the power of play as a core part of the researcher's toolkit for engaging with publics and the transmission of knowledge is yet to be fully understood and embraced.

In the exhausted discussions about innovation being driven by a mainly STEM (science, technology, engineering and mathematics) agenda, play can provide new insights, methods and critical lenses for performing within and through research. Across the sciences and humanities, researchers often use various kinds of formal and informal types of play to redesign their methods in innovative ways (Lury & Wakeford, 2012; Hjorth et al., 2016). For example, in *Inventive Methods: The Happening of the Social*, various social science scholars discuss the application of creative practice and play to help solve a range of social issues (Lury & Wakeford, 2012). Bringing play to a notion of transmission (i.e. conveying complex ideas and new ways of doing things) is important, as play can take multiple roles as a mode of inquiry and praxis (Hjorth & Byrne, 2016), or as an interdisciplinary and poetic 'cultural probe' (Gaver et al., 1999) that allows different ways to think through a problem or issue. Play is also culturally and socially specific (Sutton-Smith, 1997), and thus bringing play to the idea of transmission requires us to think through political and contextual ways of knowing.

As we have highlighted in this book through notions such as Raessens's ludification of culture, play has recently had a renaissance. Once conflated with a child's activity (Piaget, 1999), educational tool (Vygotsky, 1978) or gameplay, it has over the last decade come to the attention of many researchers across disciplines such as art, new media and game studies (Dovey & Kennedy, 2006; Giddings, 2014; Sicart, 2014). And yet, play scholarship has a long and rich history (Huizinga, 1938 [1955]; Caillois, 2001 [1961]) that was rekindled through the work of Salen and Zimmerman (2003). As games scholar Sicart (2014) observed in his analysis of contemporary practices across design, games, architecture and art, the playful has become a pivotal attitude in contemporary life.

Across the disciplines, then, play can be understood as a creative, social, cultural and political concept and mode of inquiry and practice. As mentioned in Chapter 7, artists throughout history have deployed various modes of 'playing critically' to undermine conventions (Flanagan, 2009a). As Thomas Malaby observes, anthropology and play has seen ethnography emerge as a dominant mode for understanding game cultures in context (Malaby, 2007; Taylor, 2009). More recently, games such as *Minecraft* have become key vehicles for leveraging play through contemporary media literacy workshops (Hooper & de Byl, 2014; Hill, 2015; Ito et al., 2018). Indeed, the rise of play workshops to codesign creatively for social innovation has seen play and socially engaged art practices converge. As Grant Kester (2011: 68) suggests, there is a need to canvas techniques, tools and frameworks for art practice that reimagine the socially-engaged dimensions beyond just the *aesthetic* playfield but to actually change behaviours and motivations. Here the playful becomes a key feature in not only art practice but also contemporary media cultures more generally.

For Jungnickel and Hjorth (2014), the role of transmission and knowledge exchange is about experimentation and exploration in and around practice. Academics need new and creative modalities for knowledge transmission that move beyond books and words, to instead create and curate interventions in people's lives. One of the obvious vehicles for transmission is context – for example, moving research projects outside the limitations of the gallery and into the messy contingency of urban public spaces. As discussed in Chapters 7 and 9, this model emerged in 20th-century art through movements such as Situationist International (SI) and urban games that sought to intervene in everyday urban environments (de Souza e Silva & Hjorth, 2009). Here, the tactical role of play as a mode of critical inquiry has been pivotal. We will continue this discussion in Chapter 9 in relation to pervasive gaming.

'Game jams' and 'games for change' bring game design to the space of the social. They highlight the role of play to transform and innovate. Games have the power to create change in a variety of ways, affording safe spaces to test ideas, developing empathy through role play and connecting communities in playful, innovative and creative ways. In particular, games can nurture a sense of belonging, connecting us to cultural, social and linguistic ways of being in the world. Games for change designers John Sharp and Colleen Macklin (2019) argue that games fundamentally *change the way we see the world*. In this way, games are one of the most progressive methods for social innovation. This transformative role has taken a few directions, as we discuss below – in game jams, games for change and socially-engaged art play.

## Game Jams

Game jams began a decade ago in Scandinavia and the US, harnessed by the *Global Game Jam* (Fowler et al., 2013; Deen et al., 2014; Batchelor, 2017). They are collaborative and interdisciplinary, harnessing the research-through-design tradition. Just as games are increasingly being applied in contexts beyond entertainment, game jams also exhibit functions and ideas that differ from commercially driven game prototyping (Rouse, 2011; Scott & Ghinea, 2013). The imaginative potential of game jams has seen them become a focus for design researchers interested in the creative process (Turner & Thomas, 2013). Shin et al. (2012) review the potential of collaborative learning for game jam organizers in Japan and offer processes aimed at promoting such collaborative development. In a similar project, Goddard et al. (2014) identify participation in game jams as a constructive form of 'ludic craft' and have developed a set of guidelines to facilitate playful and gameful experiences that support design outcomes in research, education and industry settings. For many, the game jam concept has bloomed into a platform which disrupts norms, allowing for the rapid prototyping of new product ideas and disruptive innovations (Musil et al., 2010), a new way of thinking about game creation that draws on the collective and quotidian (Rouse, 2011). The codesign capacity of the game jam philosophy has spread across numerous disciplines, while in its native field of game development, it has become an important rite of passage (Turner & Thomas, 2013).

Game jams have also been increasingly deployed in health care and cultural awareness contexts (HHS, 2016). Recent examples include *The MeGa Health Jam*, a 48-hour jam that applies game technologies to challenges in the health care industry in Florida. In Europe, the game jam model has been adapted into a practice of co-creation in which patients, health workers, students and teachers participate in creating games for health (Garcia-Pañella, 2018). In the US, between 2013 and 2015 two game jams were launched to help spur the use of games to address public health challenges (HHS, 2016). In recent years, game jams have themselves become subjects of attention for their health impacts. Clinicians have analysed the stress and recovery levels of two Finnish game jam organizers to see how they dealt with the hectic weekend of game development (Bonner, 2016). More recently, game jams have been scrutinized for their association with 'crunch culture', unhealthy industry practices in which unrealistic deadlines come at the cost of employee safety and wellbeing (Kaser, 2018).

Jaffa (2016) suggests that while game jams may be valuable as tools for collaborative experimentation and growth, in their execution they often acclimatize newcomers to exploitative and predatory work practices, with participants expected to take on multiple roles in high-pressure scenarios. The games industry has long been accused of unsustainable, non-family friendly work practices. As Jaffa rightly claims, education and mentorship are not principal tenets of game jams. In defence of the game jam model, *Global Game Jam* executive director Steven Siegel admits similarities in appearance between game jams and crunch culture but argues that the two are fundamentally different. Siegel articulates game jams as 'challenge-by-choice', while 'crunch' is overtime enforced by a larger company: 'game jams are soul-giving, crunch time is soul-taking' (Gilbert, 2019: n.p.). Tackling concerns of unhealthy practices head on, *Global Game Jam* has taken steps to address these critiques. Specifically, in 2019 they engaged staff from CheckPoint, an organization that provides mental health support for the gaming community, to develop a ten-point strategy for self-care and mindfulness for the event.[2]

## Games for Change

Games for change is a movement and community of practice that is committed to deploying digital and non-digital games for social change. Communities of practice (CoP) are groups of people that have an ongoing relationship through a shared concern. In a professional sense, CoP are about sharing experiences for the learning and advancement of a particular field. In the context of G4C, it can be defined as both a philosophy of practice that focuses on social innovation and a non-profit organization which curates games that engage contemporary social issues in meaningful ways. This movement has many different streams and approaches. The organization G4C was founded in 2004 to empower:

> game creators and social innovators to drive real-world change using games and technology that help people to learn, improve their communities, and contribute to make the world a better place. We convene stakeholders through our annual G4C FESTIVAL and foster the exchange of ideas and resources through workshops and consulting projects. We inspire youth to explore civic issues and learn 21st-century and STEM skills through our STUDENT CHALLENGE and train educators to run game design classes on impact games. We incubate projects through our game design challenges and executive production expertise in coalition building. We act as an amplifier by curating games for change to the public through our games arcades and awards. (Games for Change, 2019: n.p., original emphasis)

The Games for Change group includes researchers, designers and thought leaders from a range of areas, such as design thinking (e.g. Duane Bray, IDEO), in addition to well-known game designers and thinkers, such as Jane McGonigal, Tracy Fullerton, James Paul Gee and Eric Zimmerman, to name a few. The G4C organization sees its remit to deploy the power of digital games and new media as 'effective tools to advance their cause and reach new audiences' (Games for Change, 2019: n.p.). Their projects encompass challenges, arcades, consulting and sector-building. While challenges tend to focus on educational contexts, sector-building focuses more on innovation in communities of practice around new media such as Virtual Reality (VR), Augmented Reality (AR), Extended Reality (XR) for Change (XR4C) and XR Brain Jam (for neuroscientists, social impact organizations and developers to explore possibilities in new media for education and health).

Many examples of games for change can be found, from digital appropriations of existing games like *Minecraft* to board games and physical games. An example of a digital G4C is the UN Habitat project that used *Minecraft* to help make transparent the urban planning process in developing countries such as Africa and Asia. The game, which is known in some circles as Digital 3D Lego, 'helped the project leaders create a visual representation of the field that could be easily understood by the neighborhood's residents' (Parker, 2014: n.p.). Entitled *Block by Block*, the game sought to highlight through the game space some of the challenges and realities that could not be explored in other contexts, e.g. alterative urban design solutions. Here the power of games to explore, innovate, play and take risks is highlighted.

Another example is the simulation game *PeaceMaker* (2005), which was designed to allow players to understand the Israeli–Palestinian conflict by asking them to make social, political and military decisions based on actual events. The power of games to create empathy, compassion and to engender change can be seen in the adaption of *Half the Sky: Turning Oppression into Opportunity for Women Worldwide* by Nicholas Kristof and Sheryl WuDunn (2009), which concerns translating issues related to sex trafficking and gender violence in Africa, India and Asia into a game. *Half the Sky Movement: The Game* was introduced on Facebook in 2013, giving players online tasks, such as collecting books for young girls in Kenya, that can translate into tangible results. For instance, collecting 250,000 in-game books unlocked a donation of real books for Room to Read, a non-profit organization focused on literacy and equality in developing countries. Players could also make donations to the game's non-profit partners. The game attracted 1.5 million players (Games for Change, 2014).

A key figure in the games for change movement has been Jane McGonigal, whose book *Reality Is Broken: Why Games Make Us Better and How they Can Change the World* (2011) argues that combining game design and positive psychology can enhance human happiness and motivation, by providing a sense of meaning and facilitating the development of community. McGonigal's own games include *World Without Oil* (2007), which sought to inspire social and collaborative solutions to fossil fuel use by imagining a post-oil future.

For Asi Burak, the president of the Games for Change organization, the future (and success) of serious gaming depends on two things: attracting the best designers and providing everyday players with the tools for social-impact games. He argues that '[g]aming is social, participatory and has learning at its core. … These are powerful things for social impact, and it makes sense for us to take full advantage of it' (Parker, 2014: n.p.). Indeed, games for change can provide many alternative solutions to social, economic and political problems by using the power of games for playful creativity and risk-taking. In the next section we explore several games for change approaches through workshops conducted in Australia and Japan (by Hjorth, Davies, Onicas and Leong; see Hjorth et al., 2018) as part of a project that sought to test and evaluate the role of games for social inclusion and innovation.

## Games for Change Workshops

The purpose of the games for change workshops was to engage different cohorts in a series of playful activities directed towards social change, and to reflect upon

**Figure 8.2** Iteration and codesign are two key features of the games for change workshops. Here coloured post-it notes are being used to give structure to group themes. Photo: Adelina Onicas.

play methods from game design as a way to enable participants to think differently about everyday experiences and attitudes. They explored the power of games to *innovate*, to *provoke*, to create *empathy* and to *change the way people see the world* (Figure 8.2). The workshops also provided an overview of how games and play can be used as an innovative form of storytelling, and invited discussion about what types of games we like to play and why, especially in terms of the meanings and feelings we experience.

In the workshops, groups were asked to reflect upon the difference between playing and making games. While playing games can help us to *think about thinking*, making games can help us to *think about how others think* (Sharp & Macklin, 2019). Participants were then asked to design a game in response to their current research projects. We deployed game techniques to get students to engage differently with the curriculum, whether that be the environment, sustainable development goals (SDGs), or other context-specific projects. For example, in the Japanese context, issues such as ageing populations and sustainability came to the forefront, while in Australia, concerns around climate change and environmental damage were highlighted (Figure 8.3).

## Ecology workshop

This project involved codesigning card games with primary school students to address real-world environmental problems. In the two-hour workshop with Grade 4 students (9–10 years old) in both Australia and Japan, participants learnt about the

**Figure 8.3** Images from the Ecology workshop. Photos: Hugh Davies.

process of game designing and what makes a 'good' game. They reflected on the key characteristics of game design:

1.  Rules (what you can and can't do in the game)
2.  Actions (what does the game ask you to do?)
3.  Goals (what is the aim of the game?)
4.  Objects (what are the things you need, e.g. dice?)
5.  Playspace (where do you play the game?)
6.  Players (what types of play, experiences and meanings does the game offer?)

The class was asked to reflect upon various types of ecosystem problems (e.g. plastic bags are bad for the environment) and *how they could solve the problem* (e.g. replace with recyclable paper bags). They then took these reflections and worked in small groups to collaborate and design a game. They looked at examples of how common board games like *Monopoly (Earthology)* and card games like *Uno (Go Eco)* could be transformed into environmental games.

Drawing from Macklin's notion of iteration and Flanagan's critical play game design cycle, which integrates designing for *values* (such as empowerment), *diverse play styles* and *subversion*, we asked groups to brainstorm and then delegate a member with a task that corresponded with their skills (i.e. drawing, writing, planning, making of artefacts). They worked together to design inspiring games that teach – through game play – players to be mindful of the environment (Figure 8.4). They then tested the game with feedback from other groups. Both *testing* and *iteration* were

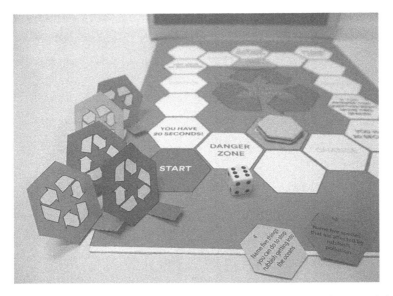

**Figure 8.4**  Example from the Ecology *primary* school workshop. Photo: Adelina Onicas.

explored as important parts of game designing. Each group then played each other's games to see what elements could be improved upon and then tweaked (or iterated) their designs after critical reflection.

## Socially-engaged art play: *The Social Play Toolkit*

With the rise of socially-engaged art practice, the role of play and games for social innovation has become part of the social innovation toolkit. Increasingly, artists use game design and play techniques as a series of methods, form of inquiry and cultural probe. In this section, we reflect upon a socially-engaged exhibition entitled *The Art of Play* (2016) that coalesced game and play techniques through an installation combining LEGO and *Minecraft* (Figure 8.5 and 8.6).

Audience members were invited to create their own 'encounter', i.e. play with the LEGO and make their own thing. They were then asked to photograph their creations and upload to Instagram using the hashtag #theartofplay. The encounters were then printed out and pinned onto the wall. Over the time of the exhibition the encounters filled the wall, transforming audience into player into artist.

Along with socially-engaged art play in the exhibition space, we also ran a series of workshops that sought to engage education groups in the codesign of their own social play toolkits. In particular, the workshops and toolkits asked participants to reflect on their digital play and how it connected to non-digital play, so as to better understand the diverse modalities of playfulness in everyday life. We set the

**Figure 8.5** *The Art of Play* participatory exhibition (2016). Photo: J. Forysth.

**Figure 8.6** Encounters from *The Art of Play* that then become the artwork on the wall. Photos: Adelina Onicas.

workshops up in three different contexts – the gallery, urban public space and class-room – to reflect on the various forms of performative spaces and play.

Over two years, as we explored different contexts for the social play workshops – public, private, formal and informal – the need for more work around coalescing these different 'worlds' became apparent. The development of *The Social Play Toolkit* – first developed for the Young and Well Cooperative Research Centre in 2017[3] and then later in 2018 for more general pedagogical contexts – sought to reconcile the different vocabularies and practices around conceptualizing play creatively in both mediated and physical worlds. In particular, we worked with schools to coalesce informal and formal methods for play in and across digital and non-digital contexts. The importance of reflecting upon the dimension of informal/formal and digital/non-digital elements would become amplified in our later research concerning COVID-19 home schooling.

In these workshops, we familiarized participants with urban and physical games such as *PacManhattan*[4] (where people dressed as *PacMan* and the in-game ghosts become 'avatars' for players geolocated elsewhere in New York and are chased around the city), flash mobbing and the massively multiplayer thumb-wrestling game (a thumb-wrestling exercise for groups). We introduced them to the New Arcade – also defined as the new 'indie scene' (Juul, 2014) – which seeks to highlight the importance of the body in game play. The New Arcade draws on the New Games Movement in terms of recalibrating the relationship between digital and non-digital forms of player embodiment.

Participants collaborated in small groups to redesign, test and play a digital game they had adapted into a physical corporeal game. This process involved a lot of translation work and critical thinking. In the workshops, the spaces (gallery, classroom, park) were transformed into game design incubators. These codesigned iterations became part of the *The Social Play Toolkit*.[5]

*The Social Play Toolkit* describes ways of codesigning with young people to connect formal and informal contexts and techniques for social play across digital and material worlds. The iterative process sought to engage with the importance of 'the social' that is crucial to understanding play. That is, playing is *social*. Building from Lury and Wakeford's *Inventive Methods* (2012), Marres, Guggenheim and Wilkie (2018) note that 'inventing the social' requires innovative methods that engage with the complexity of the social to develop impactful processes. For Marres (2017), drawing from Science and Technology Studies (STS), such experiments are an interdisciplinary way to reframe settings and participation.

**Figure 8.7** Students transform exhibition gallery space into a playful encounter. Photo: Larissa Hjorth.

**Figure 8.8** Primary school children codesigning a digital game for material, social play. Photo: Larissa Hjorth.

By implementing this interdisciplinary and creative approach through collaborative experimentation, our workshops sought to consider and activate different modes of play enacted in formal and informal, public and private spaces – what we call social play. Our activities served as a series of user-led experiments into how play can inform contemporary literacies and move across diverse spaces – galleries, public spaces and classrooms (Figure 8.7 and 8.8). Through the process, the research question became: how can we design tools that stimulate alternative models of knowledge transmission and foster diverse modalities of play across different spatial contexts?

Play, on numerous levels, became crucial in this reconfiguration, and integral to the process of transforming conventional research into translatable outcomes. Participants took home their designed board games and were encouraged to continue iterating, and *The Social Play Toolkit* was given to the schools for other teachers to use in class (Figure 8.9). Thus, through the workshop technique we effectively codesigned a toolkit that served as a cultural probe for interrogating how play is defined, performed and elicited. The aim was to provide an open access resource for schools to develop social play activities in the classroom as well as offer a broader academic framework that speaks to the importance of games and play in education settings.

What became apparent was that in gallery environments the workshops often tested the etiquette of the space through 'noisy' behaviour, while in public spaces, boundaries between the students and the public were frequently challenged, which transformed the ways in which the play was enacted. In classrooms, there was a constant negotiation of the formal and informal literacies associated with play. Each space framed the informal and formal dimensions of social play in different ways, which impacted on participants' reflections and the design of the games.

In classrooms, we could access tools and materials to make board games, while in public spaces, the students had to design quick ephemeral games *in situ* and adapt to a dynamic environment populated with 'familiar strangers'.

**Figure 8.9** *The Social Play* Project.

**Figure 8.10** Examples from the Ecology Games for Change workshop. Photo: Hugh Davies.

Moreover, students often felt self-conscious performing play in the gallery and in public places, but this was counteracted once the play became a group activity.

In the school contexts, children were more likely to view social play in a different light, as informal play often happens in the schoolyard, while 'educational' play is more commonly situated in the classroom. Students also enjoyed experimenting with the non-digital dimensions of play and the challenge of adapting these aspects into a digital game. Here, the differences between inside and outside forms of play became central. What was social play in the classroom? And how could social play be used to coalesce digital and non-digital spaces?

In our various game workshops across numerous contexts we sought to explore the ways in which students could be empowered through game design to confront an issue that was important to them. For some, that involved taking a digital game like *Crossy Roads* and making it into a physical game about people, control and play. For others in the classroom setting, it was about designing ecological games that borrowed from classic board games like *Monopoly* and got players to think about their consumption in terms of environmental damage (Figure 8.10 and 8.11). Many of the games borrowed from different tropes of activist games, game jams and games

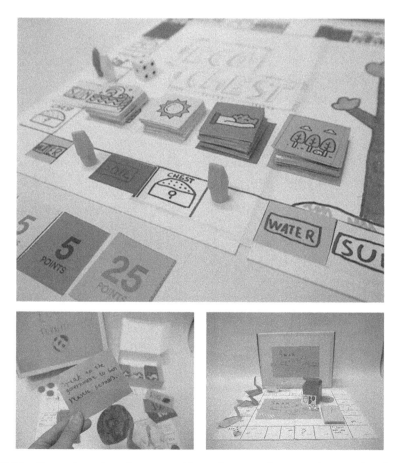

**Figure 8.11**  Examples of environmental board games from a primary school workshop. Photos: Hugh Davies.

for change. They moved across digital, material and social worlds in creative and often unexpected ways, demonstrating the power of games and critical play design for social innovation and inventive thinking.

## Conclusion

In this chapter we have explored some of the ways in which serious games can be deployed as playful interventions in social, political and health contexts, but also the power of play to activate creativity and innovation, and formal and informal forms of literacy, across digital and non-digital worlds. We began the chapter by reflecting on the role of play for social innovation before turning to discussions around game jams and games for change. We then outlined some examples of serious games at the intersection of socially-engaged art projects and community workshops – in primary schools, gallery spaces and communities. In the next chapter we continue expanding on the capacity of games for change by exploring the role of pervasive games. As we show, pervasive games have played a key role in the reconfiguration of urban environments as places for play.

## Further Reading

Dörner, R., Göbel, S., Effelsberg, W., & Wiemeyer, J. (2016). *Serious Games: Foundations, Concepts, Practice*. New York: Springer.

Flanagan, M. (2013). *Critical Play: Radical Game Design*. Cambridge, MA: The MIT Press.

Flanagan, M., & Nissenbaum, H. (2016). *Values at Play in Digital Games*. Cambridge, MA: The MIT Press.

Gray, K. L., & Leonard, D. J. (2018). *Woke Gaming: Digital Challenges to Oppression and Social Injustice*. Seattle, WA: University of Washington Press.

McGonigal, J. (2015). *Reality Is Broken: Why Games Make Us Better and How They Can Change the World*. Cambridge, MA: The MIT Press.

## Notes

1   https://tiltfactor.org/games/
2   See https://globalgamejam.org/news/looking-after-your-mental-health-ggj
3   See https://www.vichealth.vic.gov.au/programs-and-projects/young-and-well-cooperative-research-centre
4   www.pacmanhattan.com/
5   https://dcp-ecp.com/projects/social-play-tool-kit

# 9
# Pervasive Games and Urban Play

Pervasive games and forms of play have existed for many decades and arguably centuries – what has brought them to wide attention in the past two decades?

What defines the first and second generations of pervasive games?

What was the underlying ethos of the New Games Movement?

Describe some of the positive aspects of reimagining cities as playscapes. Can you think of any negative implications?

**Pervasive games** are playful experiences that go beyond the traditional confines of play. They take place in the physically embodied world. However, unlike most physical games played within defined borders, such as fields, courts, boards, and during specific timeframes, such as bouts, matches and rounds, pervasive games deliberately defy imposed limits, taking everyday reality as their temporal and spatial domain. This expansion and blurring of the boundaries of game space creates an ambiguity between in-game world and out-of-game world that, in turn, alters the players' perception of place – both during and potentially after the game (Davies, 2007). To achieve this, pervasive games often involve the use of locative technologies and mobile devices, and the layering of technology and real-world locations. The result is a multidimensional and expanded field of play.

The term 'pervasive game' does not describe a discrete or clearly defined game type but is instead an amorphous catch-all beneath which a myriad of game types can be found. Over the past two decades, many sub-genres of pervasive gaming have emerged, including role-playing games (RPG) and **Live Action Role Play** (LARP), both involving game worlds being played out in physical contexts. Other interrelated versions of pervasive games included Location-Based Games (Björk et al., 2001), Alternate Reality Games (Szulborski, 2005), Big Games (Lantz, 2006), Ubiquitous Games (McGonigal, 2006), Mobile Games (Rodriguez, 2006), Urban Games (de Souza e Silva & Hjorth, 2009), Mixed Reality Games (Crabtree et al., 2004) and Transmedia Games (Dena, 2009) (see Figure 9.1). While encompassing distinct differences, all of these diverse game types are united by their focus on urban play within physical geographies and reimagining the use of public space.

In their survey of the field of pervasive games, Kasapakis and Gavalas (2015) note a generational shift in technologies, development and understanding of pervasive games over the past two decades. This chapter approaches the field by dividing its recent history into two separate generations (see Table 9.1). The first generation centres on the emergence of pervasive games around the turn of the millennium. These games were typified by radically disruptive and edgy immersive experiences that sought to blur reality and fiction. This period was characterized by experimentation in new game types emerging across a range of arts and entertainment contexts.

The second generation of pervasive games from the 2010s onwards brought a more measured and sophisticated tone to the genre. Fields like civic engagement, health promotion and education began to deploy pervasive games to explore spatial and social dimensions of learning. This period also saw an institutionalization of

**Figure 9.1** Ecology of first-generation pervasive games. Image: Hugh Davies.

pervasive games, not just by large companies such as Niantic with their augmented reality (AR) games *Ingress* (2013) and *Pokémon GO* (2016), but also by local government and city council initiatives as part of **Smart City** programs that saw opportunities in coalescing play with quotidian ubiquitous computing. As we shall discuss, the rise of smartphones and Smart Cities – i.e. urban areas that integrate electronic, networked and sensing technologies – has seen a growth in the possibilities of pervasive games as part of mainstream culture. The close link between mobile media and play, in terms of casual, augmented reality and location-aware games, will in turn be the particular focus of the final part of the book (Mobilities).

We begin this chapter by contextualizing pervasive and urban games in terms of their shared philosophical and political histories. Outlining the rise of pervasive games in terms of key areas of influence, this chapter then investigates two eras: first generation (2000–2010) and second generation (2010–2020). We revisit the practices of initiatives such as the New Games Movement, which sought to highlight the ways in which spaces are socially and culturally constructed, questioning inequality and activating attitudinal and behavioural change in everyday life. We also explore examples of pervasive games to flesh out the ways in which play can rescript a sense of place and emplacement across digital and physical worlds.

## Beginnings

From the outset, an enduring concern driving the development of pervasive games globally has been the reimagining of the city as a location of public play. Such ideas draw from a long history of theory and practice around urban studies before the appearance of pervasive games. Philosophies of urban wayfaring were initiated by the French essayist and painter Charles Baudelaire (1821–1867) and cultural critic Walter Benjamin (1892–1940). Both figures were instrumental in exploring how space and identity were being transformed in and through the modern city. Inventions such as boulevards (first pioneered by Baron Hausmann in Paris from 1853–1870) saw the city transformed into a spectacle, as streets were widened to allow for new ways of moving, seeing and experiencing the urban environment.

Understanding pervasive games – especially the role of play to transform spaces and places – draws from several movements especially around 1960, when cities such as Paris became sites for public protesting against wars (i.e. in Vietnam and Algeria) and streets were transformed into spaces for transgression, expression and experimentation. The French Situationist International (SI), a group of social revolutionaries comprised of avant-garde artists, intellectuals and political theorists, were key in these transgressive ways of exploring the city. In particular, the SI developed concepts such as *dérive* (drifting) to reimagine new ways of traversing the city that challenged traditional modes of urban movement (de Souza e Silva & Hjorth, 2009).

According to SI leader Guy Débord, *dérive* is a 'technique of rapid passage through varied ambiences', involving 'playful-constructive behavior and awareness of psychogeographical effects' (Knabb, 1981: 50–54). Psychogeography sought to uncover the emotional, sensorial and psychological resonances of the geographic environment. Débord remains a key figure in the prehistories of pervasive games for his reimagining of the limits of play as part of everyday life.

So too, as discussed in Chapter 8 and detailed in the next section, the New Games Movement in the United States also sought to transgress the normative functions of public spaces and turn them into sites for the promotion of social justice. Both movements toyed with the concept of spaces as socially constructed – a notion deeply explored in the work of Henri Lefebvre (1991 [1974]). Central to Lefebvre's work was the idea that urban space was much more than just the physical and geographic, but rather an interconnected network of perceived, conceived and lived spaces. These notions of space recall the earlier figure of the **flâneur**, coined by Baudelaire and Benjamin. Coming to symbolize both bourgeoisie society and the new emerging 20th-century capitalism, the *flâneur* was an allegorical male who wandered and consumed the city with a distracted gaze, playing the part of both the distanced critic and immersed spectator (de Souza e Silva & Hjorth, 2009). For Boutin (2012), the *flâneur*'s mythic existence has become a catalyst for artistic reflection that (re)produces and reinvents the city through ambulatory practice, as both Michel de Certeau (1984) and Henri Lefebvre (1991 [1974]) had theorized. De Certeau's important work explored the significance of everyday life in how we understand the world, especially the repetition of practice and the tensions around institutional frameworks he called 'strategies' and pedestrian 'tactics'. This technique can be witnessed in the aforementioned wandering through city spaces called the *dérive*.

The rise of the internet and mobile devices brought about a shift in the focus of urban studies and various perspectives on the constructedness of urban spaces. Throughout the 1990s, wireless technologies became ubiquitously embedded into cityscapes, making digital accessibility pervasive and normalized. Examining how the rise of internet-enabled networked mobile devices creates new and dynamic relationships between physical and digital spaces, de Souza e Silva deploys the term 'hybrid spaces' to describe 'mobile spaces, created by the constant movement of users who carry portable devices continuously connected to the Internet and to other users' (2006: 262). Within the Latin American context, de Souza e Silva finds the strongest examples of this blurring between the physical and the digital in mobile and locative games such as *Alien Revolt* (2005) (see Chapters 10 and 11 for a more detailed discussion of locative and mobile games).

For de Souza e Silva and Hjorth (2009), movements such as those of the SI are re-enacted through contemporary everyday movements between online and offline spaces. This quotidian movement can be interpreted through the concept of digital wayfaring (Hjorth & Pink, 2014), an experience that is further complicated within mobile location-based pervasive games. Digital wayfaring acknowledges that the digital is imbricated in our social and material worlds as we move through, and make sense of, the world. Within the domain of play, de Souza e Silva and Hjorth characterize the *flâneur* and its contemporary manifestation in Robert Luke's notion of the 'phoneur' as the 'ludic character *par excellence*' (de Souza e Silva & Hjorth, 2009: 607). Other playfully mobilized archetypes have since emerged with the figure of the *gameur*, as proposed by Moore (2011), the *cyberflâneur*, as discussed by Morovoz (2013), and the *playeur*, as introduced by Evans and Saker (2019).

More recently, urban wayfaring and playful methodologies of experiencing and exploring the city as a playground have become mainstreamed through the global popularity of augmented reality games such as *Pokémon GO* (Davies & Innocent, 2017; Hjorth & Richardson, 2017; Leorke, 2018) and *Harry Potter: Wizards Unite*. In Chapter 11, we will discuss and unpack the phenomenon of *Pokémon GO* in detail. Such games also remind us of the importance of the New Games Movement in the evolution of what would become pervasive games. We discuss this in the following section, and then move onto understanding the genre in terms of first and second generations.

## Shared Histories

Pervasive games drew influence from a number of movements, one in particular being the New Games Movement, which emerged as a countercultural response to the Vietnam War and civic unrest in the late 1960s. Its large-scale games facilitated playful embodied experiences and public spectacles that did not pit players against each other in zero sum scenarios; instead, they sought to build trust and community between participants. It was envisaged that the connections created through physical play could lead to new ways of living (Pearce et al., 2007). However, within the New Games Movement competing agendas existed between the ambitions of activist and counterculture provocateur, Stewart Brand, and those of later participants, including Pat Farrington and Bernie De Koven. These differences were reflected in the games they created.

Brand's first multiplayer game was titled *Slaughter*. Involving four moving balls and two moving baskets, up to 40 players competed with each other on a large wrestling mat. The experience was described as 'intense, energetic, with much body contact' (Fluegelman, 1976: 9), exemplifying the kind of fun but antagonistic games that Brand was known for. Brand's next game, *Earthball*, involved a battle for the control of the planet. Featuring a large canvas ball from military training exercises that was painted to resemble the Earth, Brand would announce the game rules via megaphone: 'There are two kinds of people in the world: those who want to push the Earth over the row of flags at that end of the field, and those who want to push it over the fence at the other end. Go to it' (Fluegelman, 1976: 9). Players moved the Earth Ball from one side to another yet whenever a team neared a goal, it was noted that players from the winning team would defect to help the other side. The first *Earthball* game was played for an hour, without a score, thwarting zero-sum game mechanics with the players' goal emerging as not to win, but simply to play (Fluegelman, 1976: 7–8).

Arriving to the New Games Movement in the early 1970s, Pat Farrington, George Leonard and Bernie De Koven added a deeply humanistic element to Brand's work, making the games all-inclusive, intrinsically social and based on trust. De Koven, famous for his 'deep fun' philosophies discussed in his book *The Well-Played Game* (1978), designed across digital and physical worlds. Farrington felt that games could encourage players to celebrate their abilities, rather than compete with each other, contributing to a style of 'soft touch games' that aimed to develop trust and cooperation (Mäyrä, 2008: 148). George Leonard also brought the Eastern philosophy of cooperation to the movement, while De Koven advocated collaborative games codesigned with players using recycled materials (De Koven, 2004). Bringing an iterative design approach to the already established New Games Movement, De Koven sought to explore how players might engage with forms of activism and environmentalism through games, but more importantly, highlighted how people accounted for the ways they interacted with each other (De Koven, 1978). Over three decades later, against the contemporary backdrop of climate change, global conflict, political upheaval and complex gender issues, Pearce et al. (2007) recommended revisitation of the New Games Movement and its methods, as a means of constructing shared contexts for meaningful play in virtual and real-world spaces.

In Table 9.1, pervasive games have been chronologically organized in terms of first and second generation. While the first generation saw these game types as a more subversive and subcultural activity, second-generation games received more mainstream understanding and usage. For some, this mainstreaming meant an emptying out of the political power of games to question and challenge normalized ways of experiencing and moving through the city, especially as it becomes increasingly networked. For others, second-generation games like *Pokémon GO* highlight the role of games to illustrate and illuminate existing inequalities across race, class, gender and age. We discuss these issues in more detail in Chapter 11.

## First Generation

The introduction of mobile and locative devices through the 1990s was more than a technological and communicative shift. The inherent possibilities of these devices fuelled experimental and artistic practices, giving rise to forms of play that radically extended games into new contexts and spaces. From this perspective, pervasive games emerged as disruptive experiments that challenged the concepts of games,

**Table 9.1** Pervasive games of the first generation (2000–2010) and second generation (2010 onwards)

| First Generation | | | |
|---|---|---|---|
| **Game** | **Year** | **Type** | **Designer** |
| Augmented Reality Quake | 2000 | Augmented Reality Game | Wayne Piekarski |
| Botfighters | 2001 | Pervasive Assassin game | It's Alive Mobile Games AB |
| The Beast | 2001 | Alternate Reality Game | Microsoft Game Group |
| Prosopopeia | 2001 | Pervasive LARP | Martin Eriksson & team |
| Noderunner | 2002 | Scavenger Hunt | Med44 |
| Human Pac-Man | 2003 | Pervasive LARP | Mixed Reality Lab |
| Mogi | 2003 | Location-Based Game | Newt Games |
| Can You See Me Now? | 2003 | Mixed Reality Game | Blast Theory |
| Uncle Roy All Around You | 2003 | Mixed Reality Game | Blast Theory |
| PacManhattan | 2004 | Pervasive Street Game | Frank Lantz NYU |
| I Love Bees | 2004 | Alternate Reality Game | 42 Entertainment |
| StreetWars | 2004 | Pervasive Assassin Game | Aliquo & Yutai |
| The Lost Experience | 2006 | Alternate Reality Game | ABC (US), Channel 4 (UK), Channel 7 (AUS) |
| Cruel 2 B Kind | 2006 | Pervasive Assassin Game | McGonigal & Bogost |
| Why So Serious | 2007 | Alternate Reality Game | 42 Entertainment |
| Insectopia | 2007 | Location-Based Game | GAME studio |
| Second Generation | | | |
| **Game** | **Year** | **Type** | **Designer/s** |
| Jeune Institute | 2011 | Distributed Narrative | Jeff Hull |
| The Darkest Puzzle | 2011 | ARG | Psykrom |
| Cicada 3301 | 2012– | ARG | Unknown |
| Zombies, Run! | 2012 | Exergame | Six to Start |
| The Walk | 2013 | Exergame | Six to Start |
| Hello Lamp Post | 2013 | Playable City work | Pan Studio |
| Ingress | 2013 | Locative ARG | Niantic |
| Shadowing | 2014 | Playable City work | Chomko & Rosier |
| Pokémon GO | 2016 | Pervasive game | Niantic |
| XonKon | 2016 | Pervasive game | Davies & Innocent |
| The Strangers at Honja Factory | 2017 | Playable City work | One Im & Hitchcock-Yoo |
| TiMER | 2019 | Locative experience | Davies & Innocent |
| Harry Potter: Wizards Unite | 2019 | Pervasive game | Niantic |

play and everyday life (McGonigal, 2006). Although the appearance of pervasive games in the late 1990s and early 2000s was something of a global phenomenon, their development and emergence differed according to location. As we discuss in the final part of the book, pioneering games such as Japan's *Mogi* (2003) (Licoppe &

Inada, 2006) further developed networked capacities that would become integral to mainstreamed second-generation games such as *Pokémon GO* (2016).

In the UK, pervasive games became aligned with art collectives and theatre groups. Performance collectives such as Blast Theory and Forced Entertainment began to connect critical media and mobile-enabled locative games with renewed concerns about public interventions into city spaces, first articulated by the SI in the 1960s (de Souza e Silva & Hjorth, 2009). These theatre groups developed mixed-reality performances and immersive theatre experiences with ambitions of layering alternative meanings and narratives into the participants' experience of public space (Benford & Giannachi, 2011).

Blast Theory games included *Can You See Me Now?* (2003), an urban chase game where performers on the streets of a city use handheld computers, Global Positioning Systems (GPS) and walkie-talkies to chase online players who move their avatars through a virtual model of the same space (Benford et al., 2006) (Figure 9.2). *Uncle Roy All Around You* (2003) was another Blast Theory creation that saw players journey through city streets to find a fictional character called Uncle Roy (Benford et al., 2004). Through this period, an aesthetic distinction grew in pervasive games between their existence as competitive city-based activities or as experiences that could create social and spatial connection between individuals and the places in which they lived.

The UK also boasted long histories of *letterboxing*, an outdoor treasure hunt activity that combines elements of orienteering, art and problem solving, and dates back to the 1850s (Montola et al., 2009). Letterboxers would hide small, weatherproof

**Figure 9.2** Player in *Can You See Me Now*? A collaboration between Blast Theory and the Mixed Reality Lab, University of Nottingham, 2003. Reproduced with permission of Blast Theory.

containers in publicly accessible locations, then distribute clues and instructions for finding the boxes in printed catalogues or by word of mouth. In the rise of pervasive games in the early 2000s players began to use GPS to discover these hidden boxes and clues were distributed on websites and the activity evolved into geo-caching. Today geo-caches can be found in urban and rural locations globally.

In the US, pervasive games emerged as both physical Street Games and also as **Alternate Reality Games (ARGs)**, which were largely online collaborative experiences that blurred the lines between reality and fiction. Alternate Reality Games are collaborative rather than competitive experiences that enjoin groups of players to work together in order to solve puzzles and unravel mysteries by working as 'collective detectives' (McGonigal, 2003a). A founding example of an ARG is a game that came to be known simply as *The Beast*. Created by a team working in the Microsoft Game Group, *The Beast* was designed to provide clues across a variety of media forms, including websites, posters, film trailers, answering machines and emails. The game encouraged players to collaborate in solving a vast puzzle across the internet and real world.

As the mystery of *The Beast* unravelled, it became clear that it was part of the marketing campaign for the 2001 film *Artificial Intelligence: AI*. A defining feature of ARGs is that they tend not to present themselves as games, sometimes with the explicit declaration 'this is not a game' (Szulborski, 2005). The result, according to McGonigal (2003b), is a kind of 'Pinocchio effect', whereby the games appear not to recognize their own status as fiction. ARGs have since been used as viral marketing campaigns to promote feature films, television programmes and computer games. Key ARG promotion examples include *I Love Bees* (2004), created as a promotion for the videogame *Halo 2* (2004), *The Lost Experience* (2006), created for the television series *Lost* (2004–2010), and *Why So Serious* (2007), created for the Batman feature film *The Dark Knight* (2008).

Another popular US pervasive game genre is the long tradition of assassination-style games that evolved into pervasive games with the arrival of mobile technologies. *Assassin*, also often called *Killer*, is a game tournament that has been popular among US high school and college students for decades (Duggan, 2017). Players armed with nerf guns, water pistols, alarm clock 'bombs' or other harmless weapons assassinate their assigned victims in games that take place over several days. As security concerns and a broader fear of terrorism in public space heightened following the 9/11 terrorist attacks on the World Trade Center and the Pentagon, assassination-style games were increasingly discouraged by police and city councils in the US.

Nonetheless, in 2004, game designers Franz Aliquo and Liao Yutai took the basic game concept and turned it into *StreetWars*, a three-week 24/7 pervasive game involving water guns, which toured many cities around the world. In 2006, game designers Jane McGonigal and Ian Bogost devised a killer/assassin variant, called *Cruel 2 B Kind* (2006), which worked like a verbal form of rock–paper–scissors, with players offering a greeting ('Welcome to New York'), paying a compliment or blowing a kiss (McGonigal, 2011: 189–197). Subtitled 'a game of benevolent assassination', *Cruel 2 B Kind* was devised to increase 'positive social interactions' by repurposing the game mechanics of a more competitive and antagonistic experience. These multi-day or multi-week games were often presented in play festivals such as *Come Out and Play* in New York and *Hide and Seek* in London. In these gatherings, experimental games were premiered alongside flash mob activities such as *Pillow Fight Club* (a giant public pillow fight), and socially playful theatre enacted by groups like New York's *Improv Everywhere*, with invitingly self-explanatory works such as *The No Pants Subway Ride* (2002), which is still an annual participatory event to this day.

These pervasive games and related activities, which are, broadly speaking, inclusive and transparent in their intentions for social enjoyment, are also known as Big Games, Street Games or Smart Street Sports. Sometimes, they also consist of recreations of computer games in physical space. A key example of this is *PacManhattan* (see Figure 9.3). Set in the street grid around Washington Square Park in the Greenwich Village area of Manhattan, the game was created as a postgraduate project by a group of students at New York University in 2004. Other examples of videogames translated to urban environments include *Augmented Reality Quake* developed in Australia (Thomas et al., 2000) and *Human Pac-Man* presented in Germany (Magerkurth et al., 2005). In these games, a variety of sensors, head-mounted devices, wearable computers, wireless and Bluetooth technology see players take on familiar in-game characters and avatars, within physical urban space.

In Scandinavia, pervasive games combined the assassination and alternate reality game types prevalent in the US but were distinctive in their association with Live Action Role Play (LARP), a form of real-world role-playing game in which participants physically portray their characters. A key example is *Prosopopeia* (2001), a pervasive LARP event based on an alternate reality aesthetic. As with an ARG, the game involved messages received across a range of mediums, including phone messages,

**Figure 9.3**  Player of *PacManhattan* in New York (2004). Photographer: Ehud Kenan.

websites, documents and clues in physical locations. A key distinction between pervasive LARPs and ARGs lies in the players' own performance and subjectivity. While in LARPs, players role-play a character performance, in ARGs players enact a 'performance of belief', a kind of uncritical embrace of the game's fiction in order to increase levels of their own immersion (McGonigal, 2006).

As we will discuss in further detail in Chapter 11, locations such as Japan and Scandinavia, with their innovative mobile technology industries, witnessed some of the first pervasive games. A notable instance is *Botfighters* (2001), a location-aware mobile game where players near to each other can initiate player-vs-player fights (Figure 9.4). When escaping a battle or chasing an opponent, the player must physically move in order to change the device location. The game mechanics strongly encouraged keeping the game active 24 hours a day. It was also in the Scandinavian context, in particular Finland, that some of the earliest defining pervasive games scholarship began to take shape.

Much of the power of pervasive games lay in their ability to toy with conventions around the magic circle, a concept we have explored in previous chapters. In *Exploring the edge of the magic circle: Defining pervasive games*, Montola argues

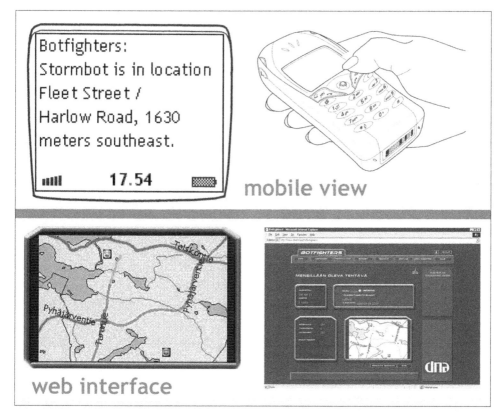

**Figure 9.4** *Botfighters* interface. Image: Olli Sotamaa (2002). Reproduced with permission of Olli Sotamaa.

'(p)ervasive gaming is a genre of gaming systematically blurring and breaking the traditional boundaries of the "magic circle" of play' (2005: n.p.). For both Huizinga (1938 [1955]) and Salen and Zimmerman (2003), the primary function of the magic circle is to prevent the game world and everyday reality from transgressing their respective domains. Conversely, for Montola and others, the very purpose of pervasive games has been to challenge these spatial and conceptual limits.

Much of the early academic work into pervasive games was conducted through the 2000s within the Integrated Project on Pervasive Games (IPerG), a pervasive games design research group that defined pervasive games as 'a radically new game form that extends gaming experiences out into the physical world' (IPerG, 2008). Emerging from the EU-funded research project which explored the technical and design aspects of pervasive games, Montola, Waern and Stenros's book, *Pervasive Games*, defines the genre as expanding the 'contractual magic circle of play spatially, temporally, or socially' (2009: 21). This definition still functions to describe the role of pervasive games today.

Likewise, in Europe, LARP games developed into a unique subculture with high production values, rigorous theoretical discourses and non-commercial spirit (Stenros et al., 2009). Differing agendas between more commercial and market-driven experiences, such as ARGs and transmedia promotional games, as opposed to the more socially and community-focused experiences of Big Games, Urban Games and Mixed Reality Games became more pronounced. Comparable tensions occurred within critical games developed in the late 1960s onwards by The New Games Movement, which aimed to use public play as social commentary and tactics of resistance by reversing social expectations and normative practices. Throughout the 2010s multiple types of pervasive games arose with regional nuances. Late in the decade, smartphone devices like the iPhone appeared. This technology advancement, along with a maturation of the form, brought a second generation of pervasive games.

## Second Generation

As the 2010s drew to a close, industrial and academic interest in pervasive games began to transform. The ubiquity of smartphone devices had brought more sophisticated mobile technologies but also more restrictive publishing regimes. The artists who had led early developments in the field could now only publish in the walled gardens of app stores (Davies & Balmford, 2020). While ARGs and distributed narratives continued with heightened conspiracy elements, such as with the Jejune Institute (2008–2011), *The Darkest Puzzle* (2011) and *Cicada 3301* (2012 onwards), the appealing 'newness' of pervasive games had dissipated; they were no longer discussed in radical and avant-garde terms. The exploration of pervasive games moved into more formal civic, health and educational settings.

With the field stabilized, this period also presented an opportunity for academics to review the landscape of pervasive games, taking stock of trends, definitions and themes (Montola, 2011; Valente & Feijó, 2013; Kasapakis & Gavalas, 2015). Pervasive games also conveyed more serious and practical dimensions. The social and spatial aspects of these game types saw them developed and applied to address a series of real-world problems, such as promoting sustained healthy behaviours (Miller et al., 2013), increasing social interactions (Santos et al., 2019) and facilitating intergenerational play (Comunello & Mulargia, 2017).

Human–computer interaction (HCI) endeavours in the first generation of pervasive games had led researchers and game makers to develop pervasive play that required less focus and attention on the mobile phone. For example, Soute et al. (2010) pioneered a sub-category of pervasive games coined Head Up games (HUG), such as *Camelot* (2006), *Stop the Bomb* (2007) and *HeartBeat* (2008), each featuring dedicated hardware built from the ground up (Keyson et al., 2011). The aim of these games and interfaces is the promotion of outdoor social interaction while keeping the player's head 'up' for natural outdoor navigation and interaction. This trajectory of research saw the emergence in the second generation of exergames, pervasive games that emphasized physical exercise (Mueller et al., 2016). Related games in this genre are the mobile games by British studio Six to Start, including *Zombies, Run!* (2012), a fitness work-out game complete with zombie chases and motivational missions, and *The Walk* (2013), a techno-thriller narrative that encourages people to walk 10,000 steps per day.

Beyond their implementation in institution contexts, the subjective affordances of pervasive games emerged as experiences that were able to offer 'new ways of experiencing place, identity and play' (Hjorth, 2011: 360). Meanwhile, with the rise of ubiquitous technologies in smart cities, pervasive games and modes of play became increasingly important as activities for critical reflection (Nijholt, 2017). Much of the first generation of pervasive games already discussed was occupied not with what was able to be achieved, but what would be achievable once the promise of ubiquitous technology had been fulfilled. This looming future had prompted McGonigal to ask whether ubiquitous computing is 'There Yet?' (McGonigal, 2006). By the second generation of pervasive games, the infrastructures of ubiquitous computing and advanced smartphone devices had been fully realized. As a result, city councils globally became interested in the role and value of play in urban living, and were keen to explore ways in which new technologies could help to increase efficiency within smart cities planning (Fischer & Hornecker, 2012).

The notion of the 'playable city' developed as a creative counterpoint to the narrative of the smart city, with playable cities emphasizing serendipity, hospitality and openness over order, efficiency and finance (Fischer & Hornecker, 2012). Concepts of the playable city were championed by organizations, including Watershed's *Playable City* in Bristol and Urban Play in Amsterdam, initiatives that evidenced a more general interest in conceiving the city as a playground (Nijholt, 2017).

Bristol's *Playable City* initiative set about integrating participatory installations in the city streets. Some of the projects include *Hello Lamp Post* (2013), a project that invites text-based conversation with street furniture like lamp posts, post boxes and bus stops (Figure 9.5). Participants text numbers found on these objects as SMS codes, leading the object to respond with a series of questions via text messages. The next person to sign in for a conversation with that object can learn about previous replies, ultimately allowing for the sharing of stories about the lives of the city's inhabitants. At face value, the work can bring about closer community connection while simultaneously hinting at deeper concerns around information privacy in the encroaching context of the Internet of Things (IoT). Within smart cities, sensing technologies like IoT have become integral, and yet the social and ethical dimensions of such media are still unresolved. As Foth, Brynskov and Ojala (2015) note, smart cities involve contested interfaces, vulnerable agencies and new forms of place-making that require us to rethink digital citizenship.

The work *Shadowing* (2014) sees streetlights equipped with infrared cameras recording the shadows of pedestrians passing beneath and replaying them back to future passers-by. Pedestrians who encounter the shadow-projecting feature of the streetlights begin to play with the database of previously captured shadows and introduce their own shadows to the system (Nijholt, 2017). The playful participation that the work invites, and the underlying surveillance technology that it presents, offers a critical take on the smart cities narrative by alluding to the shadowing or shadowiness of data collection.

**Figure 9.5** *Hello Lamp Post* (2013) by studio PAN was the winner of Watershed's *Playable City* Award. Reproduced with permission of Watershed and Playable Media.

As noted by Nijholt (2017), a crucial feature of the playable city's movement is that it does not outright embrace the ubiquitous technologies on which the works are based but implicitly invites participants to consider the opportunities and dangers they offer. The works illuminate the presence of smart technologies while allowing citizens some agency in the design, adaptation and (real-time) control of their environments using smart sensors and actuators. As Nijholt remarks:

> Making a city playable or playful by installing and offering authorized smart entertaining technology may make citizens happier and more satisfied with their environment. It helps to provide citizens with entertaining and healthy experiences that improve their quality of life. (2017: 17)

However, Nijholt also calls for experiences that are more than responsive and reactive and allow the participant to be part of codesigning the playability of their environment. This adds value to the experience by turning locals from passive consumers into creative users and designers of 'playfulness'. As discussed in previous chapters, the cities' playability can be understood as part of the rise of the 'playful attitude', especially in and around digital media practices in everyday life (Sicart, 2014).

Now boasting projects in Tokyo, Recife, Seoul, São Paulo, Austin, Melbourne and Lagos, the Playable City network has indeed become a global network. It has seen the inclusion of works such as *The Strangers at Honja Factory* (2017) by artists Do One Im and Eunju Hitchcock-Yoo, which combines street performance and digital technology to enable intimate communication and creativity between participants and spaces. Also relevant are the works of Troy Innocent that use QR coded designs located around the city inviting players to be attuned to the spatial, social and cultural codes of urban places. Games by Innocent and Davies, such as *XonKon* (2016) and *TiMER* (2019), work to evoke coded, historical, marginalized and other hidden layers within city spaces.

The notion of a 'Playable City' reinvigorates the desire to re-map urban infrastructures into spaces of play. While some pervasive games present radical strategies and confronting tactics to enjoin players to rethink city space, the playable cities collectives have cultivated more subtle and inviting approaches to the genre. This has involved activities that are familiar to everybody and have less risk of tension, such as childhood games, group sport performance and examples from the New Games Movement under Farrington and later De Koven, who each sought to develop inviting and creative games and to foster inclusive modes of play. The pervasive game within the playable city framework is one that connects community and is widely accessible.

Within such logics, pervasive games and the work of the New Games Movement align to the art world concept of *Relational Aesthetics* (1998), as proposed by French critic and curator Nicolas Bourriaud. Relational Aesthetics, according to Bourriaud, describes emergent arts activities that involve audience participation to activate the work. Like many games, pervasive games fall into this category. These connections are made explicit in Pamela Lee's 'New games' (2009), which considers how emergent gaming experiences such as pervasive games can operate as a kind of communal 'happening' (a 1960s impromptu event), and Brian Schrank's *Avant-Garde Videogames* (2014) that explores the relationship between life, art, play and reality in the work of 20th-century artists and contemporary pervasive game makers.

Having moved from the margins to the mainstream, pervasive game experiences are now ubiquitous. However, while play has become a standard feature of city spaces – as invoked by possibilities in so-called *Playable Cities* that span radical, utopian, corporate and pessimistic discourses (Leorke, 2018) – it is still a contested concept. For example, some cities in Asia are highly regulated and people are not allowed to play in ways that are deemed 'right' in European contexts. Indeed, reflecting upon the role of play within the city is still a highly debated and complex notion that highlights uneven interpretations of how public space should be used, how space is differently experienced by a diversity of individuals, and what existing uses or understandings of place are reinforced or upset by locative play (Lammes & Wilmott, 2016; Hjorth & Richardson, 2017; Sicart, 2017).

Today, academics and game designers alike agree that ample opportunities for playful interventions in the urban fabric remain and that pervasive games offer a promising means to achieve this (Lefaivre & Döll, 2007). However, while notions like Society 4.0 (automated societies) and the smart city continue to prosper in expanding urban contexts, pervasive games have the power to question inequalities in contemporary embodiment and place-making. Play in public space is an inherently political act (Flanagan, 2009a; Keogh, 2016). As Miguel Sicart (2014) has highlighted, many of the Scandinavian festivals and events that aim for inclusive and open access feature pervasive game types that reveal the inequities of public playfulness, especially when players are required to challenge conventional ways of being in urban spaces. Although lived spaces – urban and otherwise – have rapidly evolved in the past century, both the tensions as well as the radical potentialities of playful wandering remain intact.

## Conclusion

Cities often tend to have officially designated areas for play and entertainment, such as children's playgrounds, sports fields or open areas reserved for other outdoor activities. Pervasive games seek to upset these conventions by reimagining the entire cityscape as a place of play. Pervasive games offer us new ways to become wayfarers in the city, uncovering different cartographies and positionalities. This expansion and blurring of the boundaries of gamespaces creates an ambiguity between an in-game world and out-of-game world that can alter players' perceptions of space and place. However, just as cities are contested spaces in which gender, class, generational and racial differences are heightened, play in cities can both reinforce and subvert these inequalities – something we discuss in further detail in Chapter 11.

Introducing the field of pervasive games, this chapter has shown how their creators have sought to expand the field of play. Outlining the diverse ecology of pervasive game types and dividing them into two generations corresponding to the first and second decades of the new millennium, this chapter also considered how the histories of pervasive gaming draw on theories and practice from urban studies and earlier imaginings of the city as a location of public play. The rise of pervasive games must be contextualized in terms of the modernization of the city, the development of the bourgeoise and their manifestation of identity through movement.

As we traced through phenomenon such as the New Games Movement and SI, pervasive games grew out of political turmoil and subversive artists wanting to reclaim the city in new and community-engaged ways. Differences in the first and second generation of pervasive games are shown to be more than temporal, but reflect advancements in mobile devices, shifting ideas about ubiquitous technology, and an expanded understanding of the purpose and potential of urban play. As we have framed through first and second generations of the genre, pervasive games have grown from a subcultural to mainstream activity.

The next chapter begins the final part of the book, where we focus more specifically on mobile games and play. We expand on this chapter's discussion of the role of games in place-making, in addition to addressing the intersection of mobile media studies and game studies, and the increasing ubiquity of casual mobile gaming as a modality of ambient and haptic play that echoes the rhythms of everyday life.

## Further Reading

Garcia, A., & Niemeyer, G. (Eds.) (2017). *Alternate Reality Games and the Cusp of Digital Gameplay*. London: Bloomsbury.

Hjorth, L., & Pink, S. (2014). New visualities and the digital wayfarer: Reconceptualizing camera phone photography and locative media. *Mobile Media & Communication*, *2*(1), 40–57. https://doi.org/10.1177/2050157913505257

Leorke, D., & Owens, M. (Eds.) (2020). *Games and Play in the Creative, Smart and Ecological City*. London: Routledge.

Nijholt, A. (2017). *Playable Cities: The City as a Digital Playground*. New York: Springer.

Stokes, B. (2020). *Locally Played: Real-world Games for Stronger Places and Communities*. Cambridge, MA: The MIT Press.

# Part IV
## Mobilities

# 10

# The Rise and Rise of Mobile Games

Over the past decade mobile games have radically transformed the games industry and market. In what ways, and why are they so popular and ubiquitous?

Mobile games have often been derogatively described as 'casual' games? Has their status as trivial timewasters changed over the past decade?

Why is it important to understand the connection between mobile media studies and game studies? What does each disciplinary field offer for the analysis of mobile games?

How is the evolution of the touchscreen smartphone fundamental to the development of mobile games? How does the haptic interface transform the game experience?

What does the locative functionality of mobile media offer in terms of game mechanics and gameplay?

As an interface encompassing various converging platforms and contexts, mobile media devices such as iPhones and Android phones, the PlayStation Portable (PSP), Nintendo DS and 3DS, and an increasing array of tablets, are clearly becoming important spaces for gaming and playful social activities more broadly. With the increasing ubiquity of web-capable smartphones and tablets, app-based ecologies and trends towards gamification – that is, the use of games and playful apps to boost consumption of products and services – mobile games are now an intrinsic part of 21st-century popular culture. Seventy-three per cent of all mobile app revenue comes from games, and the mobile gaming industry is now valued at over US$64 billion (Influencer Marketing, 2018) which comprises nearly 50% of the global games market (Influencer Marketing, 2018).

While not all mobile games have enjoyed the success of *Angry Birds*, mobile gaming has provided many designers and programmers – and, consequently, players – with more flexibility and innovation around game genres, gameplay, and the aesthetics and affordances of game environments. Across the expanding variety of platforms, media, contexts and modes of presence, mobile games are being played by a growing number of people in a range of contexts: young and old, male and female, individuals, families and social groups, at home, on the move, at work. Not only have we witnessed an increase in the popularity of casual games across web-based media, the spectrum of gaming has also shifted to include playful social media and location-based apps. As Jesper Juul (2009) suggests, this 'casual revolution' has seen games and other forms of playful media now both reflect and modify the complex practices and relationships that constitute contemporary life. In this context, and cutting across cultures, generations and media interfaces, mobile games can no longer be considered as trivial; similarly, players can no longer be simplistically typecast as 'casual' or 'hardcore'.

This chapter provides a critical overview of mobile gaming. We first discuss the interrelation between mobile media studies and games studies, before exploring the emergence of app-based media ecologies and the problematic nomenclature of 'casual games'. The proliferation of mobile apps has effectively worked to interweave the previously disparate domains of online social networking and mobile gaming, furthering the 'ludification' of culture – the translation of interpersonal, social and communicative practices into 'playful' activities. We then briefly discuss the rise of location-based games (which will be discussed further in Chapter 11). On the one hand, casual or 'occasional' mobile games – played for minutes at a time and at irregular intervals – can be seen as a form of portable home entertainment that cocoons the player in public places, facilitating a radical mobilization of personal space and privacy. On the other hand, location-based mobile games generate 'palimpsestic' or layered experiences of place and presence, requiring the player to integrate their own situated and embodied perception of the world with dynamic Global Positioning System (GPS)-enabled information, embedded within an augmented and networked game reality. In the final sections of this chapter we focus on the use and affects of haptic touchscreen games and the interrelation between social media and mobile games.

## Game Studies and Mobile Media Studies

Over the past 15 years we have witnessed the expansion of the mobile phone into mobile media. Sustained by a fertile app-based media ecology, mobiles have now become, in conjunction with an increasingly diverse array of functionalities, game consoles in their own right, and enablers of 'playful' media practices more broadly.

Today, as fully-fledged web-capable media interfaces, mobile media devices couple the communicative capacity of the mobile phone with the participatory social web, combine the affordances of mobility and online sociality with games, and merge the portability of the digital camera with the capacity to playfully edit, remix and share creative content with online communities while on the move, effectively transforming the mundane snapshot into a primary mode of everyday communication and vernacular creativity (Burgess, 2010). Far exceeding its role as a communication device, the mobile phone is now a multimedia technology *par excellence*, with a plethora of uses that operate across aural, textual and visual economies and literacies. It is here, at the nexus of everyday media practice, sociality and gameplay, that the perspectives of mobile media studies and game studies come together.

In many ways the growth of mobile media is characterized by the rise of the active, creative and networked user, and instrumental in the coalescence of media and communication practices. We now communicate through and with media, via online gameworlds, and creating and sharing mobile camera photos in the form of visual messages on Instagram or Snapchat, for example. Mobile devices reside within a multi-platform and transmedia landscape; they are 'containers' of discrete and connected virtual worlds, and conduits of playful and creative sharing and networking. They have emerged in tandem with, and are thoroughly embedded in, participatory and spreadable media culture (Jenkins, 2006a; Jenkins et al., 2013) and the networked communication and produsage that sustains it (Bruns & Jacobs, 2006).

Mobile media are also part of an ascendant trajectory within participatory media culture – the ludification of culture first identified by Raessens (2006) in the inaugural issue of *Games and Culture* over a decade ago. As we have noted in previous chapters, in his contribution to MIT's Playful Thinking Series, Sicart (2014) observed that a 'playful attitude' or lusory sensibility now characterizes much of contemporary media practice. This playfulness can be seen in the seamless integration of games and creative mobile apps into our everyday lives and modes of communication, coalescing with the rise of social media services that prompt users to upload and share their own creative small media content (Hjorth & Richardson, 2014). In these contexts, it is difficult to overstate the cultural significance of the mobile interface.

In 2018, one-third of mobile app downloads across Android and iOS were games, and these capture nearly 75% of consumer spend. Globally, every year we spend 20% more money on mobile games (over US$70 billion in 2017) than all other game categories combined (including consoles, other handheld games and computer gaming) (Takahashi, 2018b; Perez, 2019). In tandem with these developments, researchers of media and culture have turned their attention to analysis of the mobile as an interface for play, highlighting the importance of combining (and contrasting) the approaches of mobile media studies, mobile communication studies and game studies (de Souza e Silva, 2009; Hjorth & Chan, 2009; Moore, 2011; Farman, 2012; Frith, 2013; Hjorth & Richardson, 2014).

Like the methods of game studies (see Chapter 2), mobile media and communication research, and mobile games research in particular, is interdisciplinary by necessity. Just as researchers of mobile media and communication are – increasingly and necessarily – informed by the now well-established field of game studies, they, in turn, provide critical insight into the prolific rise of mobile gaming as a pervasive and manifold media and communication practice in everyday life. For example, within the field of mobile communication, critical accounts of mobile phone use are deeply implicated in debates around various forms of work–life relations that cut across gender, space, labour, technology and capital within contemporary globalization. Indeed, the rise of the mobile phone as a symbol and practice is permeated by gendered genealogies and the contested and entangled negotiation of private (domestic) and public (work) domains (Wajcman et al., 2008). These factors continue to impact and influence users' perceptions and experience of mobile games; in particular, the ongoing gendered articulation of technology 'revealed' by mobile communication research is apparent in one of the biggest conflations surrounding mobile media and games – namely, that women engage in 'trivial' casual mobile and social gaming, while men engage in 'serious' or **hardcore gaming**.

At the same time, mobile media and communication scholars adopt and adapt games studies concepts and perspectives. As identified by Raessens (2014) and others (Roig et al., 2009; Hjorth & Richardson, 2020), the concepts of play and ludology are an effective lens through which to 'see' and critically interpret media and communication practices anew. It is clear that the rise of mobile media as significant spaces for gaming and playful social activities, in combination with the affordances of locative technologies and the mobile web, have changed the way games are made and played. Many of the medium-, design- and genre-specific characteristics of games are translated and adapted into the development and analyses of mobile communication and media use, such as the embodied and affective aspects of gameplay and game mechanics, and the key attributes of play more generally. As we outline below and in Chapter 2, research in this area has been usefully taken up by mobile media scholars and in discussions concerning the haptic effects of touchscreen interfaces (Parisi, 2008; Richardson & Hjorth, 2017). Regardless of the trajectories of influence, such work reveals a productive cross-fertilization between the disciplinary fields of mobile media and communication and game studies, particularly in terms of the role of mobile apps across communication and play practices.

## Not Just Casual, Not Just Games: The Rise of App-based Media Ecologies

Mobile gaming, like casual play, is as diverse as it is divergent. They are both inherently informed by the local and social. With mobile games, especially utilizing locative media, we see how places can be rendered into playful spaces. Mobile games also highlight deep-running ambivalences between work/life and casual/hardcore dichotomies that are being amplified within the broader 'appification' of media culture. Until recently, mobile phone gaming was largely dismissed as 'casual' – typically defined in terms of non-immersive shallow gameplay that was interruptible, non-narrative and played for minutes at a time. Yet just as the constitution of mobile gaming has evolved, expanded and deepened, so too has the notion of casual play. Most notably, the proliferation of app-based ecologies across devices has extended the dimension of play to include playful and creative activities, games across multiple genres, contexts, and levels of haptic and temporal investment.

Early mobile gaming, often called portable or hand-held gaming, was played on dedicated devices of Japanese origin, from Nintendo's Game & Watch, Game Boy series, DualScreen (NDS) and 3D-enhanced DualScreen (3DS) to Sony's PlayStation Portable (PSP). Although there was some attempt to design mobile handsets with gaming platforms (e.g. the Nokia NGage in 2003), it wasn't until the release of the first-generation iPhone in 2007, and launch of the App Store soon after, that a smartphone became a game platform in its own right.

For some, there is an argument to be made that the first mobile internet in Japan in 1999 – imode – was a precursor and template for smartphone ecology, especially in terms of its focus upon mobile games. Prior to 2002, early mobile phone gaming was initially limited to preloaded offline games such as *Tetris*, and subsequently, as mobile developers and providers experimented with distribution models, to a narrow spectrum of games made available through provider portals. Since 2008 and the launch of the App Store, mobile applications have extended the dimensions of play to include programs and services that are not simply defined by the term 'casual' or even by the term 'game'.

Indeed, the iPhone and App Store have in many ways set the standard as the mobile exemplar of the ludic turn in contemporary culture, as mobile devices become a conduit and container of both games and numerous playful and often user-generated applications. More broadly, the iPhone's appification of media practices and user-generated produsage can be linked to the commercialization and professionalization of amateur cultural practices and leisure (Stebbins, 2004; Taylor, 2012). Upon the initial release of the iPhone in 2007, Joel Mace and Michael West identified three major differences that distinguished it from competing mobile phone products: the large capacitive touch screen and keyboard, integration into the already existing iTunes store (as a high-end model of the iPod with phone capability), and the inclusion within the device of Apple's Web browser, Safari (Mace & West, 2008). In 2008, Apple also released the software development kit (SDK), soon to be followed by the opening of an online App Store one day before the iPhone 3G became available (Mace & West, 2010). As Mace and West document:

> In the first six months, the store attracted more than 15,000 applications and 500 million downloads, and three months later (April 2009) those figures had doubled to

30,000 and 1 billion, respectively; in November 2009, the figures reached 100,000 and 2 billion – the most popular were customized interfaces for existing web-sites (eBay, MySpace), locative web-enabled services and standalone applications (especially games). (2010: n.p.)

By early 2011 this number increased to 10 billion, and in mid-2013 Apple counted down to the 50-billionth download. Today, those numbers have risen significantly – thousands of apps are released for iOS and Android devices every day; the App Store now houses 1.85 million apps, and users have cumulatively downloaded 180 billion of them, while Google Play has 2.56 million available apps and 84.3 billion total downloads (Clement, 2020).

The mobile phone is now a key global platform for mobile games, redefining game audiences by putting 'a gaming platform in the hands of millions of people who had never considered (and likely will never consider) themselves gamers' (Consalvo, 2012b: 184). Like being 'online', playing games has become normalized, insinuated alongside the numerous other navigational, informational, productivity and social media app-based activities within one's mobile mediascape. For Consalvo, the pervasive incorporation of play activities into our everyday lives means that mobile phone gamers 'defy categorization', indicating the need to move beyond conventional categorizations of casual (mobile) and hardcore gaming (Consalvo, 2012b: 193).

Casual mobile gaming is often characterized as a mode of engagement that requires only sporadic attention up to a threshold of around five minutes, hence the popular notion that casual games are the mobile phone's predominant game genre, and the labelling of casual gamers, who play at most for five minutes at a time and at irregular intervals, as a key market in the mobile games industry. In the words of *The New York Times Magazine* critic Sam Anderson (2012), such games could aptly be termed 'stupid games' – games that have been around since *Tetris* was released with the Nintendo Game Boy in 1989. Anderson suggested that such games:

are designed to push their way through the cracks of other occasions. We play them incidentally, ambivalently, compulsively, almost accidentally. They're less an activity in our day than a blank space in our day; less a pursuit than a distraction from other pursuits. (2012: n.p.)

Yet at the same time, Anderson narrates his own struggle with the addictive, distractive and time-intensive lure of mobile games, lamenting that it interfered with the business of everyday life, when he should have been 'doing the dishes' or 'bathing my children'. It is a revealing story, one that belies the more common interpretation of casual and 'stupid' gaming as a trivial or in-between activity with none of the stickiness and investment of console and PC games.

As defined over a decade ago by Coulton, Pucihar and Balmford (2008: 1), hardcore gamers play differently: they play for extended periods, embrace the challenges, complexities and high levels of skill and functionality demanded by the gameworld and interface, and play games as a 'lifestyle preference or priority'. This mode of play is contrasted with low-level skills required of mobile games, and those who play them often describe the activity as peripheral, providing a 'fun' and incidental distraction. Those who play casual mobile games deliberately avoid the embodied attachment of dedicated gameplay, so that they are perpetually ready to resume the 'real business' of life. In many cases, casual players describe themselves as 'non-gamers', are unable to accurately document how much time they actually spend playing and are frequently surprised by the extent of their investment.

Yet increasingly, the casual/hardcore dichotomy provides an incomplete interpretation of 'small' or app-based gaming on mobile devices. In *A Casual Revolution*, Juul (2009) suggests that the stereotypes of the hardcore and casual gamer oversimplify the often complex and variable modalities of play. Similarly, Kallio, Mäyrä and Kaipainen (2011) stress the importance of the 'variability of meanings' attached to gameplay, the situatedness and contextuality of gaming, and the 'layered and overlapping character of game mentalities' which are particularly relevant now that mobile gaming is permeating everyday spaces and cultures. Indeed, as smartphones accompany us everywhere and anywhere, with an ever-growing app ecology populated by mobile games, the capacity for casual gameplay increases exponentially. As Taylor notes in her study of the professionalization of game playing as part of the broader commodification of lifestyle, the somewhat pejorative term 'casual' often disguises the substantial investments made by some casual gamers, and oversimplifies an increasingly diverse and rapidly developing medium of gameplay (Taylor, 2012).

Nevertheless, the games industry's attempts to define generic gamer markets in terms of temporal and financial investment have worked to reinforce distinctions between 'hardcore' and 'casual' gameplay (with the recent addition of the 'mid-core' demographic who play frequently but are not loyal or dedicated to particular games). On his *Gamasutra* blog, game developer Kevin Gliner (2013) argued that such a superficial reading of gamer audiences is problematic because it fails to recognize the spectrum of individual game practices. First, such categories can only be applied *in situ* – in the context of a specific game product; that is, there are 'different people for different products, and one game's hardcore player is another's casual player' (Gliner, 2013: n.p.). Second, they assume that a game can be defined in terms of a certain type of play-mode, instead of treating casual and hardcore play as compatible in the same game. Third, and most importantly, the identification of generic gamer markets relies on a narrow understanding of player behaviour – that an individual seeks the exact same play experience every time (Gliner, 2013). As one commenter on Gliner's blog describes:

> I like really deep, really engaging games … but not when I'm waiting at the dentist's office or some such. You can alter the design of a game for how you want a player

to engage with it, but that's not a demographic target. I've been playing *Bad Piggies* a lot lately, but not at home. I only touch it when I'm waiting somewhere for a short time. When I actually sit down to play, it'll be an MMO, or a shooter, or a strategy game, or whatever. Casual vs. hardcore is often a situational thing rather than a demographic one. (Gliner, 2013: n.p.)

Thus, gameplay is situated and variable across genres and modalities of play; gamers can adeptly choose – and spontaneously oscillate between – different levels of attention, distraction, engagement and investment depending on where they are and what they are doing. The term **casual gaming**, like mobile gaming, designates a range of activities and practices both inside and outside the home. Ironically, despite the potential physical and network mobility afforded by mobile devices, studies show that mobile games are often played in the bedroom (Chan, 2008). In other words, while the domestic increasingly becomes unbounded and mobile (Bakardjieva, 2006; Lim, 2006) portable media devices modify domestic spaces and practices as they become progressively more homebound, and app-based media ecologies – often playful and sometimes also creative – are embedded within conflicting practices of familiarity, belonging and being 'alone together' (Turkle, 2012). By contrast, when gameplay is situated in public places, the particular ways we engage with mobile games determine (and are determined by) degrees of attention, practices of viewing, and the motility and mobility of the pedestrian body. As we have documented elsewhere, the activity of mobile gaming in urban space often takes place while waiting (for a friend, at a bus stop, or for a journey to end) and becomes a way of managing the corporeal agitation of impatience, aloneness and boredom in public, effecting a mobilization of private space that can be deployed *in situ* while 'being-with-others' (Hjorth & Richardson, 2020).

Significantly, too, app-based ecologies of gaming are also transforming the way established online and console games are played, and how players engage in paratextual practices around the game. As Christian Christensen and Patrick Prax document in the context of *World of Warcraft*, customized apps enable gamers to add 'multiple new dimensions to the gaming experience' (Christensen & Prax, 2012: 731). In order to understand the cultural and experiential effect of these developments, they suggest that games and gameplay can effectively be rethought in terms of Taylor's notion of assemblage, which accounts for the way 'many varying actors and unfolding processes make up the site and action' of contemporary gaming (Taylor, 2009).

The app *World of Warcraft Mobile Armory* (Blizzard Entertainment) allows WoW gamers to view characters, access guild stats, auction and bid for items, participate in guild chat or initiate one-on-one conversations with fellow guild members. Thus, as Christensen and Prax argue, players have mobile and ubiquitous connection to WoW 'without participation in what most gamers would consider to be the central skill elements of the game' (Christensen & Prax, 2012: 737), thereby modifying the temporal, spatial and social experience of gameplay. Player reviews commend the app for facilitating game-engagement 'on-the-go', enabling the negotiation of time zones (e.g. so gamers in Australia are not left with the 'dregs' in auction houses) and providing always-on pathways of communication between guild members.

It is clear that the various modalities of mobile gaming cannot be simplistically captured under the 'casual' rubric; rather, they are part of a broader 'assemblage' of play that is cross-platform and transmediatic, dedicated and occasional, domestic and peripatetic. They are also situated, contextual and paratextual, and reside in the interstices of everyday life. In the following section we provide a brief overview of the locative capacity and functionality of mobile games, a topic we will return to in greater detail in Chapter 11.

## Locative Mobile Media Games

Location-based, navigational and image-capture technologies now dynamically frame and mediate the ways we traverse, experience, share and think about place. That is, the digital mapping and representation of place increasingly pervades our geosocial, interpersonal and embodied experience. As Jason Farman comments, the seamless integration of locative mobile media into our day-to-day activities comprises 'the new interface of everyday life'; moreover, he argues, the 'process of inhabiting multiple spaces simultaneously has moved into the sphere of the quotidian and often goes unnoticed' (Farman, 2012: 87). Over the past decade we have seen a proliferation of **location-based games** and playful apps that invite us to upload and share our personal and local content in-the-moment, thereby enacting a layered and multifaceted experience of place, presence and communication.

As we outlined in the previous chapter, historically, location-based games – variously referred to as urban games, big games, pervasive games and mixed-reality games – emerged out of avant-garde new media art, and involved creative experimentation with emerging media interfaces, platforms and networks. Such work deliberately sought to challenge or disrupt the mundane and familiar by transforming public spaces into playful places. Yet although location-based social games were once considered experimental in their enablement of geosocial play practices, they have more recently been mainstreamed (Wilken, 2012), normalized and commodified, part of the more general cultural shift towards 'gamification'. This trend is exemplified by the mobile app *Foursquare*, a 'playful' service (with a purported 30 million users) that integrates user-generated first-hand recommendations of 'the best places to go' with wayfinding, friend-networks and consumer rewards. Similarly, *MyTown*, a location-based social game, reportedly enables players to 'virtually' buy their favourite stores and places (at the same time earning cash to spend in real locations), turning the 'real world' into a Monopoly game.

Despite the cultural turn towards gamification, creators of urban and 'community' games, such as UK new media group Blast Theory, continue to deliberately 'hack' public space, inviting players to undergo a de-familiarization of their everyday perceptions and experiences of the urban environment. In this way, as we explore further in the next chapter, location-aware and hybrid reality mobile games can transform urban spaces into participatory gameworlds, a potential seen in 'sandbox' games that enable an emergent mode of play that often embeds player-centred design, relies on generative player feedback and content contribution, and is situated within the localized contexts of place and community. New York game designer Frank Lantz, who was involved in the *PacManhattan* project, argued that such games will play a pivotal role in the future of gaming.

In his analysis of *Geocaching*, Farman (2012) describes the mixed or augmented realities of pervasive location-based games where bodies, networks and material space converge. Played in over 200 countries, *Geocaching* is a treasure hunt game requiring game players to hide geocache containers marked with GPS data in public places; players then 'use their mobile devices (from GPS receivers to iPhones) to track down the container, sign the log, and leave tradable and trackable items in the cache' (Farman, 2009: 1). In such games we must seamlessly accommodate both immediate and mediated being-in-the-world. Eric Gordon and Adriana de Souza e Silva (2011) have argued that such hybrid practices generate what they term 'net locality'. Net locality, or 'net-local public space', is populated by those engaging in location-based activities with mobile devices, those (both co-present and online) inhering or participating in this network activity, and those non-participants who are co-located in the urban setting. While urban spaces have always been mediated by technologies, Gordon and de Souza e Silva suggest that net localities 'produce unique types of networked interactions and, by extension, new contexts for social cohesion', such that 'co-presence is not mutually opposed to networked interaction' and distinguishing between them at any one moment becomes increasingly difficult (Gordon & de Souza e Silva, 2011: 91).

Location-based mobile games thus require the player to integrate their own situated and embodied perception of the world with dynamic GPS-enabled information, embedded within an augmented and networked game reality. As our attentional foci in such quotidian spaces becomes split and diversified, the actual/virtual dichotomy previously used to differentiate between offline/online practices is thoroughly disassembled into complex and dynamic modes of 'presencing'. Here, presence can be broadly defined in Alva Noë's terms as access: that which is more-or-less available or accessible to our perceptual awareness (Noë, 2012). Such a definition of presence does not prioritize face-to-face modes of communication, or preclude networked, dispersed or asynchronous pathways of connection. Urban spaces are now filled with mobile media users who create communicative pockets of coexisting modalities of presence: co-located presence, telepresence, absent presence, distributed presence and ambient presence (Hjorth & Richardson, 2020), all of which demand different modes of embodied being-in-the-world. In this way, location-based mobile games and applications can be said to add a complex dimensionality to place and space.

As we have suggested in previous chapters, traditional critiques of computer and videogames argue that the 'magic circle' defines the parameters of gameplay, marking off a temporary world wherein particular game rules apply. In this view, to play a game means, materially or conceptually, 'entering' the magic circle of the game. Yet increasingly, online multiplayer games, mobile location-based and hybrid reality games erode the notion of a magic circle or dedicated gamespace. A number of theorists have proposed alternative corporeal and ontological metaphors for game worlds as substitutes for the magic circle (Castronova, 2005; Nieuwdorp, 2005; Copier, 2009), such as the porous membrane or permeable window.

In a way similar to Taylor's notion of assemblage, Copier (2009) argued a decade ago for the network trope as a descriptor of the contemporary game experience, one that still holds currency today. She suggests that the metaphor of the magic circle 'hides the ambiguity, variability, and complexity of actual games and play', and advocates instead that 'we shift our focus from a study of games in culture to study of gameplay as one of the play elements and producers of culture. A network perspective allows us to understand how every game and game experience is negotiated spatially, temporally and socially' (Copier, 2009: 169). For Copier, the composite, interconnected and dynamic ontology of the network trope provides a more authentic figuration of the game environments specific to mobile, location-based and social media gaming, and also helps us to interpret the 'playful turn' in contemporary new media culture and the infiltration of a ludic sensibility into the mobilities and practices of everyday life.

Location-based mobile games also highlight the cultural specificity of network localities, online participation and privacy. For example, the uptake of social networking service Jiepang in Shanghai, China, reflects a Chinese notion of privacy that is informed by *guanxi* (social relations based on trust and reciprocal interpersonal obligations), which is vastly different from Western concerns about surveillance and stalking in the context of *Foursquare* (Hjorth et al., 2012). As Christian McCrea (2011) points out, individual and governmental patterns of mobile media ownership and use can have distinct trajectories; both consumption and production of media are very much informed by the local, and mobile gaming is played out differently across culturally diverse contexts, reinforcing the importance of considering situatedness and context in any analysis of games and cultural play.

Mobile gaming has many histories subject to intersecting contextual trajectories – socio-linguistic, geographical, technocultural, medium- and platform-specific. That is, the definition and constitution of 'mobile gaming' depends largely upon one's historical epoch and cultural region, in terms of broader technological, economic and transnational flows, the collective gaming habits, attitudes and uptake within one's cultural milieu, and more narrowly upon one's individual game experiences and preferences within these contexts. As we argue in the following section, however, mobile games and app-based media ecologies are closely tied to the rise of haptic touchscreens, affording an intrinsically intimate and tactile form of play both within and across cultures.

## Haptic Play

As discussed in Chapter 2, haptics are very important to the affordances of mobile games. In his description of mobile games as 'stupid games', Anderson (2012) attributes their rise to the affordances and app ecology of the iPhone and subsequent touchscreen phones. The implications of the haptic mobile interface – intimate, tappable, pinchable and intuitive – combined with its portability, have had a significant impact on game design and development, and rendered games mimetic and thus accessible to everyone. In *Abstracting Craft*, McCullough (1996) insightfully argued that our deepest engagement is through touch; indeed, the primacy of touch and the importance of the hand-screen relation is obvious in game design, echoed in Nintendo's labelling of the 'Touch Generation'. Moreover, as van den Boomen (2014) articulates, our experience of any media interface mobilizes bodily metaphors or metonyms, and we use numerous and familiar somatic metaphors to conceptually and perceptually manage our engagement with mobile media and games.

An overwhelming number of games and apps available on mobile phones and tablets are mimetic to some degree; that is, they simulate embodied experience (e.g. moving a block or sling-shotting a bird) and, ideally, they are designed so that they can be used immediately and intuitively rather than requiring instruction. As Keogh notes, mimetic interfaces call upon bodily habits and memories that 'more closely align to those already learned through the player's everyday existence' (2018: 64). Haptic touchscreens, such as the iPhone, are devices that have what is called a post-WIMP interface (Jacob et al., 2008). WIMP stands for Window, Icon, Menu, Pointing Device, the standard tools for navigation and control of a desktop computer interface. Touchscreens are specifically designed for use with the finger, or fingers for multi-touch sensing, and because the screen is capacitive, it depends on electrical conductivity that can only be provided by bare skin (or specially designed styluses). As Jacob et al. (2008) point out, post-WIMP interfaces require a somatic and visceral understanding of naïve physics. For example, primary bodily sensations such as inertia and springiness can be found in many touchscreen applications and games and provide the illusion that screen objects have mass and exist in a 'real world'.

Naïve physics can also include our body-memory of hardware such as the keyboard and joystick which are then simulated in the touchscreen graphic user interface (GUI). Thus, after habitual use, the mobile touchscreen as game interface becomes kinaesthetically familiar, affording a sensory knowing of the fingers that correlates with what appears on the small screen. This is nowhere better exemplified than in mimetic games which enfold the player into a temporary and incomplete simulation of real-world physics, like turning a page in the origami-like discovery aesthetic of *Tengami*, or 'finger-bombing' in *Angry Birds* (Parisi, 2008). That is, the kinetic experience of tangibility, concreteness and elasticity become 'condensed in the hand' (Kirkpatrick, 2009: 134). Other games, such as *The Room* and *Monument Valley*, call upon our embodied memories of three-dimensional geometric worlds. Indeed, creators of *The Room* describe it as a 'physical puzzler inside a beautifully tactile 3D world', while *Monument Valley* challenges the player with 'ingenious puzzles that involve lifting and spinning the environment'. With mobile games, there is a fundamental and irreducible relation between bodily dexterity (knowledge in the hands and fingers) and our habits of perceptual orientation and movement; we use numerous and familiar whole-body metaphors to conceptually and perceptually manage our engagement with mobile games.

For Eikenes and Morrison (2010), as we come to habitually use such interfaces, we effectively develop a new kind of 'motion literacy' specific to devices that combine touchscreen with accelerometer or position-recognition functionality, such as the smartphone and tablets. A type of kinetic and motile learning is required that works to overcome or adapt to the imprecise control we have over objects and actions in and on the screen. This is possible because of our ability to take on an 'as if' structure of embodiment. As Jeff Rush (2011) notes, the way in which mimetic touchscreen games such as *Angry Birds* engender 'a heightened sense of the linkage between two different orders of reality, real physical gesture and its on-screen representation' works to attach a 'kinetic materiality' to the action and movement that takes place on the screen, creating moments of tangibility and concreteness (Rush, 2011: 245). That is, there is something of the kinetic experience of releasing an elastic band that effectively becomes 'condensed into the hand' (Kirkpatrick, 2009: 134). In part, this is achieved by what Skalski et al. (2011) call kinesic natural mapping, where bodily movement corresponds in an approximate (or 'as-if') way to onscreen action, an effect enabled by the way touchscreens can deploy physical analogies; natural mapping works to 'complete' being in a mediated space, facilitating an immersive experience. The sounds that accompany haptic games also effectively simulate (or stimulate) tactile feedback and increase the sense of 'being-in' a discrete and tangible gameworld.

Throughout our research, participants have frequently described the sensory pleasure this experience engenders. One participant described her 'obsession' with *Godus* (a world-builder that enables detailed sculpting of multiple layers of land, with each configuration being unique to the player), explaining that she played the game intensively for over a year: 'there was something about the way you could sculpt the land, and set your little workers to build or mine, that was really satisfying'. These new sensory literacies and pleasures are not just important at the level of somatic attachment to one's device, for the haptic and aural intimacy of mobile games also becomes material to our social and personal intimacies. Another participant recalled and then performed how she would share *Angry Birds* gameplay with her partner in the evenings. This involved lying together on the couch or bed, passing her iPhone between them (the only rule being that the device had to be relinquished to the other if a 'life' was lost). They thus enacted a ritual of closeness and being-together that is bound up both in the simplicity and 'swapability' of the game, and in the very materiality and co-touchability of the interface. For others, the closeness of shared play was also experienced through a sense of networked co-presence, such as the sense of connection that is realized in playing online games with physically distant friends and family, as if 'touching' the same game. In this way, touchscreen game-play expresses not only a way of being in the world, but also a way of *being together* through 'mediated social touch' (Paterson, 2007: 131).

As we outlined in Chapter 2, researchers have sought and developed a range of innovative methods and conceptual frameworks to account for 'the body's new-found centrality to the play experience' (Parisi, 2015: 6), approaches now coalescing in the subdiscipline of haptic media studies and the application of haptic ethnography.

## Social Mobile Media Games

Over the past five years or so, and in tandem with the emergence of app-based media ecologies, we have seen the convergence of mobile games with both locative media and online social networking, and the translation of interpersonal and communicative practices into 'playful' activities. Each day millions of people log onto social media at work, school, home and on the move as a way to connect, share content and play with friends. Made-for-mobile social media are a routine part of our everyday activities, sitting alongside – and often integrated with – numerous mobile games and apps on our mobile screens. Social networking and media services such as Facebook and YouTube are now fully integrated into smartphones and mobile devices. In 2012, for example, Facebook made a strategic 'shift to mobile', with chief financial officer (CFO) David Ebersman revealing that the social networking service aimed to become 'the default social infrastructure for mobile games' (Rose, 2013: n.p.). Today, many social mobile games, such as *Words With Friends*, are accessible through Facebook, while numerous mobile games link gamer data and player statistics to users' social media networks.

Similar developments are apparent in the evolution of mobile social media platform Kakao, originating in South Korea. Available for all different mobile platforms, Kakao is an example of one of the first purpose-built social mobile media. Unlike Facebook, which initially privileged the personal or desktop computer as the primary interface, having to adapt to keep up with the move to mobile devices, Kakao speaks to the growing population globally whose only or main experience of 'being online' is via the mobile phone (such as Japan and China). Kakao features an instant messaging service for group and one-on-one text, photo and video communication, that also incorporates a games suite (KakaoTalk), a photo album service with an inbuilt suite of filters (KakaoAlbum), and a blog-style service enabling users to upload and share their 'daily life stories' (KakaoStory). Kakao thus allows users to move in and out of online and offline modes, and between social and game worlds, while on the move. While initially functioning as a Mobile Instant Messaging (MIM) system, KakaoTalk has seen rapid growth through the uptake of convergent social-locative media games like *I Love Coffee*. In South Korea, once dominant PC-based **massively multiplayer online games** (MMOGs) are being eclipsed by social media games like *I Love Coffee* and played predominantly by female players. Unlike the first epoch of social media games epitomized by *Mafia Wars* and *FarmVille*, games like *I Love Coffee* have been so successful because they are made especially for the smartphone context.

## Conclusion

Mobile gaming presents a convergence of locative, social and mobile media; it is a lens through which we can see the changing nature of mobility, play and communication as it moves through broader sociocultural, technological and economic dynamics. In the context of social, cultural, media and game scholarship, the transformative effect of mobile gaming – discrete, app-based, location-based and networked – demands a reconceptualization of the fundamental principles and terminologies underlying theories of play, sociality and gaming. Terms like 'videogame', 'avatar', the 'magic circle', 'simulation', 'immersion' and 'gamespace', which demarcate gameplay from broader social and non-game contexts, are clearly no longer adequate to describe the intimacy and porosity of mobile, location-based and social gameworlds.

Within the various assemblages of mobile gaming, we see new types of intimacy and communicative practice emerging around gameplay, new ways in which co-present forms of play and place-making are enacted while on the move, and the dynamic and ongoing transformation of the mobile screen as a portal that seamlessly insinuates games and cultural play into our everyday lives. This merger of play and daily life is also an aspect of augmented reality (AR) and locative mobile media games, which we turn to in the next chapter.

## Further Reading

Hjorth, L., & Richardson, I. (2014). *Gaming in Social, Locative and Mobile Media*. Basingstoke: Palgrave.

Hjorth, L., & Richardson, I. (2020). *Ambient Play*. Cambridge, MA: The MIT Press.

Jin, D. Y. (2016). *Mobile Gaming in Asia: Politics, Culture and Emerging Trends*. New York: Springer.

Juul, J. (2009). *A Casual Revolution: Reinventing Video Games and Their Players*. Cambridge, MA: The MIT Press.

Paul, C. A. (2020). *Free-to-Play: Mobile Video Games, Bias, and Norms*. Cambridge, MA: The MIT Press.

Willson, M., & Leaver, T. (Eds.) (2016). *Social, Casual and Mobile Games: The Changing Gaming Landscape*. New York: Bloomsbury Academic.

# 11

# Augmented Reality Games and Playful Locative Media

---

Mobile games and playful apps are increasingly embedded in our everyday lives. Describe some of the ways 'mobile media play' is part of your daily practices.

Why is mobile gaming considered a form of ambient play?

How do augmented reality games change our experience of presence, both in terms of our interaction with others and our perception of public space and the environment?

In what ways do AR games further dissolve the boundaries of the magic circle?

Why do you think *Pokémon GO* was so popular? Why do some describe it as the 'perfect storm'?

---

This chapter explores the cultural and perceptual effects of augmented reality (AR) gaming as a form of play in public spaces increasingly embedded in the routines of everyday life. First, we provide a general introduction to mobile play in public spaces in relation to AR games, and then focus on a detailed case study of the *Pokémon GO* phenomenon in both historical and culturally-specific contexts. *Pokémon GO* could be considered a perfect storm – coalescing the transmedia success of Pokémon, the ubiquity of location-aware mobile devices, and decades of locative and AR experimentation by new media groups and urban installation artists. Our more focused exploration in this chapter considers how *Pokémon GO* provides a lens through which we might critically interpret the entanglements of mobile games, playful imaginaries and the politics of everyday life. This chapter continues key arguments made in the previous chapters concerning the way location-based mobile games and augmented reality games challenge the distinction between 'play' and 'everyday life', and the evolution of mobile gaming into a significant form of contemporary play.

## Mobile Play in Public Spaces

Our engagement with mobile screens is quite different from the singular attention we give to other screens, such as television, cinema and even home computers. As we move about in the urban environment, this is a necessity, as our attention is split between the mobile interface and what's around us. We attend to our phones for minutes at a time, checking for messages, social media posts or a missed call, finding out where to go on Google Maps, or playing a quick level of *Kick the Buddy* while waiting for the train. Mobile phone engagement is characterized by this kind of sporadic attention and digitally informed multitasking in public spaces.

As we noted in Chapter 10, this distracted engagement is understood all too well by mobile phone game developers, who label the mobile player a casual gamer. In our ethnographic research, participants would often trivialize their mobile gameplay as an incidental distraction, an unimportant activity and a waste of time. Some were even embarrassed to admit they play such trivial games. When we asked Perth high-school student and self-professed gamer Michael if he ever played mobile games, he said 'no, I don't bother with those'; yet as he took us on a media walkthrough of his mobile phone, he explained that he would sometimes play *Jetpack Joyride* and other 'silly' games when he was on the train to and from school. His most used mobile app – like many post-millennial digital natives – was *Snapchat*, which can be described as an ambiently playful and gamified form of in-the-moment communication, enabling people to share photos and messages throughout the day and compete for the longest 'snapstreaks' (consecutive daily snaps) that can sometimes extend for many months.

Through the ubiquity of mobile media, much like the now perpetual state of being online, games and playful communication apps have become a normal and habitual part of everyday life. Importantly, like mobile media use, mobile gameplay modifies how we move through the urban environment, effectively comingling mediated and actual experience. It changes how we interact with (or ignore) each other in public spaces. As we have suggested this normalization of mobile games, together with their constant availability, renders mobile play *ambient* (Hjorth & Richardson, 2020). This term conveys how mobile media and games have increasingly infiltrated our modes of social interaction and become part of our daily routines. One of the significant effects of mobile media is the way such interfaces have changed our modalities of presence (or our sense of 'here-ness' and 'there-ness'), as both face-to-face and networked communication become increasingly entangled.

In the context of public urban space, it has previously been shown how portable music devices such as the Walkman, iPod, mp3 player and mobile phones afford a kind of *auditory privatization*, altering our behaviour towards the 'familiar strangers' that surround us (Helyer, 2007). As Michael Bull has commented: 'Mediated isolation itself becomes a form of control over spaces of urban culture in which we withdraw into a world small enough to control' (2005: 169). In a similar way, much like listening to music, mobile phone use and casual gaming are often used as proxy *Do Not Disturb* signs when we are alone in public. This kind of behaviour is now one that we all recognize, a mode of media distraction similar to reading a book or newspaper on public transport – an indicator of wanted privacy well understood by those around us. Yet while music players may work to shut out the bustling noise of urban life – that is, enabling us to disconnect – the mobile phone is also a communicative and networked device, a conduit of connectivity. The now constant and familiar noises of connection and intimacy – ringtones, bleeps, buzzes and one-sided conversations – can often be unpredictable and disruptive, puncturing the soundscapes of public spaces and places of social congregation.

For many of our research participants, mobile media use and gameplay in the public domain offers multiple affordances – relief of boredom, a sense of ambient connection and in the proximity of potential risk or discomfort (from the unwelcome intrusion of others), a strategy of protection and avoidance. Mobile gameplay, and mobile media use more generally, allows us to personalize and mobilize media entertainment as an enactment of privacy while being-with-others. At the same time, the mobile device also becomes co-opted into the labour of waiting, filling the empty times and spaces that are peppered throughout everyday urban life (Bissell, 2007).

For Jussi Parikka and Jaakko Suominen (2006), mobile media act as a 'third place' situated between public and private space; the mobile interface quite literally *mobilizes* and *activates* private and personal space in the public sphere. Yet in some ways it is a new form of an old habitual practice already common in the 19th century:

> [W]hat is new in this division of space and creation of a place of one's own? Instead of seeing this solely as a trend of digital mobile culture, we argue that this is more a phenomenon that took off with the creation of modern urban space and the new paradigms of media consumption. … [T]he pattern of mobile entertainment usage as the creation of a private sphere was already part of the railway culture of the nineteenth century – even if people consumed such media content as newspapers and books instead of digital entertainment. (Parikka & Suominen, 2006: n.p.)

What is different today, however, is the way this third space is also a meeting-place. That is, the closing-off enacted by mobile media users in public is also an opening up – an unfolding of multiplayer gameworlds, an amplified gesturing of playful communication, a way of reaching out and being present elsewhere in the network.

As we outlined in Chapter 10 and explore further below, mobile augmented reality games also involve an opening up of *hybrid space* that merges physical location and online networks, dissembling the 'magic circle' of play. Such games change our experience of urban space and place in another important way, by transforming our neighbourhoods and cities into collaborative playgrounds.

## Augmented Realities and Hybrid Presence

Recent advances and investments in virtual and augmented reality technologies have seen both rise in prominence in recent decades, but ambitions and technologies for layering virtual and actual worlds are not new. Histories of virtual reality long predate contemporary technology and can be found in the ambitions of painters from the Italian Renaissance to ancient Greece. Histories of augmented reality are much more recent (see Figure 11.1).

In 1968, Harvard professor and computer scientist Ivan Sutherland invented an augmented reality device that he called *The Sword of Damocles* with his student, Bob Sproull, but it was not until 1990 that a Boeing researcher named Tom Caudell coined the term 'augmented reality' (Arth et al., 2015). Detailed histories and applications of augmented reality (AR) can be found in Berryman's 'Augmented reality: A review' (2012) and in Arth et al.'s *The History of Mobile Augmented Reality* (2015).

Location-based services typically provide situational information about the urban environment, such that what we see on our mobile screens changes the way we navigate through and experience our immediate surroundings. In this way, 'being online'

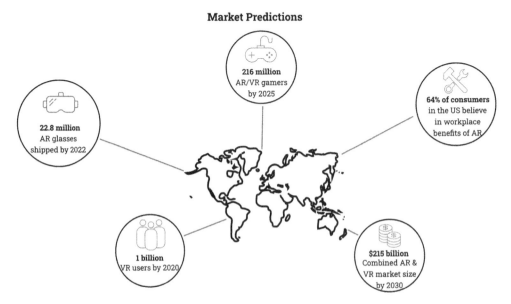

**Market Predictions**

216 million
AR/VR gamers
by 2025

64% of consumers
in the US believe
in workplace
benefits of AR

22.8 million
AR glasses
shipped by 2022

1 billion
VR users by 2020

$215 billion
Combined AR &
VR market size
by 2030

**Figure 11.1** Evolution of augmented reality. Image: GamingScan.com.

is enfolded within present contexts and activities, as we find our way through the city, search for a good place to eat, drive to a friend's house for the first time, or tag our location on location-based apps such as *Foursquare*. Location-based mobile gaming with integrated augmented reality (such that we can 'see' digital information and artefacts in the real world) is a particularly robust instance of this emergent hybrid experience.

In the game *Mogi*, for example – beta-tested successfully in Japan between 2003 and 2006 – the city of Tokyo was represented both as a map on players' mobile phones and on the web, the latter of which provided online players with an expanded view of the gamespace overlaying Tokyo, along with the geographic and gameworld location of all players (de Souza e Silva & Hjorth, 2009: 621). *Mogi* worked primarily as a collecting and trading game; both mobile and desktop players accessed live maps (of different sizes, depending on the screen interface) and collaborated with each other to accrue points by collecting virtual items. The game required players to collect virtual objects such as fruits or animals spread throughout the city of Tokyo. Using location-aware mobile phones, players and objects were visible on the cell phone screen, and players could catch objects within 400 metres, and interact with each other depending on their location. Through the game, players transformed the urban space of Tokyo into a playful and ludic space, rediscovering the city as they walked around in search of virtual objects and other players. Yet as Licoppe and Inada (2006) revealed through ethnographic methods (see Chapter 2), the game also invited stalking and often blurred the boundaries between wanted and unwanted proximity.

In games such as *Mogi* both actual and 'as-if' mobility is fundamental to our experience of hybrid space. Here, the term 'mobility' must account for the physical macro-movement of the pedestrian body which can be traced geospatially on the gamer's desktop computer, the micro-movements and motor coordination required of the mobile player, and the virtual movement and exchange of objects and creatures on gamers' mobile devices as they move through the hybrid gamespace. Licoppe and Inada described players of the game *Mogi* as 'hybrid beings' who were able to 'smoothly integrate the embodied lived experience of the body and the mediated perception of oneself and of the environment' (2006: 52). In this way, even early AR games work to seamlessly combine actual and virtual worlds as they are actively negotiated on-the-move, effectively creating a hybrid mode of being where the boundary between the game and real life collapses.

The players of *Mogi* quite often altered their passage through the city, dynamically reworking the spatial order and perceptual experience of familiar and unfamiliar urban space. A frequent player of the game described how his trips to the city became physically 'randomized' or diverted as an effect of the game, such that he 'got a chance to discover part of the city that I ignored, [motivated] to check out that parallel street I never took' (Hall, 2004: n.p.). Social designer of networked environments

Amy Jo Kim suggested that *Mogi* was ideally suited to the casual gamer: 'It nestles in your everyday life, rather than requiring you to change your behavior. ... It amplifies your ordinary behavior – it changes going on an errand into a piece of a game' (cited in Hall, 2004: n.p.). Unlike other mobile games of this era, including *Botfighters* (2001), *Noderunner* (2002), *PacManhattan* (2004) and *Conquest* (2004), which all involved open competition against other players, *Mogi* took an ambient and social approach to pervasive games by emphasizing collecting and trading, as well as communication and collaboration, allowing for broader demographic appeal (Kim, 2004; Terdiman, 2004). *Mogi* and a similar game, *Insectopia* (2007), extended traditional Japanese practices of play, such as collecting, and represent key precursors to *Pokémon GO* (2016). Such mixed-reality games, rather than creating an escape from real life through the sticky screen immersion typical of console gaming, work to integrate play and game interaction into the patterns, trajectories, mobilities and habitudes of everyday life and work.

More recently, game designer Naomi Alderman's creation *Zombies, Run!* has successfully integrated audio storytelling into location-based mobile gameplay to augment the experience of jogging in the urban environment. In developing the mixed-reality mobile app, Alderman effectively exploited both the propensity of joggers to listen to playlists and podcasts on their mobile device, and the popularity of zombie narratives in the contemporary imagination – and consequent familiarity with 'heart-pounding running sequences in zombie movies' (Alderman, 2019: n.p.). Progression in the game is cumulatively achieved the more the player runs (as the hero Runner Five) and collects items in their effort to escape the undead and successfully complete the 'mission' directive.

The game is also an example of user-generated participatory media culture, as the growing community of runners contributed to narrative elements and uploaded fanfiction and fan art that Alderman incorporated into the game. *Zombies, Run!* also maximizes the perceptual and affective intimacy of mobile media. As Alderman comments, it 'feels like the characters are whispering directly into your ear... It can get very emotional, in a really good way' (Alderman, 2019: n.p.). In effect, the mobile app coalesces location-aware technology with a popular everyday routine, embedding an established sci-fi storyworld into the habitual mobile media use of exercising city-dwellers. As we will discuss below, the grafting of a popular transmedia narrative into a location-based AR game is also a strategy effectively deployed in *Pokémon GO*.

As we have suggested, each of these games described above effectively dissolves what has been termed the magic circle of gameplay, which has traditionally been used as a way of distinguishing between acts of play and not-play, designating how a game is contained, figuratively, conceptually and in praxis. Huizinga described play as 'an intermezzo, an *interlude* in our daily lives' (emphasis original), although he acknowledged that it is also a regular event, an accompaniment or complement and 'an integral part of life in general' (Huizinga, 1938 [1955]: 9, cited in Copier, 2009: 166–167). Both players and game developers engage in strategies of containment and boundary-work around what constitutes gameplay, in order to determine where a game begins and ends. Today, these boundaries are no longer clear, shifting and dissolving as gameworlds and the everyday lifeworld come together.

Moreover, as we have explored at length in previous chapters (see, for example, Chapter 6 on paratextual play practices, and Chapter 4 on game fandom), games and playfulness are becoming increasingly intertwined with social interactivity, communities and diverse cultural practices in everyday life. The digital and material network ecologies of gameplay – from multiplayer online gaming to mobile location-based and pervasive gaming – are inextricable from the patterns and mobilities of daily activity. That is, for many of us it is impossible to say where our online player identities end and our real-life personae begin, where social interaction stops and gameplay starts, or how game spaces can be marked off from urban, public and city spaces.

As Farman notes, one of the characteristics of mobile technologies is that they have transformed our experience of presence and absence into perpetual co-presence through a form of 'social proprioception' – the ambient awareness of others in the network (Farman, 2012: 108). Indeed, as noted in the previous chapter, mobile media users and game players experience a complex spectrum of presence: *co-located* presence (while in the same physical space as others), *telepresence* (when communicating at a distance, such as skyping or snapchatting), *absent* presence (through the blog or Facebook posts of those not currently online), *distributed* presence (via online multiplayer gaming or chatrooms) and *ambient* presence (the perdurable awareness of others online). In this way, mobile apps and games can be said to add a complex *dimensionality* to place and space. The impact of these multiple ways of understanding and sensing presence is that we must now rethink the spatial and place-based experience of being-in-public, as we continue to blend online information about our immediate environment into the patterns of urban life and pedestrian movement. This is precisely what Gordon and de Souza e Silva mean by 'net locality', a fluid movement between physical and mediated proximity that 'takes the otherness of the web and places it squarely into where you are' (Gordon & de Souza e Silva, 2011: 3).

With mobile devices, net locality is with us wherever we go. It even informs our domestic life, as our homes become findable with online maps, and populated by location-based game elements, as is the case with *Pokémon GO*. While in the early stages of the internet we may have maintained a clear separation between the actual and the virtual, the online and offline, now those boundaries have collapsed. Consequently, our spectrum of attention and sense of presence has become both ambient and dispersed. Just as a range of media products and services from television broadcasts to wireless internet have previously embedded themselves into our daily lives,

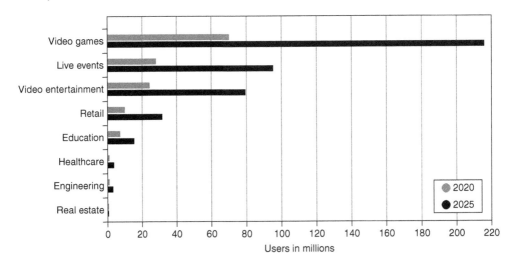

**Figure 11.2** Expected uptake of AR and VR software. Image: GamingScan.com.

it is widely predicted that augmented reality, virtual reality and other hybrid reality mediums will become normalized in quotidian terms (see Figure 11.2).

In the futures of mobile location-based and hybrid reality gaming, we are also beginning to see a mutually contingent interplay between actual and virtual domains. When we play location-based games such as *Pokémon GO* and *Harry Potter: Wizards Unite*, we enter hybrid realities that alter our movement through urban space, changing how we perceive and share experiences of and about place. Not only are urban environments being augmented and transformed into collaborative playgrounds, but the widespread use of AR games such as *Pokémon GO* is having emergent effects on the commercial potential of particular locations within cities, with possible consequences for the planning and configuration of urban spaces. As we describe below through the experiences of our participants, *Pokémon GO* serves as an example *par excellence* of location-based and augmented reality mobile gaming, as it highlights the hybrid and contextual nature of mobile play, and the way it transforms public spaces into urban playgrounds.

## Pokémon GO

Within the first weeks of its launch in July 2016, millions of people across several countries downloaded the *Pokémon GO* app onto their iOS and Android devices and entered an augmented reality. They wandered local neighbourhoods and public spaces in search of Pokémon and PokéStops, encountering the eponymous monsters in real-world settings, and competing and connecting with other players through virtual Pokémon gyms, raids and battles.

In its first month, *Pokémon GO* generated more revenue than any other mobile game to date (US$207 million), and at its peak in late 2016 was played by over 45 million people. As of mid-2019, it still captures an 84% market share of all location-based games (measured by downloads), generates around US$4 million per day, and has 5 million daily active users (DAU).[1] It has reportedly been the subject of Facebook and Instagram posts, comments or shares over 1 billion times, and over 110 million friend connections have been made through the game.[2]

Through the augmented layering of the digital onto physical place, banal and familiar surroundings are transformed into game terrain (Figure 11.3). A Pokémon monster can be found and caught in one's own bathroom; a gym or PokéStop might be situated at the local library, café or nearby graveyard. The popularity of *Pokémon GO* – touted as the first ever *really* successful location-based game – has been the subject of much criticism and celebration. As media researchers, the success and popularity of the game gives us a unique opportunity to explore the experience of *en masse* location-based mobile gameplay, and to consider how AR games afford modes of public playfulness and hybrid presence.

About three-quarters of *Pokémon GO* players are aged 18–34,[3] with a moderate leaning towards male users, an age range which reflects the way in which the game emerged out of an already-established transmedia franchise (originally created in Japan by Satoshi Tajiri in 1995), attracting a large *Pokémon* fanbase over two decades in the making. For some, *Pokémon GO* is a positive experience – the gameplay evokes 20-something nostalgia (Surman, 2009; McCrea, 2017), encourages physical exercise, facilitates 'genuine human-to-human interaction' (Wawro, 2016: n.p.) and effectively enhances our sense of wellbeing and belonging (Vella et al., 2019).

**Figure 11.3** *Pokémon GO* augmented reality view. Photo: Wachiwit/Shutterstock.com.

For others, the game forces us to reflect on the ongoing gendered, racial, socio-economic, age-based and bodily inequities of urban mobility that affect many of us on a daily basis (Isbister, 2016).

More philosophically, for game critic Bogost, there's 'something fundamentally revolting about celebrating the Pokémonization of the globe as the ultimate realization of the merged social and technological potential of modern life' (2016: n.p.). Thus, there are complications to this 'social revolution' of hybrid or augmented reality gaming within mainstream media cultures. The culture, place, identity and embodiment of the player all informs their experience of *Pokémon GO*, highlighting the uneven politics of mobile games and everyday play and their intrinsic relationship to power. We are reminded again of the irreducible variability, specificity and contextuality of all media use.

The various issues pertaining to *Pokémon GO* as a cultural moment move across many contemporary political and social debates. These include the effect of location-aware technologies in constructions of privacy (Coldewey, 2016; Cunningham, 2016), risk and surveillance (Machkovech, 2016; Mishra, 2016), and the role of mobile media in commodifying (Evangelho, 2016) and expanding the social, cultural and creative dimensions of play (Isbister, 2016; Mäyrä, 2017). *Pokémon GO* was also the focus of a recent issue of *Mobile Media & Communication* (Hjorth & Richardson, 2017), in which ten key mobile communication, mobile media and game theorists provided short commentaries on the game's actual and potential effects. The issue patently exemplifies the coming together of these disciplinary fields.

*Pokémon GO* sits at the nexus of a complex array of technological and cultural trajectories: the playful turn in contemporary media culture; the ubiquity of location-based and haptic mobile media (and apps and games); innovative game design and the integrative effects of digital mapping technologies; the intertwining of performative media games and art; our individual and collective memories of storyworlds and transmedia universes; the increasing importance of issues concerning privacy and risk in public spaces; the ongoing digital and networked augmentation of place and space; and the politics embedded in this hybrid experience of the lifeworld.

Throughout our ethnographic research, many of our participants, young and old, played the game, some lamenting that it is a simplified version of other more substantial and complex *Pokémon* games (such as those designed for the Nintendo Game Boy and DualScreen), others excited by the way it overlaid game features onto the real world. As 25-year-old Misha from Perth described:

> For me it's a bit of nostalgia and reminds me of when me and my friends used to play and trade on our Game Boys. I had the board game, posters, figurines… everything. We used to fight imaginary Pokémon battles every arvo in the local park. Now I've got the game open 24/7 on my phone, and even wander about during work breaks collecting Pokémon and tagging PokéStops. I live a fair way out of the

city, so there's not much Pokémon action when I'm at home! Though sometimes I might find one in the kitchen or toilet [laughs].

Misha's story reminds us of the inherently *spatial* and *mobile* nature of popular culture and media, and how popular culture forms have always been part of our everyday geographies (Horton, 2012: 11–12). In bringing together childhood and play studies with human geography, for example, John Horton documents how his young research participants integrated Pokémon play into the structure of their mundane spatial practices and daily space–time routines, effectively remaking their homes, local shops, and neighbourhoods as part of the Pokémon universe. In this sense, *Pokémon GO* can be seen as another instance of the way the 'stuff' of media permeates our everyday geographies, and an actualization of the location-based and augmented reality experienced by children over ten years ago. As Christian McCrea (2017) identifies, Pokémon is an expansive mobile game platform in its own right (firmly established by six generations of Game Boy and DS games) and participating in the Pokémon universe demands the 'deep agency' of players and accrual of experiential play knowledge that can potentially span several decades.

As our participants revealed in their narrations of *Pokémon GO* play, the pedestrian labour of location-based gaming, and the interweaving of digital and physical information, alters the 'spatial legibility' of urban space – or the way urban environments appear as coherent and recognizable patterns (Frith, 2014). Jon, an avid Pokémon fan and father of two young boys, relayed how the game was teaching his sons how to read and navigate maps. Georgia, a Perth-based lab technician, told us she went to places and streets she would never otherwise visit, and that she'd started to think of shops and parks in her neighbourhood as repurposed PokéStops and Gyms. This aptly conveys the key features of 'ambient play', a term that contextualizes mobile games within the routines and habits of everyday life, and as integral to our social and emotional lives.

Georgia's experience also reflects a quite extraordinary potential effect of location-based games. As some media theorists have suggested, there is evidence that games such as *Pokémon GO* may act as catalysts for large-scale changes in people's 'destination choice' or 'trip distribution' (Colley et al., 2017). In other words, such games have the potential to motivate 'people to do something they rarely do: substantially change where they choose to go' (Colley et al., 2017: n.p.). Lammes and Wilmott (2018) have explored the way location-based games – such as *Zombies, Run!* – effectively turn maps into 'navigational interfaces and gameboards' (p. 466), an observation that can also be applied to *Pokémon GO*. With developments in mobile technologies and the rise of collaborative platforms, making and sharing maps has taken on new playful, ambient and co-present dimensions.

In the second iteration of *Pokémon GO*, in which player cooperation has been designed into the game, social interaction and physical activity have become a key feature of play. Interestingly, this version of *Pokémon GO* has seen significant uptake by older adults, giving us insight into practices of intergenerational play as well as quotidian forms of digital health. In the streets of Badalona, north of Barcelona (Spain), it is not uncommon to see a digital wayfarer in the form of a *Pokémon GO* player. For some players, it has become intimately interwoven with practices of inter-generational care and the daily routines of pedestrian mobility. In these contexts, as the dust settled on the *Pokémon GO* craze and it became habitualized or forgotten as 'old' media, more compelling phenomena began to emerge of its deployment as a tool for enhancing social and physical wellbeing among middle-aged and elderly adults (Hino et al., 2019). Augmented reality, virtual reality and game technologies are increasingly being used to innovate in health solutions, especially to create mul-tisensorial tools for ageing well and ameliorating against the effects of dementia and phobia (Jakob & Collier, 2017; Gromer et al., 2019). In the context of this uptake, we suggest that rather than developing new and untested mobile apps to deal with health issues in the digital age, strategic care practices can be leveraged by way of the social and embodied affordances of 'old' and more established games like *Pokémon GO*. Moreover, we can learn from the lived experiences of such modalities of play through ethnographic approaches (see Chapter 2).

The positive health dimensions of mobile location-based games have been the subject of numerous studies. *Pokémon GO*, in particular, has been explored as a vehi-cle for intergenerational literacy, sharing and informal health practices (Lindqvist et al., 2018; Militello et al., 2018). As Tim Althoff, Ryen White and Eric Horvitz (2016) note, games like *Pokémon GO* encourage physical activity as part of the game-play, and increased exercise has been documented particularly in low-activity par-ticipants (Althoff et al., 2016; Hino et al., 2019). Hino et al. (2019), for example, conducted a ten-month ethnographic study in Yokohama (Japan) to investigate the ways *Pokémon GO* was used by middle-aged and older adults as part of their exercise routines. In another clinical study in Japan, Kato et al. (2017) explored how *Poké-mon GO* encouraged patients suffering *hikikomori* (a severe form of social isolation that can involve years of living in one room) to venture outside. Here the game allows players to enter a revisioned world-as-playground mediated by the screen, engaging with familiar routines of gameplay in public places previously perceived as risky or strange.

Yet while *Pokémon GO* play may address the importance of exercise in ameliorat-ing against mental health issues, it doesn't necessarily remedy the problem of social isolation within the culturally specific context of Japan, as people may play near one another without communicating. As one participant in the Kato et al. study noted, 'Most people are independently staring at their own individual screens in parks. We Japanese, unlike Westerners, don't chat with strangers!' (Kato et al., 2017: 75). *Hikikomori* has often been associated with the negative effects of videogaming. The condition appeared at the same time as videogames became popular in Japan. It also emerged at the end of the economic downturn during the late 1980s, in which the salaried tradition of employment ceased to be a secure career option for men. As psychotherapists note (Kato et al., 2017), although using AR games like *Pokémon GO* may encourage people to overcome physical seclusion through the familiar tropes of games and gameplay, such interventions must be employed in conjunction with other therapeutic techniques that foster sociality.

One of our research participants, Sofia, is a 67-year-old widow and nurse who has lived in the Catalonian town of Badalona all her life. Sofia is especially close to her 7-year-old grandson, Diego. They do many activities together, constantly sharing intergenerational skills, and it was Diego who first introduced Sofia to *Pokémon GO*. As they walked the streets of Badalona together, he would show her the digital overlays and virtual objects perceived through the game, and how to flick the haptic screen to capture Pokémon, effectively reinventing Sofia's everyday experiences of familiar and mundane spaces. She would wander the streets catching Pokémon, and trips to the market or shops became *Pokémon GO* adventures in which she would navigate alternative routes so as to encounter more of the virtual creatures. In effect, Sofia became a digital wayfarer (Hjorth & Pink, 2014).

A term coined by Hjorth and Pink, 'digital wayfaring' adapts Tim Ingold's work to convey how digital online networks of information and communication become imbricated and habituated in our movement through urban space. As we move from place to place, Ingold argued, we develop an embodied sense of knowing and being in the world – that is, we literally and dynamically make meaning as we walk and travel through the environment. Today, our knowledge and experience of place is augmented by an increasing array of geo-locative mobile apps, and thus are simultaneously material and digital. In augmented reality games such as *Pokémon GO*, the experience of digital wayfaring is further compounded, as locations are transformed into sites of collaborative and competitive play, and familiar terrain (our own homes, neighbourhoods and cities) are remade into playspaces.

Throughout our study of *Pokémon GO* players, it also became clear that the uptake of *Pokémon GO* by elderly populations points to the importance of taking haptic play seriously. Like many mobile touchscreen games, *Pokémon GO* is fundamentally mimetic; that is, the gameplay calls upon or simulates our embodied memory of familiar actions and real-world physics, such as throwing a ball, and ideally such games are designed so that they can be grasped immediately and intuitively rather than requiring specific expertise. A number of researchers have described the pleasure and intimacy of mimetic mobile gameplay (Richardson & Hjorth, 2017; Keogh, 2018), and this is also true of *Pokémon GO*. The game demands particular haptic gestures (e.g. the flicking of the Poké Ball or tagging PokéStops) that invite the knowing body to translate lived experience to the medium of the screen – the game is literally 'felt' through the body. Moreover, as Apperley and Moore (2018) insightfully observe, in networked and locative touchscreen games such as *Pokémon GO*, the haptic effects generate a kind of 'affective resonance', or a shared and empathic connection to other bodies; that is, the 'shared experience of touch, gesture, comportment and movement that is established and structured through the playful enactment of the *Pokémon GO* app … [induces] a wider and dispersed collective affinity and co-presence' (Apperley & Moore, 2018: 7). Citing Hjorth and Richardson (2020), Apperley and Moore note that this 'haptic effect' is a key dimension of the ambient play afforded by the game.

As a location-based AR game, *Pokémon GO* play is also felt through the body in another way – by embedding pedestrian mobility and co-located player interaction into the game's mechanics. It is not by accident that haptic games like *Pokémon GO* are being taken up by a broad spectrum of players, including the elderly, as the haptic and location-aware functionalities privilege mimetic touch and physical mobility (rather than the audiovisuality typical of many media interfaces), and the experience of playing becomes literally corporealized as a novel remaking of the urban environment, in conjunction with the new communicative possibilities of mobile play. By coalescing multisensorial modes of embodied perception, *Pokémon GO* play illustrates the possibilities of AR touchscreen games for generating new ways of being in the world through haptic screen cultures.

As our research also highlights, it is important that we observe and understand the daily routines and authentic technology uses of people *in situ*, and focus more carefully on the social dimensions of ageing well, rather than simply intervening reactively with new technologies and apps. We can learn a lot from 'old' or existing media experiences like *Pokémon GO*, and how they can be reinvented, demonstrating the need to discern embodied habitudes of socio-technical practice in designing for digital health solutions. The beneficial social and corporeal effects are authentic and potentially enduring precisely because the gameworld is already established and embedded into collective media practices and the urban environment, and because the gameplay fits comfortably into the rhythms and patterns of daily life. Here, haptic mobile media, digital wayfaring and location-based AR gaming come together in ways that can offer inventive approaches to quotidian health challenges.

Mobile augmented reality games present a spectrum of affordances: hybrid modalities of experience (through the coalescence of digital, networked and physical ways of knowing); digital wayfaring (as this hybrid experience generates a new kind of collective place-making); haptic play (through the tactile intimacy of the touchscreen and 'feel' of the game); ambient play (as the game becomes diffused through the embodied routines of everyday life) and social play (via the embedment of collaborative action in the game's mechanics). Understanding and interpreting the implications, significance and possibilities of mobile and location-based AR games across diverse populations and user demographics requires a robust grasp of these affordances, and the manifold ways we embody and enact quotidian media practices.

In these contexts, it is important to highlight the uneven ways players occupy the game space and how gameplay is embedded in cultural and locational specificity. That is, certain bodies have more leeway to deviate from normalized socio-cultural practices, while, as Katie Salen (2017) argues, some don't. Salen considers the potential disempowerment and marginalization that affects players of AR games and mobile location-based apps such as *Pokémon GO*. That is, *Pokémon GO* requires users to explore their (sub)urban environments, and thus it is a form of gameplay underscored by issues of racial inequity and the relative freedom people have to move playfully through their neighbourhoods and cities.

Salen asks, what can *Pokémon GO* teach us about mobility, accessibility, race and privilege? It is clearly more dangerous for some bodies to be in some places at certain times, and there are undoubtedly different levels of risk at work that act upon our bodies differently depending on our age, gender, ethnicity or social milieu. There have been many alarming stories of *Pokémon GO* players subjected to overt prejudice from police and local residents.[4] As Omari Akil ponders:

> [C]ombining the complexity of being Black in America with the real world proposal of wandering and exploration that is designed into the gameplay of *Pokemon GO*, there was only one conclusion. *I might die if I keep playing…*
>
> The [game] asks me to put my life in danger if I chose to play it as it is intended… (Akil, 2016: n.p.)

In their study of the racial and ethnic bias of *Pokémon GO*, Colley and his co-authors examine how the game's data and code, which 'augment' reality, often 'reinforces preexisting power structures' and 'geographic contours of advantage and disadvantage', as PokéStops and game resources are distributed more densely in wealthier areas with predominantly white non-minority populations (Colley et al., 2017: n.p.). In these contexts, as appealing as it may be to enter and share an augmented reality, *Pokémon GO* may not be an open-ended playground full of creative possibility, but rather a transformation of the local environment into a game resource, where urban spaces are made relevant and virtually affluent by the extent to which they are populated by game currency, objects and rewards. For Sicart (2017), while *Pokémon GO* may open up new possibilities for design and play in augmented reality, we should be wary of the potential for corporate appropriation of public spaces enabled by the game. These debates have a long history in and around locative media. As de Souza e Silva (2017) points out, *Pokémon GO* recalls issues relating to mobility, sociability, spatiality and surveillance that are characteristic of many previous hybrid reality games and mobile location-based applications.

Similarly, Dal Yong Jin (2017) considers the economies of web-based media and the commodification of digital games, arguing that *Pokémon GO* generates value to developers and companies through the free immaterial labour of players, intensifying the

**Figure 11.4**    *Pokémon GO* players at Siam Paragon in Bangkok, Thailand. Image: sharppy/Shutterstock.com.

'new capitalism' that increasingly typifies our use of online services and applications. In a more positive light, Frith (2017: 53) explores the 'commercial potential of augmented reality', and how *Pokémon GO* can be used by businesses to attract foot traffic through the placement of 'lures', revealing how digital 'objects' can influence our movement and behaviour in the physical world, as we enact the pedestrian labour of location-based gaming (Figure 11.4).

These ambiguities around play, commerce and labour have indeed been amplified by the gamification of contemporary life, and the way social and reward-based game mechanics are embedded into business software applications and self-monitoring apps, primarily for increased profit and productivity. It could be argued that *Pokémon GO* typifies both gamification principles (i.e. the player accrues items and gains rewards the more they play, and the more they play with others) and playbour (i.e. the player is co-opted into generating game content and 'works' to enrich the game experience).

Such dialectics of exploitation and empowerment are pertinent to *Pokémon GO* and location-aware mobile games more broadly. On the positive and potentially subversive side, players can use such games to activate communities of interest in local contexts, organize urban events and public demonstrations of play. On the negative side, many *Pokémon GO* players have unknowingly shared private information that we would assume is secure. For example, iOS users logging into *Pokémon GO* through Google also shared their Gmail account information, a security breach since rectified. Indeed, in the case of games such as *Ingress, Foursquare* and *Pokémon GO*, we can acknowledge that there are both benefits and risks in the accrual and deployment of user data *en masse* in the service of an enriched AR game experience.

Despite these issues, *Pokémon GO* has nevertheless been an undeniably popular and transformative game. Its effects are clearly significant, as the game weaves in and out of players' daily routines and pedestrian trajectories, and impacts upon their interaction with the familiar strangers populating urban streets. As we suggested in the previous chapter on mobile play, there is no doubt that even the most casual mobile games change what we pay attention to, and the experience and duration of that attentiveness. Even more poignantly, our involvement with location-based hybrid reality games such as *Pokémon GO* require us to adopt an *as-if* type of experience, inviting us to move through the environment *as-if* it were game terrain or an urban playground. In this respect, *Pokémon GO* is not just a casual mobile game, for while we might play it in the midst of other daily activities, it also palpably intervenes in and modifies our social, material and embodied being-in-the-world.

## Conclusion

This chapter has explored how augmented reality games are instances of the way the *stuff* of media permeates our everyday urban geographies. We have considered the complex relations between mobile media, urban space, pedestrian bodies and play. We first focused on mobile play in public spaces, and how location-based mobile gaming can be seen as a kind of playful space-making that reorients our movement through the urban environment. We then explored such practices through the example of *Pokémon GO*, and how for millions of people around the world the bodily experience of public space has been notably altered by this mobile game based on a popular transmedia storyworld.

In the next chapter we conclude and summarize the findings of the book. In particular, we focus on the uptake and transformative potential of games in light of our recent experiences of the COVID-19 pandemic. We reflect upon where games and gaming cultures are now, and where they might be going in the future.

### Further Reading

Farman, J. (2012). *Mobile Interface Theory: Embodied Space and Locative Media*. London: Routledge.

Geroimenko, V. (2019). *Augmented Reality Games I: Understanding the Pokémon GO Phenomenon*. New York: Springer.

Leorke, D. (2018). *Location-based Gaming: Play in Public Space*. Basingstoke: Palgrave Macmillan.

Sicart, M. (2017). Reality has always been augmented: Play and the promises of *Pokémon GO*. Mobile Media & Communication, 5(1), 30–33.

# Notes

1  https://www.businessofapps.com/data/pokemon-go-statistics/
2  https://videogamesstats.com/pokemon-go-statistics-facts/
3  https://videogamesstats.com/pokemon-go-statistics-facts/
4  https://www.vox.com/2016/7/11/12149664/pokemon-go-augmented-reality-racist; https://www.
   usatoday.com/story/tech/news/2016/08/09/pokemon-go-racist-app-redlining-communities-color-
   racist-pokestops-gyms/87732734/; https://www.opendemocracy.net/en/digitaliberties/pok-
   walking-while-black-pok-mon-go-and-america-s-e-q/

# 12
## Conclusion: Themes and Futures

Play and gaming are deeply connected to the things that matter and impact our lives. This means, ultimately, that gaming is a civic space, political domain, media sphere and site of critical work, while simultaneously being a place of leisure, even rest and respite. Gaming cannot be set off to the side, a quirky outpost functioning as an academic novelty. It is a huge – indeed for many, the *most significant* – space where people engage directly in core cultural issues and debates. It shapes and deeply impacts mainstream conversations and culture. Games *matter* (Taylor, 2018b: 13–14).

As we finished this book, the world underwent unprecedented social and economic transformation. The coronavirus pandemic forced entire societies and their citizens to self-isolate and learn new habits of physical distancing, and people increasingly turned to mobile and online networks as primary conduits of communication and interaction. Interestingly, though not surprisingly, in 2020 we witnessed a surge in screen-based activities and social media engagement. The role of online networks in all facets of our everyday lives became heightened, illustrating how the digital reflects social, cultural, environmental and material concerns.

In the US, overall videogame internet traffic increased 75% following the imposition of restrictions on urban and suburban movement in the first half of 2020, a trend replicated across the world in countries with prolific game cultures (M.B., 2020). During the same period, Steam, one of the dominant online retailers of videogames, peaked at 20.3 million concurrent players, an 11% increase, while Twitch has seen its average viewership double (M.B., 2020). According to Nielsen, consumers now spend US$120 billion per year on videogaming globally, compared to roughly $30 billion on recorded music and $42.5 billion at the box office (WePC, 2020). In 2019, Netflix CEO Reed Hastings stated that the most significant challenge to their dominance in the entertainment industry comes not from other streaming services, such as Amazon Prime, but from games such as *Fortnite*, as viewers turn *en masse* to playing and watching games (Koss, 2020). By 2021, it is predicted that around one-third of the world's population will regularly play games, with mobile gaming comprising over half of generated revenue (Koss, 2020).

Undoubtedly, people are playing lots of games together, for longer durations, and more often – from casual puzzle games like *Words With Friends* to deeply immersive online worlds like *Subnautica*, *Final Fantasy XIV* and *Overwatch*. In this shift, the role of massively multiplayer online games (MMOs) is significant, as they have long been vibrant 'third places' where people engage in a lively spectrum of social interaction. As discussed in a number of chapters throughout the book, although gamespaces may at times be fraught with prejudice and bullying antics, they are fundamentally *places* where we can meet and make friends, form communities and friendships. Playing and talking together through games, especially during times of enforced physical separation, fosters and maintains deep connections across generations and cultures.

As the heightened threat of viral contagion gripped the popular imaginary, the debates around screen time, and especially games, also shifted. The World Health Organization (WHO), which last year officially registered game addiction as a mental health disorder, have now recognized the communicative power and global reach of games.[1] WHO's global strategy ambassador Ray Chambers recently tweeted his support of #PlayApartTogether, an initiative of games industry leaders, including Twitch, Riot Games and Amazon Appstore. Members of the programme are disseminating key messages throughout their massive user networks, encouraging everyone to follow the WHO coronavirus guidelines.[2] Gamers pass these messages on, reminding each other to wash their hands and stay safe, and offering support to physically isolated players in quarantine.

This phenomenon highlights a well-versed argument in media and game studies – that we need more nuanced ways to understand the role of games in our everyday lives, beyond dystopian versus utopian polemics. As international media and game scholars have identified, for children and adults alike, videogames have ongoing positive effects on wellbeing – they are spaces of collaborative effort and creativity, and of real social connection and inclusion (McGonigal, 2010; Giddings, 2014; Livingstone, 2020). Games that welcome younger players, such as *Minecraft* and *Roblox* – each with more than 100 million monthly active users amassing over one billion hours of playtime – not only facilitate sociality, but also function as familiar and importantly 'normal' spaces for children and young people to talk about, or escape from, current social, political or health crises. As Livingstone (2020) has identified, for children to have healthy relationships to technology, parents need to see the internet and videogames not as the enemy; rather, they can be a space to explore and establish intergenerational connection, co-learning and sociality. Playing and talking together on screens can help to bond and connect, rather than distance, the generations.

Especially now, games are important not only as spaces for friendly sociality and play, but also because they allow us to explore, take risks, empathize and build a sense of community, caring and belonging. During the pandemic, people not only played more games longer, but the content and messaging also shifted. A *Minecraft* community of players recreated, at scale, the hospitals built in Wuhan following the COVID-19 outbreak as a 'tribute to the builders and hospital workers on the front line' (M.B., 2020). Even the place-based game *Pokémon GO*, with game mechanics largely dependent on pedestrian movement through the urban environment, altered its game play to allow players to hatch eggs and play raids from home (Wood, 2020).

Exploring games both during and post-pandemic can provide much insight into how we are critically reflecting on and recalibrating our relationship to people, media and the world, and reveals the power of games for social connection and change that spans generational and cultural differences and distances. As we have identified throughout the book, games and game cultures are barometers of contemporary society and quotidian practices; they reflect *digital, material, spatial* and *social worlds*. In the following section we conclude the book by revisiting the core themes outlined in the introduction in relation to the potential futures for games and game studies.

## Book Themes and Game Futures

> The future of entertainment is gaming. And the future of gaming is community. (Koss, 2020: n.p.)

In this book we have explored the diverse ways games and gaming cultures have manifested globally. As we have described through empirical case studies and analyses of scholars and critics, games are ubiquitous and embedded in everyday life, yet also play across a spectrum of socio-economic, cultural, linguistic, material and digital complexities. From the outset, we suggested that understanding games and game cultures today requires acknowledging the significant role of play and the playful attitude – as part of both ludification and gamification – in contemporary societies. We identified six key interlacing themes that thread their way through each of the chapters and parts of the book.

The theme **Mainstream and Independent** concerns the unevenness of diversity and inclusion that resonates across the games industry and its attendant communities. These issues were touched on in a number of chapters but were the particular focus of Chapter 3: Game Industries and Interfaces. Here, we provided a brief history of dominant game companies, platforms and interfaces, and the more recent emergence of indie game makers who are now tackling gender and racial inequity and representation in the ever-changing landscape of media and game content creation. Today, game developers and scholars alike see a promising future where people of diverse genders, ethnicities and abilities are empowered and equitably represented, enhancing innovation and the game experience for the benefit of players, communities, economies and media cultures more broadly.

Over the past decade, we have also seen games becoming increasingly more **Live and Social**. In Chapter 4: Game Communities and Productive Fandom, we explored the significance of fan cultures, sociality and player creativity that surround games and game genres. In this and other chapters, we showed how playful game-related activity is not confined to the 'magic circle' of gameplay. Indeed, it is now recognized that social interaction is fundamental to the success of many games, whether in the form of discussion forums and commentary, user-generated and user-created content (such as modding), game guilds, cosplay events, or in-game collaborative play and social networking. As noted above, games are important third places where people meet, nurture long-lasting friendships and form persistent communities. In Chapters 5 and 6, we examined how communities also coalesce around the live broadcasting and streaming of gameplay and revealed how watching games as-they-are-played has become a prominent new form of media entertainment in its own right. Both forms of play engender new ways of engaging with games and collapse the institutional and material boundaries that separate games, media entertainment and sport. Commentators across both the sports and games industries predict that people's engagement with live gameplay will continue to increase, evidenced by the prolific rise of eSports tournaments and audiences, and the cumulative popularity of Twitch.

In the introductory chapter, we described what is termed the ludification of culture – that is, our cultural turn towards a 'playful attitude' in our media practices and mediated interaction with others. Encapsulated by the key theme **Ambient and Playful**, the processes of ludification and gamification are perhaps the most prevalent features of contemporary media culture, and the ambient and playful theme weaves its way throughout every chapter of the book. In particular, Chapters 4 and 6 discussed the significance of user-created content production (in the form of modding, livestreaming and Let's Play) as an integral part of playful media practices and the 'paratexts' that surround and inform gameplay. In Chapters 10 and 11 we focused on the 'ambient' quality of mobile and location-based games, and documented through our ethnographic research how they have become thoroughly embedded in our everyday routines. More broadly, playful media in the form of creative and social mobile apps are now a mundane and sedimented aspect of the way we interact with family, friends and network publics, and they will undoubtedly continue to inform and channel our modalities of communication into the future.

The success of ambient mobile media and games is in part attributable to the ubiquity of touchscreen and haptic interfaces and their intimate affordances. The theme **Mobile and Haptic** captures this effect, and was the particular focus of Chapter 2, in terms of new research methods emerging from haptic media and game studies, and Chapter 10 on mobile games. In Chapter 2 we identified how haptic technologies, such as vibrating game controllers and mobile touchscreens, have required researchers to develop innovative methods and new techniques that are able to document the movement and perception of the user's body. The mimetic quality of mobile touchscreen games – that is, their simulation of real-world effects, activities and physics – is discussed at some length in Chapter 10, and the way such games are designed to be intuitive and immediately playable for the non-expert player is described in Chapter 11 in terms of the uptake of *Pokémon GO* by older adults. More broadly, the mobile affordances of pervasive and augmented reality games are the topic of both Chapters 9 and 11, where we investigated the capacity of locative media interfaces such as mobile phones to enable 'hybrid' experiences that intermix actual and virtual reality. For some game critics and forecasters, this hybrid potential – allowing players to move about and engage with the 'real world' – is what assures the future of AR games in contrast to VR games, despite considerable investment into the latter by media giants Facebook, Google and Microsoft (Koss, 2020).

One of the more positive and enlivening aspects of games, game cultures and game development lies in their capacity to motivate and mobilize social and political change. The theme of **Innovation and Intervention** is addressed in many of the chapters, including the aforementioned discussion of indie game developers with progressive agendas of inclusion and diversity. It is the particular focus of Part III: Artful Interventions, as each of the three chapters explore, respectively: the fertile and often transgressive merger of games and art; the deployment of games as vehicles of social transformation and 'critical play'; and the historical and current manifestation of urban and pervasive games that turn public spaces into collaborative playgrounds. In these chapters, we show how game artists and innovators engage in public debates and intervene in normative perceptions and assumptions about the world, and how they use games as a mode of critical commentary on cultural practices and urban life, to get us to 'think differently' about social and political issues and imagine alternative futures.

As games have emerged as one of the most transformative and significant mediums in contemporary culture, technological change has evolved in tandem, with reciprocal effects. Correspondingly, research methods in game studies have undergone radical revision. The theme of **Methods and Data**, which runs through many of the chapters, aims to document some of these changes, from haptic approaches (as previously mentioned) to big data analytics. Methods are the specific concern of Chapter 2, where we provided an overview of quantitative, qualitative and mixed methods, along with haptic and practice-led methodologies, and the role of datafication and gamification in terms of how we conceptualize and practise research about games, gameplay and game cultures. Game methods are also featured in other chapters: in Chapter 3, we looked at Chee's ethnographic and codesign approach to gender inequality in an AAA game company, which sought to engage employees in a process of 'co-futuring' towards best practices in diversity and inclusion; in Chapter 6, we explored research on game livestreaming in particular cultural contexts, which involves rethinking how we can capture games as both archival and live experiences; in Chapter 8, we described several projects that seek to deploy games as a form of research intervention, both in the primary school context and through an art exhibition. Such a wide spectrum of research methods exposes the increasing complexity of games, their embedment across all aspects of contemporary life, and the need to keep our methods *dynamic* and *agile* so we can continue to effectively capture their impact and deploy them as a form of intervention now and into the future.

As we hope to have shown throughout our book, *games matter*. Play theorists have long argued that our capacity to play defines us as social and empathic beings. As a predominant form of collective play, videogames have become enduring cultural interfaces and social domains – with all the complexity and possibility that implies. For media and cultural researchers, exploring gamespaces, gameplay and game cultures during times of significant change and upheaval can offer us crucial insights into how we recalibrate our lives and develop the new critical literacies we require, enabling us to better understand and negotiate consequential shifts in our collective *Zeitgeist*. In response to the unprecedented climactic, political and health challenges we face in the new millennium, and as the social becomes increasingly and necessarily digital, we are optimistic that games, game players and their broader communities can become exemplars of creativity, innovation, diversity, empathy and collective resilience.

## Notes

1  https://www.usatoday.com/story/tech/gaming/2020/03/28/video-games-whos-prescription-solace-during-coronavirus-pandemic/2932976001/
2  https://www.businesswire.com/news/home/20200328005018/en/Games-Industry-Unites-Promote-World-Health-Organization

# Glossary

**AAA (Triple A Game)**   Large commercial game studios and the games they make. AAA games can be understood as the game equivalent of the Hollywood blockbuster film.

**Appification**   The transition of digital information interfaces from web portals to dedicated applications or 'apps'.

**AR (Augmented Reality)**   The projection of virtual elements over the top of reality via a visual interface such as a mobile device in order to seamlessly integrate virtual and actual worlds.

**ARG (Alternate Reality Games)**   Games that are delivered across multiple media types and that deny their own status as games. In doing so these games aim to blur the line between in-game reality and the real world.

**Art Games**   Games that are made as works of art for aesthetic, conceptual and contemplative purposes as opposed to fulfilling traditional game ambitions such as competition or entertainment.

**Avatar**   A digital representation of a player within the virtual world of a game.

**Big Data**   The unprecedented and growing abundance of digital data within contemporary networked society.

**Casual Gaming**   A mode of game interaction that is typically non-immersive, shallow, interruptible, non-narrative, and played for minutes at a time. Casual game players often do not describe themselves as game players and are often regarded by hardcore gamers as not 'real' gamers. See 'hardcore gaming' for antonym.

**Codesign**   The process of collaborative design. For example, rather than a design professional creating a product in isolation, they may collaborate with an end user to ensure they produce a product with intimate knowledge and input from its intended audience.

**Co-presence**   The phenomenon of being with others in digital space; co-located presence refers to being in physical space with others.

**Datafication**   The transformation of a wide range of phenomena into quantifiable data that can be used in a variety of ways.

**eSports (Electronic Sports)**   The popular phenomenon of competitive and athletic videogame play that takes place before large audiences who are located in offline and online spaces.

**Fandom**   Communities with shared interests and knowledge on specific topics such as television shows, film genres, book series, games, music, etc.

**Fanfiction**   Unofficial fiction created by fans that uses and expands upon the characters and worlds of existing (usually copyright) media narratives.

**Fantasy sports**   Internet-based games where participants compile imaginary teams made up of actual sports stars and use the real-life statistics to determine which team in a fantasy league is winning.

**Flâneur**   An imaginary figure evoked to symbolize the experience of 'taking in' one's urban surroundings and atmosphere through the simple act of strolling. Originating with the writings of Charles Baudelaire, the term in its native French means 'lounger' or 'saunterer'.

**Game Jam**   The rapid design and prototyping of a game by a community of game designers and/or non-gamers.

**Gamification**   The application of game elements and design principles into non-game contexts such as fitness and work productivity, to make the activity more engaging, playful and playable.

**Hardcore Gaming**   Deeply committed game play often involving high skill levels in complex game environments sometimes lasting for hours at a time. See 'casual gaming' for antonym.

**LARP (Live Action Role Play)**   A mode of game play where players take on and perform their in-game characters and play in real-world settings.

**Let's Play (LP)**   a video recording of gameplay uploaded post-production to the web, often accompanied by the gamer's humorous or entertaining voiceover and an inset of their face or upper body and reactions as they play.

**Livestreaming**   Practices of live broadcasting game play and game commentary simultaneously, usually through dedicated platforms such as Twitch.

**Location-based Game (LBG)**   A mobile game that employs the locative functionality of the mobile media interface.

**Ludification**    The myriad ways in which multiple aspects of everyday life are becoming more playful and gameful.

**Machinima**    A combination of 'machine' and 'cinema', machinima denotes the use of videogame software to produce cinematic imagery.

**Magic Circle**    An often invisible and imaginary boundary that demarcates game space or play space from the everyday world. The magic circle is also often rendered visible through lines on lawn or chalk on pavement, such as a sports oval or basketball court.

**MMOGs (massively multiplayer online games)**    online networked games that allow large numbers of players to play together in a virtual game space simultaneously.

**Modding**    Modifications to a videogame by players, artists, fans or hackers. 'Mods' can range from simple adjustments and customizations in visual design and game play to total code and/or design overhauls in which entire games are recreated. 'Modding' is the process of creating mods and 'modders' are the people who make them.

**New Games Movement**    A countercultural response to the Vietnam War and civic unrest in the late 1960s, initially led by Stewart Brand, which led to large-scale games focusing on playful embodied experiences and public spectacles with the intention of advocating social play and community building.

**Parasociality**    Relationships between fans and media figures that are typically one-sided (fan projected) and imagined.

**Paratext**    often user-generated media content and activities (such as fanfiction, cosplay, game walkthroughs, etc.) that circulate around a core media text or game.

**Pervasive Game**    A game type that uses the real world as its game board. Pervasive games are said to be socially, spatially or temporally expansive, and as such, they often dissolve the 'magic circle' that separates the real world from the world of the game.

**Produsage**    A term coined by Bruns and Jacobs (2006); a portmanteau of 'production' and 'usage', denoting the way we simultaneously consume and create media content through repurposing, remixing and redistribution.

**Serious Games**    Games that are created to address issues in the real world. While serious games may be entertaining, their primary purpose is to educate, train or enact social or political change.

**Smart City**    A city or urban space that uses ubiquitous computing and sensory technologies to collect and process information towards delivering civic services and information more efficiently.

**Spreadable Media**    A term coined by Jenkins et al. (2013) to describe the way media content is created and dispersed across multiple platforms and pathways of distribution. The notion of spreadable media dissolves traditional broadcasting binaries between content makers and audiences.

**VR (Virtual Reality)**    A computer-generated simulation that delivers a highly immersive experience of a complete, yet entirely virtual world.

# References

Aarseth, E. (2001). Computer Game Studies, year one. *Game Studies*, *1*(1). Available at: www.gamestudies.org/0101/editorial.html

Abt, C. C. (1970). *Serious Games*. New York: The Viking Press.

Adamus, T. (2012). Playing computer games as electronic sport: In search of a theoretical framework for a new research field. In J. Fromme & A. Unger (Eds.), *Computer Games and New Media Cultures: A Handbook of Digital Games Studies* (pp. 477–490). New York: Springer.

Akil, O. (2016). Warning: Pokémon GO could be a death sentence if you are a black man. *Huffington Post*. Available at: www.huffingtonpost.com/omari-akil/warning-pokemon-go-is-death-sentence-black-man_b_10946826.html

Alderman, N. (2019). Turn your run into a thriller. *Behind the Scenes*. Apple App Store. https://apps.apple.com/nz/story/id1297896684

Althoff, T., White, R. W., & Horvitz, E. (2016). Influence of *Pokémon GO* on physical activity: Study and implications. *Journal of Medical Internet Research*, *18*(12), e315. Available at: www.jmir.org/2016/12/e315/

Anderson, B. (1983 [2006]). *Imagined Communities: Reflections on the Origin and Spread of Nationalism*. London: Verso.

Anderson, C. A., & Bushman, B. J. (2001). Effects of violent video games on aggressive behaviour, aggressive cognition, aggressive affect, physiological arousal, and prosocial behaviour: A meta-analytic review of the scientific literature. *Psychological Science*, *12*(5), 353–359. doi: 10.1111/1467-9280.00366

Anderson, S. (2012). Just one more game… *The New York Times* (reprints), 4 April. Available at: www.nytimes.com/2012/04/08/magazine/angry-birds-farmville-and-other-hyperaddictive-stupid-games.html

Ang, C. S., Zaphiris, P., & Wilson, S. (2010). Computer games and sociocultural play: An activity theoretical perspective. *Games & Culture*, *5*(4), 354–380. doi: 10.1177/1555412009360411

Anthropy, A. (2012). *Rise of the Videogame Zinesters: How Freaks, Normals, Amateurs, Artists, Dreamers, Drop-outs, Queers, Housewives, and People Like You Are Taking Back an Art Form*. New York: Seven Stories Press.

App Store Preview (2020). *Ahead of the game: How female-focused Runaway Play is sparking a movement*. Available at: https://apps.apple.com/au/story/id1496438398

Apperley, T. (2013). The body of the gamer: Game art and gestural excess. *Digital Creativity*, *24*(2), 145–156. doi: 10.1080/14626268.2013.808967

Apperley, T., & Moore, K. (2018). Haptic ambience: Ambient play, the haptic effect and co-presence in *Pokémon GO*. *Convergence*, *25*(1), 6–17.

Arth, C., Grasset, R., Gruber, L., Langlotz, T., Mulloni, A., & Wagner, D. (2015). *The History of Mobile Augmented Reality: Developments in Mobile AR over the Last Almost 50 Years*. Institute for Computer Graphics and Vision, Graz University of Technology, Austria. Available at: https://arxiv.org/pdf/1505.01319.pdf

Arvers, I. (2010). Cheats or cheats or glitch? Voice as a game modification in machinima. In N. Neumark, R. Gibson, & T. van Leeuwen (Eds.), *VOICE: Vocal Aesthetics in Digital Arts and Media* (pp. 225–240). Cambridge, MA: The MIT Press.

Atcheson, S. (2018). Embracing diversity and fostering inclusion is good for your business. *Forbes*, 25 September. Available at: https://www.forbes.com/sites/shereeatcheson/2018/09/25/embracing-diversity-and-fostering-inclusion-is-good-for-your-business/#d3fd2da72b1c

Atherton, R., & Karabinus, A. (2019). Professional practice, amateur profile: Mapping amateur game design communities. 1–8. *Proceedings from the 37th ACM International Conference*. New York: ACM Press. doi: 10.1145/3328020.3353941

Au, W. J. (2002). Triumph of the mod. *Salon.com*. Available at: http://dir.salon.com/story/tech/feature/2002/04/16/modding/index.html

Baer, R. (2005). *Videogames in the Beginning*. Springfield, NJ: Rolenta Press.

Bakardjieva, M. (2006). Domestication running wild: From the moral economy of the household to the mores of a culture. In T. Berker, M. Hartmann, Y. Punie, & K. Ward (Eds.), *Domestication of Media and Technology* (pp. 62–78). New York: McGraw-Hill International.

Balnaves, M., Willson, M., & Leaver, T. (2012). Entering Farmville: Finding value in social games. In C. Anyanwu, K. Green, & J. Sykes (Eds.), *Communicating Change and Changing Communication in the 21st Century: Australian and New Zealand Communication Association Conference*, 4–6 July, Adelaide, Australia.

Banks, J. (2013). Introduction: Co-creating matters. In J. Banks (Ed.), *Co-creating Videogames* (pp. 1–10). London: Bloomsbury Academic. doi: 10.5040/9781472544353.0005

Banks, J., & Cunningham, S. (2016). Creative destruction in the Australian videogames industry. *Media International Australia*, *160*(1), 127–139. doi: 10.1177/1329878X16653488

Banks, J., Cunningham, S. D., & Woodford, D. (2013). Innovation and workplace culture in the Australian interactive entertainment industry: The Halfbrick story. In *DiGRA 2013: DeFragging Game Studies*, August, Atlanta, GA.

Batchelor, J. (2017). The Global Game Jam is a counter-movement to increased nationalistic tendencies. *Games Industry*, 19 January. Available at: https://www.gamesindustry.biz/articles/2017-01-19-the-global-game-jam-is-a-counter-movement-to-increased-nationalistic-tendencies

Benford, S., Crabtree, A., Flintham, M., Drozd, A., Anastasi, R., Paxton, M., Tandavanitj, N., Adams, M., & Row-Farr, J. (2006). Can you see me now? *ACM Transactions on Computer–Human Interaction* (pp. 100–133) *(TOCHI)*, *13*. New York: ACM Press.

Benford, S., Flintham, M., Drozd, A., Anastasi, R., Adams, M., Row-Farr, J., Oldroyd, A., Sutton, J., & Park, A. (2004). Uncle Roy All Around You: Implicating the city in a location-based performance. In *ACE04*. New York: ACM Press. Available at: www.performancestudies.pl/dydaktyka/files/ace2004.pdf.

Benford, S., & Giannachi, G. (2011). *Performing Mixed Reality*. Cambridge, MA: The MIT Press.

Bennett, A., & Kahn-Harris, K. (2004). *After Subculture: Critical Studies in Contemporary. Youth Culture*. Basingstoke: Palgrave Macmillan.

Bennett, L. (2014). Tracing textual poachers: Reflections on the development of fan studies and digital fandom. *The Journal of Fandom Studies*, *2*(1), 5–20. doi: 10.1386/jfs.2.1.5_1

Berryman, D. R. (2012). Augmented reality: A review. *Medical Reference Services Quarterly*, *31*(2), 212–218. doi: 10.1080/02763869.2012.670604

Billings, A., & Ruihley, B. (2013). Why we watch, why we play: The relationship between fantasy sport and fanship motivations. *Mass Communication and Society*, *16*(1), 5–25. doi: 10.1080/15205436.2011.635260

Billings, A., Ruihley, B., & Yang, Y. (2017). Fantasy gaming on steroids? Contrasting fantasy sport participation by daily fantasy sport participation. *Communication & Sport*, *5*(6), 732–750. doi: 10.1177/2167479516644445

Bissell, D. (2007). Animating suspension: Waiting for mobilities. *Mobilities*, *2*(2), 277–298. doi: 10.1080/17450100701381581

Bittanti, M. (2009). Game art: (This is not) A Manifesto, (This is) A Disclaimer. In M. Bittanti & D. Quaranta (Eds.), *Gamescenes: Art in the Age of Videogames* (pp. 7–14). Monza: Johan & Levi Editore.

Björk, S., Falk, J., Hansson, R., & Ljungstrand, P. (2001). Pirates! – Using the physical world as a game board. Paper presented at *Interact 2001, IFIP TC.13 Conference on Human–Computer Interaction*, 9–13 July, Tokyo, Japan.

Blight, M. G. (2016). 'Relationships to video game streamers: Examining gratifications, parasocial relationships, fandom, and community affiliation online'. *Theses and Dissertations* 1255. Available at: https://dc.uwm.edu/etd/1255

Boellstorff, T., Nardi, B. A., Pearce, C., Taylor, T. L., & Marcus, G. E. (2012). *Ethnography and Virtual Worlds: A Handbook of Method*. Princeton, NJ: Princeton University Press.

Bogost, I. (2010). Cow Clicker: The making of obsession. *Videogame Theory, Criticism, Design*. Available at: www.bogost/com/blog/cow_clicker_1.shtml

Bogost, I. (2011). Gamification is bullshit. Available at: www.bogost.com/blog/gamification_is_bullshit/

Bogost, I. (2016). The tragedy of *Pokémon Go*: What it takes to attract money. *The Atlantic*, July. Available at: www.theatlantic.com/technology/archive/2016/07/the-tragedy-of-pokemon-go/490793/

Boluk, S., & Lemieux, P. (2017). *Metagaming: Playing, Competing, Spectating, Cheating, Trading, Making, and Breaking Videogames*. Minneapolis, MN: University of Minnesota Press.

Bonner, H. (2016). How does a 48-hour game development event affect the body? *First Beat*. Available at: https://www.firstbeat.com/en/user-stories/firstbeat-at-global-game-jam/

Bourriaud, N. (1998). *Relational Aesthetics*. Paris: Presses du Reel.

Boutin, A. (2012). Rethinking the *flâneur*: *Flânerie* and the senses. *Dix-Neuf*, *16*(2), 124–132. doi: 10.1179/dix.2012.16.2.01

Bowker, G. C., & Star, S. L. (1999). *Sorting Things Out: Classification and its Consequences*. Cambridge, MA: The MIT Press.

boyd, d., & Crawford, K. (2011). Six provocations for big data. In *A Decade in Internet Time: Symposium on the Dynamics of the Internet and Society*, September. Available at: https://papers.ssrn.com/sol3/pape''s.cfm?abstract_id=1926431

Branson, D. M. (2018). *The Future of Tech is Female: How to Achieve Gender Diversity*. New York: New York University Press.

Bridle, J. (2011). *The new aesthetic*. Available at: https://jamesbridle.com/works/the-new-aesthetic

Brock, T. (2017). Roger Caillois and e-sports: On the problems of treating play as work. *Games and Culture*, *12*(4), 321–339.

Brown, N., Billings, A. C., & Ruihley, B. (2012). Exploring the change in motivations for fantasy sport participation during the life cycle of a sports fan. *Communication Research Reports*, *29*(4), 333–342. doi: 10.1080/08824096.2012.723646

Bruns, A., & Jacobs, J. (Eds.) (2006). *Uses of Blogs*. London: Peter Lang.

Bruton, M. (2019). The West eyes eSport greatness: But can it catch South Korea? *OZY*, 8 November. Available at: https://www.ozy.com/the-new-and-the-next/how-western-esports-teams-are-leveling-up/227771/

Bull, M. (2005). The intimate sounds of urban experience: An auditory epistemology of everyday mobility. In K. Nyíri (Ed.), *A Sense of Place: The Global and the Local in Mobile Communication* (pp. 169–178). Vienna: Passagen.

Burgess, J. (2010). Remediating vernacular creativity: Photography and cultural citizenship in the Flickr photosharing network. In T. Edensor, D. Leslie, S. Millington, & N. Rantisi (Eds.), *Spaces of Vernacular Creativity: Rethinking the Cultural Economy* (pp. 116–126). London: Routledge.

Burgess, J., & Green, J. (2009). *YouTube: Online Video and Participatory Culture*. Cambridge: Polity Press.

Burroughs, B., & Rama, P. (2015). The eSports Trojan horse: Twitch and streaming futures. *Journal of Virtual Worlds Research*, 8(2), 1–5. doi: http://dx.doi.org/10.4101/jvwr.v8i2.7176

Burrows, L. (2013). Women remain outsiders in video game industry. *Boston Globe*, 27 January. Available at: https://www.bostonglobe.com/business/2013/01/27/women-remain-outsiders-video-game-industry/275JKqy3rFylT7TxgPmO3K/story.html

Burwell, C., & Miller, T. (2016). Let's Play: Exploring literacy practices in an emerging videogame paratext. *E-Learning and Digital Media*, 13(3–4), 109–125. doi: 10.1177/2042753016677858

Busch, T., Chee, F., & Harvey, A. (2017). Corporate responsibility and gender in digital games. In K. Grosser, M. A. Kilgour, & L. McCarthy (Eds.), *Gender Equality and Responsible Business: Expanding CSR Horizons* (pp. 31–45). London: Routledge.

Caillois, R. (2001 [1961]). *Man, Play and Games*. Trans. M. Barash. Chicago, IL: University of Illinois Press. First published in French (1958).

Campbell-Kelly, M. (2003). *From Airline Reservations to Sonic the Hedgehog: A History of the Software Industry*. Cambridge, MA: The MIT Press.

Candy, L., & Edmonds, E. (2018). Practice-based research in the creative arts: Foundations and futures from the front line. *Leonardo*, 51(1), 63–89. doi: 10.1162/LEON_a_01471

Cannon, R. (2007a). Introduction to game modification. Paper presented at *Plaything: The Language of Gameplay 2*. Available at: https://web.archive.org/web/20040309221102/http://www.dlux.org.au/plaything/media/rebecca_cannon_web.pdf

Cannon, R. (2007b). Meltdown. In A. Clarke & G. Mitchell (Eds.), *Videogames and Art* (pp. 38–53). Bristol: Intellect.

Cassell, J., & Jenkins, H. (1998). *From Barbie to Mortal Kombat: Gender and Computer Games*. Cambridge, MA: The MIT Press.

Castronova, E. (2005). *Synthetic Worlds*. Chicago, IL: University of Chicago Press.

Cerini, M. (2018). Pleasure principle: Meet the Chinese artist breaking taboos for fun, not politics. *CNN*, 23 March. Available at: https://edition.cnn.com/style/article/lu-yang-art-basel-hong-kong/index.html

Cermak-Sassenrath, D. (2018). *Playful Disruption of Digital Media*. Singapore: Springer.

Chan, D. (2008). Convergence, connectivity, and the case of Japanese mobile gaming. *Games and Culture*, 3(1), 13–25. doi: 10.1177/1555412007309524

Chan, D. (2009). Beyond the 'Great Firewall': The case of in-game protests in China. In L. Hjorth & D. Chan (Eds.), *Gaming Cultures and Place in Asia-Pacific* (pp. 141–157). London: Routledge.

Chee, F., Hjorth, L., & Davies, H. (2021, forthcoming). A participatory ethnographic approach to promoting diversity in the games industry. *Feminist Media Studies*.

Chess, S. (2017). *Ready Player Two: Women Gamers and Designed Identity*. Minneapolis, MN: University of Minnesota Press.

Christensen, C., & Prax, P. (2012). Assemblage, adaptation and apps: Smartphones and mobile gaming. *Continuum: Journal of Media & Cultural Studies*, 26(5), 731–739. doi: 10.1080/10304312.2012.706461

Christy, T., & Kuncheva, L. I. (2014). Technological advancements in affective gaming: A historical survey. *GSTF Journal on Computing*, 3, 1–10. Available at: https://lucykuncheva.co.uk/papers/tclkIJC14.pdf

Clement, J. (2020). Number of apps available in leading app stores 2020. *Statista*. Available at: https://www.statista.com/statistics/276623/number-of-apps-available-in-leading-app-stores/

Code, B. (2017). Is game design for everybody? Women and innovation in video games. *Kinephanos* (Special Issue: Gender Issues in Video Games), July, 169–184. Available at: https://www.kinephanos.ca/Revue_files/2017_Code.pdf

Cohen, S. (1984). *Zap, the Rise and Fall of Atari*. New York: McGraw-Hill.

Coldewey, D. (2016). Senator Al Franken questions Niantic over Pokeprivacy policy. *TechCrunch*, 13 July. Available at: https://techcrunch.com/2016/07/12/sen-al-franken-questions-niantic-over-pokeprivacy-policy/

Colley, A., Thebault-Spieker, J., Yilun Lin, A., Degraen, D., Fischman, B., Hakkila, J., Kuehl, K., Nisi, V., Nunes, N. J., Wenig, N., Wenig, D., Hecht, B., & Schöning, J. (2017). The geography of *Pokémon GO*: Beneficial and problematic effects on places and movement. *CHI 2017*, 6–11 May, Denver, CO.

Comunello, F., & Mulargia, S. (2017). My Grandpa and I 'gotta catch 'em all': A research design on intergenerational gaming focusing on *Pokémon Go*. In J. Zhou & G. Salvendy (Eds.), *Human Aspects of IT for the Aged Population, Vol. 10298. Application, Services and Contexts* (pp. 228–241). Cham, Switzerland: Springer International.

Consalvo, M. (2012a). Confronting toxic gamer culture: A challenge for feminist game studies scholars. *Ada: A Journal of Gender, New Media, and Technology*, 1. doi: 10.7264/N33X84KH

Consalvo, M. (2012b). Slingshot to victory: Games, play and the iPhone. In P. Snickars & P. Vonderau (Eds.), *Moving Data: The iPhone and the Future of Media* (pp. 184–194). New York: Columbia University Press.

Consalvo, M. (2017). When paratexts become texts: De-centering the game-as-text. *Critical Studies in Media Communication*, 34(2), 177–183. doi: 10.1080/15295036.2017.1304648

Consalvo, M., & Dutton, N. (2006). Game analysis: Developing a methodological toolkit for the qualitative study of games. *Game Studies*, 6. Available at: http://gamestudies.org/06010601/articles/consalvo_dutton

Consalvo, M., & Harper, T. (2009). The sexi(e)st of all: Avatars, gender, and online games. In N. Panteli (Ed.), *Virtual Social Networks: Mediated, Massive and Multiplayer* (pp. 98–113). Basingstoke: Palgrave.

Copier, M. (2009). Challenging the magic circle: How online role-playing games are negotiated by everyday life. In M. van den Boomen, S. Lammes, A.-S. Lehmann, J. Raessens, & M. Tobias Schäfer (Eds.), *Digital Material: Tracing New Media in Everyday Life and Technology* (pp. 159–172). Amsterdam: Amsterdam University Press.

Corneliussen, H. (2008). *World of Warcraft* as a playground for feminism. In H. Corneliussen & J. Rettberg (Eds.), *Digital Culture, Play, and Identity* (pp. 63–86). Cambridge, MA: The MIT Press.

Costa, C., Carmenates, S., Madeira, L., & Stanghellini, G. (2014). Phenomenology of atmospheres: The felt meanings of clinical encounters. *Journal of Psychopathology*, 20, 351–357. Available at: https://www.jpsychopathol.it/issues/2014/vol20-4/SOPSI4-14.pdf#page=12

Coulton, P., Pucihar, K. C., & Balmford, W. (2008). Mobile social gaming. In *Proceedings of the 2008 Workshop on Social Interaction and Mundane Technologies* (SIMTech '08). Lancaster: Lancaster University.

Cova, B., & White, T. (2010). Counter-brand and alter-brand communities: The impact of Web 2.0 on tribal marketing approaches. *Journal of Marketing Management*, 26(3–4), 256–270. doi: 10.1080/02672570903566276

Crabtree, A., Benford, S., Rodden, T., Greenhalgh, C., Flintham, M., Anastasi, R., Drozd, A., Adams, M., Row Farr, J., Tandavanitj, N., & Steed, A. (2004). Orchestrating a mixed reality game 'on the ground'. *Proceedings of the SIGCHI Conference on Human Factors in Computing Systems (CHI '04)* (pp. 391–398). New York: ACM Press. doi: https://doi.org/10.1145/985692.985742

Crawford, C. (2003). *Chris Crawford on Game Design*. Indianapolis, IN: Peachpit.

Crookall, D. (2010). Serious games, debriefing, and simulation/gaming as a discipline. *Simulation & Gaming*, 41(6), 898–920. doi: 10.1177/1046878110390784

Cunningham, A. (2016). iOS version of *Pokémon Go* is a possible privacy trainwreck (updated). *Ars Technica*. Available at: http://arstechnica.com/gaming/2016/07/pokemon-go-on-ios-gets-full-access-to-your-google-account

D'Anastasio, C. (2019). Inside the culture of sexism at Riot Games. *Kotaku*, 19 February. Available at: https://kotaku.com/inside-the-culture-of-sexism-at-riot-games-1828165483

Davies, H. (2007). Place as media in pervasive games. *Proceedings of the 4th Australasian Conference on Interactive Entertainment* (pp. 7:1–7:4). Melbourne, Australia.

Davies, H. (2020). Spatial politics at play: Hong Kong protests and videogame activism. *Proceedings of the 2020 DiGRA Australia Conference*. February, Brisbane, Australia.

Davies, H., & Balmford, W. (2020). Tapping in: Playful mobile media art in Australia. In L. Hjorth, A. de Souza e Silva, & K. Lanson (Eds.), *The Routledge Companion to Mobile Media Art* (pp. 214–225). Abingdon, UK: Routledge.

Davies, H., & Innocent, T. (2017). The space between Debord and Pikachu. *Proceedings of the 2017 DiGRA International Conference*. Digital Games Research Association, July 2017, *1*(14). Melbourne, Australia.

de Aquino, C. T. E., & Robertson, R. W. (2018). *Diversity and Inclusion in the Global Workplace: Aligning Initiatives with Strategic Business Goals*. Basingstoke: Palgrave Macmillan.

de Certeau, M. (1984). *The Practice of Everyday Life*. Berkeley, CA: University of California Press.

Deen, M., Cercos, R., Chatman, A., Naseem, A., Bernhaupt, R., Fowler, A., Schouten, B., & Mueller, F. (2014). Game jam: [4 research]. In *CHI '14 Extended Abstracts on Human Factors in Computing Systems* (CHI EA '14) (pp. 25–28). New York: ACM Press. doi: https://doi.org/10.1145/2559206.2559225

De Koven, B. (1978). *The Well-Played Game*. Garden City, NY: Anchor Press.

De Koven, B. (2004). *Junkyard Sports*. Champaign, IL: Human Kinetics Publishers.

De Koven, B. (2013). *The Well-Played Game: A Players Philosophy*. Cambridge, MA: MIT Press.

Dena, C. (2009). 'Transmedia practice: Theorising the practice of expressing a fictional world across distinct media and environments'. PhD dissertation, University of Sydney.

de Souza e Silva, A. (2006). From cyber to hybrid: Mobile technologies as interfaces of hybrid space. *Space and Culture*, *9*(3), 261–278. doi: 10.1177/1206331206289022

de Souza e Silva, A. (2009). Hybrid reality and location-based gaming: Redefining mobility and game spaces in urban environments. *Simulation & Gaming*, *40*, 404–424. doi: 10.1177/1046878108314643

de Souza e Silva, A. (2017). *Pokémon Go* as an HRG: Mobility, sociability, and surveillance in hybrid spaces. *Mobile Media and Communication*, *5*(1), 20–23. doi: 10.1177/2050157916676232

de Souza e Silva, A., & Hjorth, L. (2009). Playful urban spaces: A historical approach to mobile games. *Simulation & Gaming*, *40*(5), 602–625. doi: 10.1177/1046878109333723

Desurvire, H., & El-Nasr, M. S. (2013). Methods for game user research: Studying player behavior to enhance game design. In *IEEE Computer Graphics and Applications*, *33*(4), 82–87, July–August. doi: 10.1109/MCG.2013.61

Djaouti, D., Alvarez, J., Jessel, J. P., & Rampnoux, O. (2011). Origins of serious games. In M. Ma, A. Oikonomou, & L. Jain (Eds.), *Serious Games and Edutainment Applications*. New York: Springer.

Donovan, T. (2010). *Replay: The History of Video Games*. Lewes: Yellow Ant.

Dovey, J., & Kennedy, H. (2006). *Game Cultures*. Milton Keynes: Open University Press.

Downey, G. (2001). Virtual webs, physical technologies, and hidden workers: The spaces of labor in information internetworks. *Technology and Culture*, *42*(2), 209–235. doi: 10.1353/tech.2001.0058

Duggan, E. (2017). Squaring the (magic) circle: A brief definition and history of pervasive games. In A. Nijholt (Ed.), *Playable Cities* (pp. 111–135). Singapore: Springer.

Dym, B. (2020). Exploring transformative fandom to broaden participation in computing. In *Companion of the 2020 ACM International Conference on Supporting Group Work*. New York: Association for Computing Machinery.

Edwards, T. F. M. (2013). *eSports: A brief history*. 30 April. Available at: http://adanai.com/eSports/

Egenfeldt-Nielsen, S. (2005). *The basic learning approach behind serious games*. Available at: https://web.archive.org/web/20120610101344/http://media.seriousgames.dk/downloads/the_basic_learning_approach.pdf

Eikenes, J. O. H., & Morrison, A. (2010). Navimation: Exploring time, space & motion in the design of screen-based interfaces. *International Journal of Design*, *4*(1), 1–16.

Emarketer. (2014). 2 billion consumers worldwide to get smart (phones) by 2016. *Emarketer*, 11 December. Available at: https://www.emarketer.com/Article/2-Billion-Consumers-Worldwide-Smartphones-by-2016/1011694

Engebretsen, M., & Kennedy, H. (Eds.) (2020). *Data Visualization in Society*. Amsterdam: Amsterdam University Press.

Ernkvist, M. (2008). Down many times, but still playing the game: Creative destruction and industry crashes in the early video game industry 1971–1981. In K. Gratzer and D. Stiefel (eds), *History of Insolvency and Bankruptcy from an International Perspective* (pp. 161–191). Huddinge: Södertörns högskola.

Evangelho, J. (2016). 'Pokémon GO' is about to surpass Twitter in daily active users on Android. *Forbes*, 10 July. Available at: www.forbes.com/sites/jasonevangelho/2016/07/10/pokemon-go-about-to-surpass-twitter-in-daily-active-users/#17eda4bd5174

Evans, L., & Saker, M. (2019). The playeur and *Pokémon Go*: Examining the effects of locative play on spatiality and sociability. *Mobile Media & Communication*, 7(2), 232–247. doi: 10.1177/2050157918798866

Farman, J. (2009). Locative life: Geocaching, mobile gaming, and embodiment. *Proceedings of Digital Arts and Culture*, December 12–15, 2009, Irvine, California, USA.

Farman, J. (2012). *Mobile Interface Theory: Embodied Space and Locative Media*. London: Routledge.

Farquhar, P. (2018). The world's biggest daily fantasy sports company DraftKings is off and running in Australia. *Business Insider*, April. Available at: https://www.businessinsider.com.au/the-worlds-biggest-daily-fantasy-sports-company-draftkings-is-off-and-running-in-australia-2018-4

Favis, E., & Park, G. (2020). A majority of game developers want to unionize. Few are convinced it will happen. *Washington Post*, 25 January. Available at: https://www.washingtonpost.com/video-games/2020/01/24/majority-game-developers-want-unionize-few-are-convinced-it-will-happen/

Fayard, A.-L., & Van Maanen, J. (2015). Making culture visible: Reflections on corporate ethnography. *Journal of Organizational Ethnography*, 4(1), 4–27. doi: 10.1108/JOE-12-2014-0040

Fischer, P., & Hornecker, E. (2012). Urban HCI: Spatial aspects in the design of shared encounters for media façades. *Proceedings of the Human Factors in Computing Systems Conference* (pp. 307–316). Texas, TX, May. doi: 10.1145/2207676.2207719

Fiske, J. (1992). The cultural economy of fandom. In L. A. Lewis (Ed.), *The Adoring Audience: Fan Culture and Popular Media* (pp. 30–49). London: Routledge.

Flanagan, M. (2009a). *Critical Play: Radical Game Design*. Cambridge, MA: The MIT Press.

Flanagan, M. (2009b). *LAYOFF*. Available at: https://tiltfactor.org/play-layoff/layoff_pressrelease.pdf

Flanagan, M. (2010). Creating critical play. In R. Catlow, M. Garrett, & C. Morgana (Eds.), *Artists Re: Thinking Games* (pp. 49–53). Liverpool: Liverpool University Press.

Flanagan, M. (2016). Game art. In G. Raiford & H. Lowood (Eds.), *Debugging Game History: A Critical Lexicon* (pp. 151–158). Cambridge, MA: The MIT Press.

Fluegelman, A. (1976). *The New Games Book*. Tiburon, CA: Headlands Press.

Forbes. (2019). What does the fantasy sports industry look like in the U.S. right now? *Forbes*, 6 November. Available at: https://www.forbes.com/sites/quora/2019/11/06/what-does-the-fantasy-sports-industry-look-like-in-the-us-right-now/#632c63507796

Foth, M., Brynskov, M., & Ojala, T. (Eds.) (2015). *Citizen's Right to the Digital City: Urban Interfaces, Activism, and Placemaking*. Singapore: Springer.

Fowler, A., Khosmood, F., Arya, A., & Lai, G. (2013). The Global Game Jam for teaching and learning. In *Proceedings of the 4th Annual Conference on Computing and Information Technology Research and Education New Zealand* (pp. 28–34). Hamilton, New Zealand.

Frasca, G. (2003). Ludologists love stories, too: Notes from a debate that never took place. *DiGRA'03 – Proceedings of the 2003 DiGRA International Conference: Level Up* (pp. 92–99). Utrecht, The Netherlands.

Freeman, G., & Wohn, D. (2017). eSports as an emerging research context at CHI: Diverse perspectives on definitions. *CHI 2017* (pp. 1601–1608). 6–11 May, Denver, CO. doi: 10.1145/3027063.3053158

Frissen, V., Beijer, S., Lammes, S., Lange, M. de, Mul, J. de, & Raessens, J. (Eds.) (2015). *Playful Identities: The Ludification of Digital Media Cultures*. Amsterdam: Amsterdam University Press.

Frith, J. (2013). Turning life into a game: Foursquare, gamification, and personal mobility. *Mobile Media & Communication, 1*(2), 248–262. doi: 10.1177/2050157912474811

Frith, J. (2014). Communicating through location: The understood meaning of the Foursquare check-in. *Journal of Computer-Mediated Communication, 19*(4), 890–905.

Frith, J. (2017). The digital 'lure': Small businesses and *Pokémon Go. Mobile Media & Communication, 5*(1), 51–54. doi: 10.1177/2050157916677861

Fuchs, M. (2005). Art games – from an artist's perspective. *Artificial.dk*, 31 December. Available at: www.artificial.dk/articles/fromanartist.htm

Games for Change. (2014). *Half the sky movement: The game*. Available at: www.gamesforchange.org/game/half-the-sky-movement-the-game/

Games for Change. (2019). *Games for Change student challenge*. Available at: www.gamesforchange.org/who-we-are/about-us/

Garcia-Pañella, O. G. (2018). *Jam today*. Available at: http://jamtoday.citilab.eu/index.php/speakers/dr-oscar-garcia-panella/

Gaver, B., Dunne, A., & Pacenti, E. (1999). Design: Cultural probes. *Interactions, 6*, 21–29. doi: 10.1145/291224.291235

Gee, J. P. (2005). Semiotic social spaces and affinity spaces: From the age of mythology to today's schools. In D. Barton & K. Tusting (Eds.), *Beyond Communities of Practice: Language, Power and Social Context* (pp. 214–232). Cambridge: Cambridge University Press.

Giddings, S. (2014). *Gameworlds*. London: Bloomsbury.

Giddings, S. (2017). The phenomenology of *Angry Birds:* Virtual gravity and distributed proprioception in videogame worlds. *Journal of Gaming & Virtual Worlds, 9*(3), 207–244. doi: 10.1386/jgvw.9.3.207_1

Gilbert, B. (2019). Gruelling, 100-hour work weeks and 'crunch culture' are pushing the video game industry to a breaking point: Here's what's going on. *Business Insider*. Available at: https://www.businessinsider.com.au/video-game-development-problems-crunch-culture-ea-rockstar-epic-explained-2019-5?r=US&IR=T

Gliner, K. (2013). Mid-core is bullshit. *Gamasutra*. Available at: www.gamasutra.com/blogs/KevinGliner/20130307/187983/MidCore_Is_Bullshit.php

Goddard, W., Byrne, R., & Mueller, F. F. (2014). Playful game jams: Guidelines for designed outcomes. In *Proceedings of the 2014 Conference on Interactive Entertainment* (pp. 1–10). New York: ACM Press. doi.org/10.1145/2677758.2677778

Golding, D., & Van Deventer, L. (2016). *Game Changers*. Melbourne: Affirm Press.

Gordon, E., & de Souza e Silva, A. (2011). *Net Locality: Why Location Matters in a Networked World*. Oxford: Wiley-Blackwell.

Gray, K. L., Buyukozturk, B., & Hill, Z. (2017). Blurring the boundaries: Using Gamergate to examine 'real' and symbolic violence against women in contemporary gaming culture. *Sociology Compass, 11*(3), n.p. doi: 10.1111/soc4.12458

Gray-Denson, K., Voorhees, G., & Vossen, E. (2018). *Feminism in Play*. Basingstoke: Palgrave Macmillan.

Gromer, D., Reinke, M., Christner, I., & Pauli, P. (2019). Causal interactive links between presence and fear in virtual reality height exposure. *Frontiers in Psychology, 10*.

Guevara-Villalobos, O. (2011). Cultures of independent game production: Examining the relationship between community and labour. *DiGRA Conference*. Available at: www.digra.org/wp-content/uploads/digital-library/11307.08157.pdf

Gundling, E., & Zanchettin, A. (2007). *Global Diversity: Winning Customers and Engaging Employees Within World Markets*. London: Nicholas Brealey Publishing International.

Hall, J. (2004). Mogi: Second generation location-based gaming. *The Feature*. Available at: www.thefeaturearchives.com/topic/Gaming/Mobi_Second_Generation_Location-Based_Gaming.html

Hallmann, K., & Giel, T. (2017). eSports – Competitive sports or recreational activity? *Sport Management Review*, *21*(1), 14–20. doi: 10.1016/j.smr.2017.07.011

Halverson, E., & Halverson, R. (2008). Fantasy baseball: The case for competitive freedom. *Games & Culture*, *3*(3–4), 286–308.

Hamari, J., & Sjöblom, M. (2017). What is eSports and why do people watch it? *Internet Research*, *27*(2), 211–232. Available at: https://www.emerald.com/insight/content/doi/10.1108/IntR-04-2016-0085./full/html

Harris, B. J. (2014). *Console Wars: Sega vs Nintendo, and the Battle that Defined a Generation*. London: Harper Collins Publishers.

Harvey, A. (2019). Becoming gamesworkers: Diversity, higher education, and the future of the game industry. *Television & New Media*, *20*(8), 756–766. doi: 10.1177/1527476419851080

Harvey, A., & Fisher, F. (2014). Everyone can make games! The post-feminist context of women in digital game production. *Feminist Media Studies*, *15*(4), 576–592. doi: 10.1080/14680777.2014.958867

Helyer, N. (2007). The Sonic Commons: Embrace or retreat? *Scan Journal*, *4*(3). Available at: http://scan.net.au/scan/journal/display.php?journal_id=105

Herman, L. (2001 [1994]). *Phoenix: The Fall and Rise of Videogames*. Union, NJ: Rolenta Press.

HHS (Department of Health & Human Services). (2016). *The CDC & HHS Health Game Jams*. Available at: https://www.hhs.gov/cto/projects/the-cdc-and-hhs-health-game-jams/index.html

Hill, R. & Vaughan, L. (2017). Design for Social Innovation Impact Evaluation Study. *Design and Creative Practice, Enabling Capability Platform*. Melbourne: RMIT University.

Hill, V. (2015). Digital citizenship through game design in Minecraft. *New Library World*, *116*(7/8), 369–382. doi: 10.1108/NLW-09-2014-0112

Hills, M. (2002). *Fan Cultures*. London: Routledge.

Hino, K., Asami, Y., & Jung, S. L. (2019). Step counts of middle-aged and elderly adults for 10 months before and after the release of *Pokémon GO* in Yokohama, Japan. *Journal of Medical Internet Research*, *21*(2), e10724. doi: 10.2196/10724

Hjorth, L. (2011). *Games and Gaming: An Introduction to New Media*. Oxford: Berg.

Hjorth, L., & Byrne, L. (2016). *Design and Play Exhibition Catalogue*. Melbourne: RMIT Design Hub.

Hjorth, L., & Chan, D. (Eds.) (2009). *Gaming Cultures and Place in Asia-Pacific*. London: Routledge.

Hjorth, L., Davies, H., Onicas, A., & Leong, J. (2018). *Social play in Kyoto: Summary report*. Melbourne: RMIT University. Available at: https://dcp-ecp.com/content/projects/45-social-games-for-change-workshop-japan/social-play-workshop-kyoto_summary-doc.pdf

Hjorth, L., Horst, H., Bell, G., & Galloway, A. (2016). *The Routledge Companion to Digital Ethnography*. London: Routledge.

Hjorth, L., & Pink, S. (2014). New visualities and the digital wayfarer: Reconceptualizing camera phone photography and locative media. *Mobile Media & Communication*, *2*(1), 40–57. https://doi.org/10.1177/2050157913505257

Hjorth, L., & Richardson, I. (2014). *Gaming in Social, Locative and Mobile Media*. Basingstoke: Palgrave.

Hjorth, L., & Richardson, I. (2016). Mobile games and ambient play. In M. Willson & T. Leaver (Eds.), *Social, Casual and Mobile Games: The Changing Gaming Landscape* (pp. 105–116). London: Bloomsbury Academic.

Hjorth, L., & Richardson, I. (2017). *Pokémon GO*: Mobile media play, place-making, and the digital wayfarer. *Mobile Media & Communication*, *5*(1), 3–14. doi: 10.1177/2050157916680015

Hjorth, L., & Richardson, I. (2020). *Ambient Play*. Cambridge, MA: The MIT Press.

Hjorth, L., Wilken, R., & Gu, K. (2012). Ambient intimacy: A case study of the iPhone, presence, and location-based social media in Shanghai, China. In L. Hjorth, J. Burgess, & I. Richardson (Eds.), *Studying Mobile Media* (pp. 43–62). London: Routledge.

Holmes, T. (2003). Arcade classics spawn art? Current trends in the art game genre. *Melbourne DAC*. Available at: www.techkwondo.com/external/pdf/reports/Holmes.pdf

Hong, R., & Chen, V. H.-H. (2014). Becoming an ideal co-creator: Web materiality and intensive laboring practices in game modding. *New Media & Society*, 16(2), 290–305. doi: 10.1177/1461444813480095

Hooper, J., & de Byl, P. (2014). Towards a unified theory of play: A case study of *Minecraft*. *DIGRA*. Available at: http://digraa.org/wp-content/uploads/2014/06/29_hooper.pdf

Horowitz, K. (2016). *The Sega Arcade Revolution: A History in 62 Games*. Jefferson, NC: McFarland and Co. Publishers.

Horowitz, K. (2018). *Playing at the Next Level: A History of American Sega Games*. Jefferson, NC: McFarland and Co. Publishers.

Horton, J. (2012). 'Got my shoes, got my Pokémon': Everyday geographies of children's popular culture. *Geoforum*, 43, 4–13. doi: 10.1016/j.geoforum.2011.07.005

Howard, S. (Ed.) (1998). *Wired-up: Young People and the Electronic Media*. London: UCL Press.

Huizinga, J. (1938 [1955]). *Homo Ludens: A Study of the Play Element in Culture*. Boston, MA: Beacon Press.

Humphreys, S. (2019). On being a feminist in game studies. *Games and Culture*, 14(7–8). doi: 10.1177/1555412017737637

Hunt, V., Yee, L., Prince, S., & Dixon-Fyle, S. (2018). Delivering through diversity, January 2018 Report. *Mckinsey and Company*. Available at: https://www.mckinsey.com/business-functions/organization/our-insights/delivering-through-diversity

Huntemann, N. B. (2010). Pixel pinups: Images of women in video games. In R. A. Lind (Ed.), *Race/Gender/Media: Considering Diversity Across Audiences, Content, and Producers* (2nd ed., pp. 250–257). Harlow, UK: Pearson.

Hutchins, B. (2008). Signs of meta-change in second modernity: The growth of e-sport and the world cyber games. *New Media & Society*, 10(6), 851–869.

Hutchins, B. (2016). Tales of the digital sublime: Tracing the relationship between big data and professional sport. *Convergence*, 22(5), 494–509. doi: 10.1177/1354856515587163

Hutchins, B., & Rowe, D. (2009). From broadcast scarcity to digital plenitude: The changing dynamics of the media sport content economy. *Television New Media*, 10(4), 354–370. doi: https://doi.org/10.1177/1527476409334016

Influencer Marketing (2018). *Influencer marketing hub*. Available at: https://influencer marketinghub.com/mobile-gaming-statistics/

IPERG (2008). *IPERG Project information*. Kista: CORDIS. Available at: https://cordis.europa.eu/project/id/004457

Isbister, K. (2016). Why *Pokémon GO* became an instant phenomenon. *The Conversation*. Available at: http://theconversation.com/why-pokemon-go-became-aninstant-pheno menon-62412

Isidore, C. (2003). The ultimate fantasy – profits. *CNNMoney.com*. Available at: https://money.cnn.com/2003/08/29/commentary/column_sportsbiz/sportsbiz/

Ito, M., Martin, C., Pfister, R. C., Rafalow, M. H., Salen, K., & Wortman, A. (2018). *Affinity Online: How Connection and Shared Interest Fuel Learning*. New York: NYU Press.

Jacob, R. J. K. et al. (2008). Reality based interaction: A framework for post-WIMP interfaces. In *CHI 2008 Proceedings: Post-WIMP* (p. 201). Florence, Italy, 5–10 April.

Jaffa, V. (2016). The myth of the Indie game success story needs to stop and here's why. *Model View Culture*, 27 April, Issue 36. Available at: https://modelviewculture.com/pieces/the-myth-of-the-indie-game-success-story-needs-to-stop-and-heres-why

Jain, S., & Lobo, R. (2012). *Diversity and Inclusion: A Business Imperative in Global Professional Services*. Berlin: Springer-Verlag.

Jakob, A., & Collier, L. (2017). Sensory enrichment for people living with dementia: Increasing the benefits of multisensory environments in dementia care through design. *Design for Health*, 1(1), 115–133. doi: 10.1080/24735132.2017.1296274

Jansson, M. (2009). Interview: Orhan Kipcak (ArsDoom, ArsDoom II) (1995–2005). *GameScenes.org*, November. Available at: www.gamescenes.org/2009/11/interview-orphan-kipcak-arsdoom-arsdoom-ii-1995.html

Jansson, M. (2012). *Everything I Shoot is Art*. Brescia: Link Editions.

Jantzen, G., & Jensen, J. F. (1993). Powerplay: Power, violence and gender in video games. *AI & Society*, 7(4), 368–385. doi: 10.1007/BF01891418

Jayemanne, D. (2017). *Performativity in Art, Literature, and Videogames*. Cham, Switzerland: Springer International. doi: 10.1007/978-3-319-54451-9

Jenkins, H. (1992). *Textual Poachers: Television Fans and Participatory Culture*. London: Routledge.

Jenkins, H. (2004). Game design as narrative architecture. In N. Wardrip-Fruin & P. Harrigan (Eds.), *First Person: New Media as Story, Performance, and Game*. Cambridge, MA: The MIT Press.

Jenkins, H. (2006a). *Fans, Bloggers and Gamers: Exploring Participatory Culture*. New York: New York University Press.

Jenkins, H. (2006b). *Convergence Culture: Where Old and New Media Collide*. New York: New York University Press.

Jenkins, H. (2007). Afterword: The future of fandom. In J. Gray, C. Sandvoss, & C. Harrington (Eds.), *Fandom: Identities and Communities in a Mediated World* (2nd ed.). New York: New York University Press. Available at: www.jstor.org/stable/j.ctt1pwtbq2

Jenkins, H. (2008). *The moral economy of Web 2.0* (Part One). Available at: http://henryjenkins.org/blog/2008/03/the_moral_economy_of_web_20_pa.html

Jenkins, H., Ford, S., & Green, J. (2013). *Spreadable Media: Creating Value and Meaning in a Networked Culture*. New York: New York University Press.

Jin, D. Y. (2017). Critical interpretation of the *Pokémon GO* phenomenon: The intensification of new capitalism and free labor. *Mobile Media & Communication*, 5(1), 55–58. doi: 10.1177/2050157916677306

Jonasson, K., & Thiborg, J. (2010). Electronic sport and its impact on future sport. *Sport in Society*, 13(2), 287–299. doi: 10.1080/17430430903522996

Jungnickel, K., & Hjorth, L. (2014). Methodological entanglements in the field: Methods, transitions and transmissions. *Visual Studies*, Special Issue: Transformations in art and ethnography, 29(2), 138–147. doi: 10.1080/1472586X.2014.887263

Jutel, T., & Schirato, T. (2008). Media interactivity and fantasy sport. *MEDIANZ: Media Studies Journal of Aotearoa New Zealand*, 11(1),1–13. doi: 10.11157/medianz-vol11iss1id57

Juul, J. (2009). *A Casual Revolution*. Cambridge, MA: The MIT Press.

Juul, J. (2014). High-tech low-tech authenticity: The creation of independent style at the Independent Games Festival. In *Proceedings of the 9th International Conference on the Foundations of Digital Games*. Liberty of the Seas, Caribbean.

Kallio, P. K., Mäyrä, F., & Kaipainen, K. (2011). At least nine ways to play: Approaching gamer mentalities. *Games and Culture*, 6(4), 327–353. doi: 10.1177/1555412010391089

Kasapakis, V., & Gavalas, D. (2015). Pervasive gaming: Status, trends and design principles. *Journal of Network and Computer Applications*, 55. doi: 10.1016/j.jnca.2015.05.009

Kaser, R. (2018). Rockstar Games controversy renews concern over 'crunch culture'. *The Next Web*. Available at: https://thenextweb.com/gaming/2018/10/18/rockstar-controversy-crunch-culture/

Kato, T. A., Teo, A. R., Tateno, M., Watabe, M., Kubo, H., & Kanba, S. (2017). Can *Pokémon GO* rescue shut-ins (hikikomori) from their isolated world? *Psychiatry and Clinical Neurosciences*, 71(1), 75–76. doi: 10.1111/pcn.12481

Katrib, R. (2011). *Cory Arcangel Catalogue*. North Miami, FL: Museum of Contemporary Arts.

Kawashima, N. (2010). The rise of 'user-creativity' – Web 2.0 and a new challenge for copyright law and cultural policy. *International Journal of Cultural Policy*, *16*(3), 337–353. doi: 10.1080/10286630903111613

Kemerer, C. F., Dunn, B. K., & Janansefat, S. (2017). *Winners-take-some dynamics in digital platform markets: A reexamination of the video game console wars*. Report. University of Pittsburgh, PA. Available at: https://www.pitt.edu/~ckemerer/Video%20Game%20Reexamination%2020170216-submitted.pdf

Kennedy, H., Poell, T., & van Dijck, J. (2015). Introduction: Data and agency. *Big Data & Society*, *2*(2). doi: 10.1177/2053951715621569

Kennedy, J. (2013). Rhetorics of sharing: Data, imagination, and desire. In G. Lovink & M. Rasch (Eds.), *Unlike Us Reader: Social Media Monopolies and Their Alternatives* (pp. 127–136). Amsterdam: Amsterdam Institute of Network Cultures.

Kent, S. (2001). *The Ultimate History of Video Games: From Pong to Pokémon and Beyond*. New York: Three Rivers Press.

Keogh, B. (2016). *Pokémon Go* and the politics of digital gaming in public. *Overland*. Available at: https://overland.org.au/2016/07/Pokémon-go-and-the-politics-of-digital-gaming-in-public/

Keogh, B. (2018). *A Play of Bodies: How We Perceive Videogames*. Cambridge, MA: The MIT Press.

Kerr, A. (2010). Beyond billiard balls: Transnational flows, cultural diversity and digital games. In C. B. Graber & M. Burri-Nenova (Eds.), *Governance of Digital Game Environments and Cultural Diversity: Transdisciplinary Enquiries* (pp. 47–73). Cheltenham: Edward Elgar.

Kerr, A. (2013). Space wars: The politics of games production in Europe. In N. Huntemann & B. Aslinger (Eds.), *Gaming Globally* (pp. 215–231). Basingstoke: Palgrave.

Kerr, A. (2017). *Global Games: Production, Circulation and Policy in the Networked Era*. London: Routledge.

Kester, G. (2011). *The One and the Many: Contemporary Collaborative Art in a Global Context*. Durham, NC: Duke University Press.

Keyson, D., Maher, M., Streitz, N., Cheok, A., Augusto Wrede, J., Wichert, R., Englebienne, G., Aghajan, H., & Krose, B. (2011). Ambient intelligence. *Proceedings of the Second International Joint Conference on AmI* 2. Amsterdam, The Netherlands, 16–18 November.

Kim, A. J. (2004). *The Network is the game: Social trends in mobile entertainment*. PowerPoint presentation at Game Developers Conference 2004, San Jose, CA.

Kirkpatrick, G. (2009). Controller, hand, screen: Aesthetic form in the computer game. *Games and Culture*, *4*(2), 127–143. doi: 10.1177/1555412008325484

Knabb, K. (Ed.) (1981). *Situationist International Anthology*. Berkley, CA: Bureau of Public Secrets.

Koenitz, H. (2014). Reflecting civic protest – the Occupy Istanbul game. *Proceedings of the 9th International Conference on the Foundations of Digital Games (FDG)*. Liberty of the Seas, Caribbean: Society for the Advancement of the Science of Digital Games. Available at: www.fdg2014.org/papers/fdg2014\_poster\_06.pdf

Koss, H. (2020). What does the future of the gaming industry look like? *Built In*, 3 February. Available at: https://builtin.com/media-gaming/future-of-gaming

Kuchera, B. (2006). Professor uses America's Army to protest war in Iraq: Players see just another griefer. *ARS Electronica*. Available at: https://arstechnica.com/gaming/2006/06/4233/

Kücklich, J. (2005). Precarious playbour: Modders and the digital games industry. *Fibreculture Journal*. Available at: https://www.researchgate.net/publication/26490724_Precarious_Playbour_Modders_and_the_Digital_Games_Industry

Kücklich, J., & Fellow, M. C. (2004). *Play and playability as key concepts in new media studies*. STeM Centre, Dublin City University (pp. 1–44).

Lamarre, T. (2017). Platformativity. *Asiascape: Digital Asia, 4*(3), 285–305. doi: 10.1163/22142312-12340081

Lamerichs, N. (2018). *Productive Fandom: Intermediality and Affective Reception in Fan Cultures.* Amsterdam: Amsterdam University Press. doi: 10.2307/j.ctv65svxz

Lammes, S., & Wilmott, C. (2018). The map as playground: Location-based games as cartographical practices. *Convergence, 24*(6), 648–665. doi: 10.1177/1354856516679596

Lange, P. G., & Ito, M. (2010). Creative production. In M. Ito & J. Antin (Eds.), *Hanging Out, Messing Around, and Geeking Out: Kids Living and Learning with New Media* (pp. 243–293). Cambridge, MA: The MIT Press.

Lankoski, P., & Björk, S. (Eds.) (2015). *Game Research Methods.* Pittsburgh, PA: ETC Press.

Lantz, F. (2006). Big Games and the porous border between the real and the mediated. *Receiver,* 16. Available at: www.receiver.vodafone.com/16/articles/index07.html

Lee, P. M. (2009). New games. *Australian and New Zealand Journal of Art, 10*(1), 34–55. doi: 10.1080/14434318.2009.11432601

Lefaivre, L., & Döll, H. (2007). *Ground-up City: Play as a Design Tool.* Rotterdam: 010 Publishers.

Lefebvre, H. (1991 [1974]). *The Production of Space.* Oxford: Blackwell.

Leorke, D. (2018). *Location-based Gaming: Play in Public Space.* Basingstoke: Palgrave Macmillan.

Lessig, L. (2008). *Remix: Making Art and Commerce Thrive in the Hybrid Economy.* Harmondsworth: Penguin.

Levy, P. (1994). *L'intelligence Collective*: *Pour une Anthropologie du Cyberspace.* Paris: La Découverte.

Licoppe, C., & Inada, Y. (2006). Emergent uses of a multiplayer location-aware mobile game: The interactional consequences of mediated encounters. *Mobilities, 1*(1), 39–61. doi: 10.1080/17450100500489221

Lien, T. (2013). No girls allowed: Unravelling the story behind the stereotype of video games being for boys. *Polygon.* Available at: https://www.polygon.com/features/2013/12/2/5143856/no-girls-allowed

Lim, S. S. (2006). From cultural to information revolution: ICT domestication by middle-class Chinese families. In T. Berker, M. Hartmann, Y. Punie, & K. Ward (Eds.), *Domestication of Media and Technology* (pp. 185–201). New York: McGraw-Hill International.

Lin, Z., & Zhao, Y. (2020). Self-enterprising eSports: Meritocracy, precarity, and disposability of eSports players in China. *International Journal of Cultural Studies, 23*(4), 582–599. https://doi.org/10.1177/1367877920903437

Lindqvist, A. K., Castelli, D., Hallberg, J., & Rutberg, S. (2018). The praise and price of *Pokémon GO*: A qualitative study of children's and parents' experiences. *JMIR Serious Games, 6*(1), e1. doi: 10.2196/games.8979

Lindtner, S., & Dourish, P. (2011). The promise of play: A new approach to productive play. *Games and Culture, 6*(5), 453–478. doi: 10.1177/1555412011402678

Livingstone, S. (2020). Parenting in the digital age. *TED Talk.* Available at: https://www.ted.com/talks/sonia_livingstone_parenting_in_the_digital_age

Llorens, M. R. (2017). eSport gaming: The rise of a new sports practice sport. *Sport, Ethics and Philosophy, 11*(4), 464–476. doi: 10.1080/17511321.2017.1318947

Locker, M. (2012). #1ReasonWhy: Women take to Twitter to talk about sexism in video game industry. *Time Newsfeed,* 27 November. Available at: http://newsfeed.time.com/2012/11/27/1reasonwhy-women-take-to-twitter-to-talk-about-sexism-in-video-game-industry/

Lowther, R. (2006). Embracing and managing diversity at Dell: Introducing flexible working and a women's network to help retain key employees. *Strategic HR Review, 5*(6), 16–19. doi: 10.1108/14754390680000921

Lupton, D. (2016a). The diverse domains of quantified selves: Self-tracking modes and dataveillance. *Economy and Society, 45*(1), 101–122. doi: 10.1080/03085147.2016.1143726

Lupton, D. (2016b). *The Quantified Self: A Sociology of Self-tracking*. Cambridge: Polity Press.

Lupton, D. (2017). How does health feel? Towards research on the affective atmospheres of digital health. *Digital Health*, *3*, April. doi: 10.1177/2055207617701276

Lury, C., & Wakeford, N. (Eds.) (2012). *Inventive Methods: The Happening of the Social*. London: Routledge.

Mace, J., & West, M. (2008). *Value creation in the mobile internet: The impact of Apple's iPhone*. Available at: www.joelwest.org/Papers/WestMace2008.pdf (accessed 10 April 2012).

Mace, J., & West, M. (2010). Browsing the Killer App: Explaining the rapid success of Apple's iPhone. *Telecommunications Policy*, *34*(5–6), 270–286. doi: 10.1016/j.telpol.2009.12.002

Machkovech, S. (2016). Armed muggers use *Pokémon GO* to find victims. *Ars Technica*, July. Available at: http://arstechnica.com/gaming/2016/07/armed-muggers-use-pokemon-go-to-find-victims/

Magerkurth, C., Cheok, A., Mandryk, R., & Nilsen, T. (2005). Pervasive games: Bringing computer entertainment back to the real world. *Computers in Entertainment*, *3*(4). doi: 10.1145/1077246.1077257

Malaby, T. M. (2007). Beyond play: A new approach to games. *Games & Culture*, *2*(2), 95–113. doi: 10.1177/1555412007299434

Mansoor, I. (2019). Twitch revenue and USAGE statistics. *Business of Apps*, 27 February. Available at: https://www.businessofapps.com/data/twitch-statistics/

Marone, V. (2015). From discussion forum to discursive studio: Learning and creativity in design-oriented affinity spaces. *Games and Culture*, *10*(1), 81–105. doi: 10.1177/1555412014557328

Marres, N. (2017). *Digital Sociology*. Cambridge: Polity Press.

Marres, N., Guggenheim, M., & Wilkie, A. (2018). *Inventing the Social*. Manchester: Mattering Press.

Marsh, J., Robinson, M., & Willett, R. (2009). *Play, Creativity and Digital Cultures*. London: Routledge.

Martin, C. B., & Deuze, M. (2009). The independent production of culture: A digital games case study. *Games and Culture*, *4*(3), 276–295. doi: 10.1177/1555412009339732

Matthew, E. (2012). Sexism in video games: There is sexism in gaming. *Price Charting*. Available at: blog.pricecharting.com/2012/09/emilyami-sexism-in-video-games-study.html

Mäyrä, F. (2008). *An Introduction to Game Studies: Games in Culture*. London: SAGE.

Mäyrä, F. (2016). Exploring gaming communities. In R. Kowert & T. Quandt (Eds.), *The Video Game Debate: Unravelling the Physical, Social, and Psychological Effects of Digital Games* (pp. 74–93). London: Routledge.

Mäyrä, F. (2017). *Pokémon GO*: Entering the ludic society. *Mobile Media & Communication*, *5*(1), 47–50. doi: 10.1177/2050157916678270

M.B. (2020). The rise and rise of videogames. *The Economist*, 19 May. Available at: https://www.economist.com/prospero/2020/03/19/the-rise-and-rise-of-video-games

McCrea, C. (2011). We play in public: The nature and context of portable gaming systems. *Convergence*, *17*(4), 389–403. doi: 10.1177/1354856511414987

McCrea, C. (2017). Pokémon's progressive revelation: Notes on 20 years of game design. *Mobile Media & Communication*, *5*(1), 42–46. doi: 10.1177/2050157916678271

McCullough, M. (1996). *Abstracting Craft: The Practiced Digital Hand*. Cambridge, MA: The MIT Press.

McDonald, H. (2013). Living in a fantasy world. *BackPageLead*. Available at: www.backpagelead.com.au/afl/9366-living-in-a-fantasy-world

McGonigal, J. (2003a). 'This is not a game': Immersive aesthetics and collective play. *Conference Proceedings: Digital Arts & Culture*. Melbourne, Australia.

McGonigal, J. (2003b). A real little game: The Pinocchio effect in pervasive play. *Proceedings of the DiGRA Conference*. University of Utrecht, The Netherlands. Available at: https://pdfs.

semanticscholar.org/2dec/697fb7ebe20f337abe40543121fea639685e.pdf?_ga=2.4081392.1322757614.1584405783-1159665543.1584097364

McGonigal, J. (2006). 'This might be a game: Ubiquitous play and performance at the turn of the twenty-first century'. PhD thesis, University of California. Available at: www.avantgame.com/McGonigal_TtitleS_MIGHT_BE_A_GAME_sm.pdf

McGonigal, J. (2010). Gaming can make a better world. *TED Talk*. Available at: https://www.ted.com/talks/jane_mcgonigal_gaming_can_make_a_better_world?language=en

McGonigal, J. (2011). *Reality Is Broken: Why Games Make Us Better and How They Can Change the World*. Harmondsworth: Penguin.

McNeill, L. (2019). Video game workers see power in a union. *New Republic*, 15 May. Available at: https://newrepublic.com/article/153892/riot-game-workers-union

Meunier, N. (2010). Homophobia and harassment in the online gaming age. *IGN*, 14 January. Available at: https://au.ign.com/articles/2010/01/13/homophobia-and-harassment-in-the-online-gaming-age

Militello, L. K., Hanna, N., & Nigg, C. R. (2018). *Pokémon GO* within the context of family health: Retrospective study. *Journal of Medical Internet Research: Pediatric Parent, 1*(2), e10679.

Miller, A., Pater, J., & Mynatt, E. (2013). Design strategies for youth-focused pervasive social health games. *IEEE*, 9–16. doi: 10.4108/icst.pervasivehealth.2013.252081

Mishra, S. P. (2016). *Pokémon Go* Australia: Aussie police issues warning to gamers to 'stay away'. Available at: www.australianetworknews.com/please-edit-pokemon-go-australia-aussie-police-issues-warning-to-gamers-to-stay-away/

MOMA (2017). *Ian Cheng: Emissaries Exhibition*. MOMA online. Available at: https://www.moma.org/calendar/exhibitions/3656

Montola, M. (2005). *Exploring the edge of the magic circle: Defining pervasive games. CD ROM Proceedings of Digital Arts and Culture (DAC)* (pp. 1–3). Melbourne, Australia.

Montola, M. (2011). A ludological view on the pervasive mixed-reality game research paradigm. *Personal and Ubiquitous Computing, 15*, 3–12. doi: 10.1007/s00779-010-0307-7

Montola, M., Waern, A., & Stenros, J. (2009). *Pervasive Games: Theory and Design Experiences on the Boundary Between Life and Play*. Burlington, MA: Morgan Kaufmann.

Moody, K. A. (2014). 'Modders: Changing the game through user-generated content and online communities'. Dissertation, University of Iowa. Available at: https://doi.org/10.17077/etd.5ak8cz3w

Moore, C. (2011). The magic circle and the mobility of play. *Convergence: The International Journal of Research into New Media Technologies, 17*(4), 373–387. doi: 10.1177/1354856511414350

Moore, T., Gibson, M., McAuliffe, C., & Edmond, M. (2020, forthcoming). Freeplay and independent games. In *Fringe to Famous: Indie and Mainstream Cultural Production in Australia*. London: Bloomsbury.

Morovoz, E. (2013). The death of the cyberflâneur. *New York Times*, 4 February. Available at: https://www.nytimes.com/2012/02/05/opinion/sunday/the-death-of-the-cyberflaneur.html

Mortensen, T. (2016). Anger, fear, and games: The long event of #GamerGate. *Games and Culture, 13*(8), 787–806. doi: 10.1177/1555412016640408

Mueller, F., Khot, R., Gerling, K., & Mandryk, R. (2016). Exertion games. *Foundations and Trends in Human-Computer Interaction, 10*(1), 1–86. doi: 10.1561/1100000041

Murray, J. (2005). The last word on ludology v narratology in game studies. *DiGRA 2005*, Vancouver, Canada, 17 June.

Musil, J., Schweda, A., Winkler, D., & Biffl, S. (2010). Synthesized essence: What game jams teach about prototyping of new software products. In *ACM/IEEE 32nd International Conference on Software Engineering*, v2, 183–186. New York: ACM Press.

Nafus, D. (2016). *Quantified: Biosensing Technologies in Everyday Life*. Cambridge, MA: The MIT Press.

Nafus, D., & Neff, G. (2016). *Self-tracking*. Cambridge, MA: The MIT Press.

Newell, A. (2018). How much money does Faker make? We break it down. *Dotesports.com*. Available at: https://dotesports.com/league-of-legends/news/faker-earnings-league-of-legends-14357

Newzoo (2019). *The Global Games Market Will Generate $152.1 Billion in 2019 as the U.S. Overtakes China as the Biggest Market*. Available at: https://newzoo.com/insights/articles/the-global-games-market-will-generate-152-1-billion-in-2019-as-the-u-s-overtakes-china-as-the-biggest-market/

Newzoo (2020). *Newzoo Global Esports Market Report 2020 | Light Version*. Available at: www.newzoo.com/insights/trend-reports/newzoo-global-esports-market-report-2020-light-version/

Nguyen, J. (2016). Praxis: Performing as video game players in Let's Plays. *Transformative Works and Cultures*, *22*, 1–28. doi: 10.3983/twc.2016.0698

Nieborg, D., & van der Graaf, S. (2008). The mod industries? The industrial logic of non-market game production. *European Journal of Cultural Studies*, *11*(2), 177–195. doi: 10.1177/1367549407088331

Nieuwdorp, E. (2005). The pervasive interface: Tracing the magic circle. *Proceedings of DiGRA 2005 Conference: Changing Views – Worlds in Play*. Vancouver, Simon Fraser University, 16–20 June.

Nijholt, A. (2017). *Playable Cities: The City as a Digital Playground*. New York: Springer.

Noë, A. (2012). *Varieties of Presence*. Cambridge, MA: Harvard University Press.

Olsson, M. (2019). 'Motivations and ownership in Fortnite communities'. Master's thesis, Malmö universitet/Kultur och samhälle.

Page, S. E. (2017). *The Diversity Bonus: How Great Teams Pay Off in the Knowledge Economy*. Princeton, NJ: Princeton University Press.

Parikka, J., & Suominen, J. (2006). Victorian snakes? Towards a cultural history of mobile games and the experience of movement. *Game Studies*, *6*(1). Available at: http://gamestudies.org/0601/articles/parikka_suominen

Parisi, D. (2008). Fingerbombing, or 'touching is good': The cultural construction of technologized touch. *Senses & Society*, *3*(3), 307–327.

Parisi, D. (2009). Game interfaces as bodily techniques. In R. Ferdig (Ed.), *Handbook of Research on Effective Electronic Gaming in Education* (pp. 111–126). Hershey, PA: Information Science Reference: IGI Global.

Parisi, D. (2015). A counterrevolution in the hands: The console controller as an ergonomic branding mechanism. *Journal of Games Criticism*, *2*(1). Available at: http://gamescriticism.org/articles/parisi-2-1/

Parisi, D., Paterson, M., & Archer, J. (2017). Haptic media studies. *New Media & Society*, *19*(10), 1513–1522. doi: https://doi.org/10.1177/1461444817717518

Parker, L. (2014). Games for change uses video games for social projects. *The New York Times*, 21 April. Available at: https://www.nytimes.com/2014/04/22/arts/video-games/games-for-change-uses-video-games-for-social-projects.html

Paterson, M. (2007). *The Senses of Touch: Haptics, Affects and Technologies*. Oxford: Berg.

Paterson, M., Dodge M., & MacKian, S. (2012). Introduction: Placing touch within social theory and empirical study. In M. Paterson & M. Dodge (Eds.), *Touching Space, Placing Touch* (pp. 1–28). Farnham: Ashgate Publishing.

Paul, C. (2011). *Cory Arcangel Pro Tools*. Catalogue. Whitney Museum of American Art, 26 May–11 September.

Paul, C. A. (2018). *The Toxic Meritocracy of Video Games: Why Gaming Culture is the Worst*. University of Minnesota Press: Minneapolis.

Pearce, C. (2009). *Communities of Play: Emergent Cultures in Multiplayer Game and Virtual Worlds*. Cambridge, MA: The MIT Press.

Pearce, C. (2010). *Play's the thing: Games as fine art. Keynote address presented at the Art History of Games Symposium, High Museum of Art's Rich Auditorium*, Woodruff Arts Center, Atlanta,

GA. Available at: https://www.youtube.com/watch?v=3x7GTjQFT18&feature=edu&list=PLA11 7E9FF1B8C375D

Pearce, C., Fullerton, T., Fron, J., & Morie, J. (2007). Sustainable play: Toward a New Games Movement for the digital age. *Games and Culture*, 2(3), 261–278. doi: 10.1177/1555412 007304420

Perez, S. (2019). Mobile games now account for 33% of installs, 10% of time and 74% of consumer spend. *Techcrunch*, 11 June. Available at: https://techcrunch.com/2019/06/11/mobile-games-now-account-for-33-of-installs-10-of-time-and-74-of-consumer-spend/

Petrova, E., & Gross, N. (2018). Four reasons people watch gaming videos on YouTube. *Think with Google*. Available at: https://www.thinkwithgoogle.com/data-collections/gamer-demographics-gaming-statistics/

Piaget, J. (1999). *Play, Dreams and Imitation in Childhood*. London: Routledge. First published in French (1951).

Pink, S. (2009). *Doing Sensory Ethnography*. London: SAGE.

Pink, S. (2015). Approaching media through the senses: Between experience and representation. *Media International Australia*, 154(1), 5–14. doi: 10.1177/1329878X1515400103

Pink, S., Sinanan, J., Hjorth, L., & Horst, H. (2016) Tactile digital ethnography: Researching mobile media through the hand. *Mobile Media & Communication*, 4(2), 237–251. doi: 10.1177/2050157915619958

Planells, J. A. (2017). Video games and the crowdfunding ideology: From the gamer-buyer to the prosumer-investor. *Journal of Consumer Culture*, 17(3), 620–638. doi: 10.1177/1469540515611200

Ploug, K. (2005). Art games as genre: An introduction. *Dichtung*. Available at: www.dichtung-digital.de/2005/2/Ploug/index.htm

Polansky, L. (2016). Towards an art history for videogames. *Rhizome*, 3 August. Available at: https://rhizome.org/editorial/2016/aug/03/an-art-history-for-videogames/

Poor, N. (2014). Computer game modders' motivations and sense of community: A mixed-methods approach. *New Media & Society*, 16(8), 1249–1267. doi: 10.1177/14614448 13504266

Postigo, H. (2007). Of mods and modders: Chasing down the value of fan-based digital game modifications. *Games and Culture*, 2(4), 300–313. doi: 10.1177/1555412007307955

Postigo, H. (2008). Video game appropriation through modifications: Attitudes concerning intellectual property among modders and fans. *Convergence*, 14(1), 59–74. doi: 10.1177/135485 6507084419

Prax, P. (2019). Is this still participation? A case study of the disempowerment of player labourers. In *DiGRA Conference*. Available at: www.digra.org/digital-library/publications/is-this-still-participation-a-case-study-of-the-disempowerment-of-player-labourers/conf/digra/2019 db/conf/digra/digra2019.html#Prax19

Preskill, H., & Beer, T.C. (2012). *Evaluating Social Innovation*. Washington, D.C.: FSG & Centre for Evaluation Innovation.

Price, L. (2014). The sims: A retrospective – a participatory culture 14 years on. *Intensities: The Journal of Cult Media*, 7(1), 135–140.

Quaranta, D. (2014). *Beyond New Media Art*. Brescia: Link Editions.

Radde-Antweiler, K., & Zeiler, X. (2015). Methods for analyzing Let's Plays: Context analysis for gaming videos on YouTube. *Gamevironments*. Available at: https://elib.suub.uni-bremen.de/peid=P00104729&Exemplar=1&LAN=DE

Raessens, J. (2006). Playful identities, or the ludification of culture. *Games and Culture*, 1(1), 52–57. doi: 10.1177/1555412005281779

Raessens, J. (2012). *Homo Ludens 2.0: The Ludic Turn in Media Theory*. Utrecht: Utrecht University Press.

Raessens, J. (2014). The ludification of culture. In M. Fuchs, S. Fizek, P. Ruffino, & N. Schrape (Eds.), *Rethinking Gamification* (pp. 91–114). Lüneburg: Meson Press.

Ramanan, C. (2017). The video game industry has a diversity problem – but it can be fixed. *The Guardian*, 15 March. Available at: https://www.theguardian.com/technology/2017/mar/15/video-game-industry-diversity-problem-women-non-white-people

Reitman, J. G., Anderson-Coto, M. J., Wu, M., Lee, J. S., & Steinkuehler, C. (2020). eSports research: A literature review. *Games and Culture*, 15(1), 32–50. doi: 10.1177/1555412019840892

Reseigh-Lincoln, D. (2017). Skins, Smurfs and *Skyrim*: A brief history of PC modding. *Techradar*, 14 August. Available at: https://www.techradar.com/au/news/skins-smurfs-and-skyrim-a-brief-history-of-pc-modding

Rey, P. J. (2012). Gamification, playbor and exploitation. *Cyborgology*, 15 October. Available at: http://thesocietypages.org/cyborgology/2012/10/15/gamification-playbor-exploitation-2/

Rheingold, H. (1993). *The Virtual Community: Homesteading on the Electronic Frontier*. Reading, MA: Addison-Wesley.

Richardson, I., & Hjorth, L. (2017). Mobile media, domestic play and haptic ethnography. *New Media & Society*, 19(10), 1653–1667. doi: 10.1177/1461444817717516

Ritterfeld, U., Cody, M., & Vorderer, P. (Eds.) (2009). *Serious Games: Mechanisms and Effects*. London: Routledge.

Robertson, A. (2014). Massacre threat forces Anita Sarkeesian to cancel university talk. *The Verge*, 14 October. Available at: https://www.theverge.com/2014/10/14/6978809/utah-state-university-receives-shooting-threat-for-anita-sarkeesian-visit

Rodriguez, H. (2006). The playful and the serious: An approximation to Huizinga's Homo Ludens. *Game Studies*, 6(1). Available at: http://gamestudies.org/0601/articles/rodriges

Roig, A., San Cornelio, G., Ardèvol, E., Alsina, P., & Pagès, R. (2009). Videogame as media practice. *Convergence: The International Journal of Research into New Media Technologies*, 15(1), 89–103. doi: 10.1177/1354856508097019

Romano, A. (2014). The sexist crusade to destroy game developer Zoe Quinn. *The Daily Dot*, 1 March. Available at: https://www.dailydot.com/parsec/zoe-quinn-depression-quest-gaming-sex-scandal/

Romualdo, S. (2015). Videogame art and the legitimation of videogames by the art world. *Proceedings from Computation Communication Aesthetics and X*, xCoAx, Glasgow, Scotland.

Rose, M. (2013). *Facebook's mobile transition is going smoothly – except for games*. 13 January. Available at: www.gamasutra.com/view/news/185788/Facebooks_mobile_transition_is_going_smoothly_except_for_games.php

Rouse, T. (2011). The Game Jam as radical practice. *Ludist*, 11 November. Available at: www.ludist.com/?p=117

Ruberg, B. (2019). *Video Games Have Always Been Queer*. New York: NYU Press.

Ruberg, B. (2020). *The Queer Games Avant-garde: How LGBTQ Game Makers Are Reimagining the Medium of Video Games*. Durham, NC: Duke University Press.

Ruihley, B. (2010). 'The fantasy sport experience: Motivations, satisfaction, and future intentions'. Dissertation, University of Tennessee. Available at: https://trace.tennessee.edu/utk_graddiss/747

Ruotsalainen, M., & Friman, U. (2018). 'There are no women and they all play mercy': Understanding and explaining (the lack of) women's presence in eSports and competitive gaming. *DiGRA Nordic '18: Proceedings of 2018 International DiGRA Nordic Conference*. Available at: www.digra.org/digital-library/publications/there-are-no-women-and-they-all-play-mercy-understanding-and-explaining-the-lack-of-womens-presence-in-esports-and-competitive-gaming

Ruppert, E. (2011). Population objects: Interpassive subjects. *Sociology*, 45(2), 218–233. doi: 10.1177/0038038510394027

Rush, J. (2011). Embodied metaphors: Exposing informatic control through firstperson shooters, *Games and Culture*, 6(3), 245–258.

Ryan, J. (2011). *Super Mario: How Nintendo Conquered America*. Harmondsworth: Penguin.

Ryan, M.-L., Emerson, L., & Robertson, B. J. (Eds.) (2014). *The Johns Hopkins Guide to Digital Media*. Baltimore, MD: Johns Hopkins University Press.

Salen, K. (2017). Afraid to roam: The unlevel playing field of *Pokémon GO*. *Mobile Media and Communication*, *5*(1), 34–37. doi: 10.1177/2050157916677865

Salen, K., & Zimmerman, E. (2003). *Rules of Play: Game Design Fundamentals*. Cambridge, MA: The MIT Press.

Salen, K., & Zimmeramn, E. (Eds.) (2005). *The Game Design Reader: A Rules of Play Anthology*. Cambridge, MA: The MIT Press.

Santos, L., Okamoto, K., Funghetto, S., Cavalli, A., Hiragi, S., Yamamoto, G., Sugiyama, O., Castanho, C., Aoyama, T., & Kuroda, T. (2019). Effects of social interaction mechanics in pervasive games on the physical activity levels of older adults: Quasi-experimental study. *JMIR Serious Games*, *7*(3). doi: 10.2196/13962

Sarkeesian, A. (2013). *Tropes vs women in video games. Part 1-2-3* (video). Available at: www.feministfrequency.com

Sawyer, B. (2007). Serious games: Broadening games impact beyond entertainment. *Computer Graphics Forum*, *26*(3), xviii–xviii. doi: 10.1111/j.1467-8659.2007.01044.x

Schell, J. (2019). *The Art of Game Design* (3rd ed.). New York: A K Peters/CRC Press.

Schirato, T. (2012). Fantasy sport and media interactivity. *Sport in Society*, *15*(1), 78–87. doi: 10.1080/03031853.2011.625278

Schirato, T. (2016). Digital media, fantasy sport and the transformation of the contemporary field of sport. *Communication Research and Practice*, *2*(4), 496–505. doi: 10.1080/22041451.2016.1259972

Schrank, B. (2014). *Avant-garde Videogames*. Cambridge, MA: The MIT Press.

Schreier, J. (2017). *Blood, Sweat, and Pixels: The Triumphant, Turbulent Stories Behind How Video Games Are Made*. New York: Harper Paperbacks.

Scott, M. J., & Ghinea, G. (2013). Promoting game accessibility: Experiencing an induction on inclusive design practice at the Global Games Jam. In *Proceedings of the 8th International Conference on the Foundations of Digital Games*, Chania, Crete, Greece, 14–17 May.

Sefton-Green, J. (Ed.) (1998). *Digital Diversions: Youth Culture in the Age of Multimedia*. London: UCL Press.

Seo, Y. (2016). Professionalized consumption and identity transformations in the field of eSports. *Journal of Business Research*, *69*(1), 264–272. doi: 10.1016/j.jbusres.2015.07.039

Seo, Y., & Jung, S. U. (2016). Beyond solitary play in computer games: The social practices of eSports. *Journal of Consumer Culture*, *16*(3), 635–655. doi: 10.1177/1469540514553711

Seth, E., Jenny, R., Manning, D., Keiper, M. C., & Olrich, T. W. (2017). Virtual(ly) athletes: Where eSports fit within the definition of 'sport'. *Quest*, *69*(1), 1–18. doi: 10.1080/00336297.2016.1144517

Sezen, T. I., & Sezen, D. (2016). Designing and playing to protest: Looking back to Gezi Games. In B. Bostan (Ed.), *Gamer Psychology and Behavior*. International Series on Computer Entertainment and Media Technology. New York: Springer.

Sharp, J. (2015). *Works of Game: On the Aesthetics of Games and Art*. Cambridge, MA: The MIT Press.

Sharp, J., & Macklin, C. (2019). *Iterate*. Cambridge, MA: The MIT Press.

Shin, K., Kaneko, K., Matsui, Y., Mikami, K., Nagaku, M., Nakabayashi, T., Kenji, O., & Yamane, S. R. (2012). Localizing Global Game Jam: Designing game development for collaborative learning in the social context. In A. Nijholt, T. Romano, & D. Reidsma (Eds.), *Advances in Computer Entertainment, Lecturer Notes in Computer Science*, Vol. 7624 (pp. 117–132). Berlin/Heidelberg: Springer.

Sicart, M. (2014). *Play Matters*. Cambridge, MA: The MIT Press.

Sicart, M. (2017). Reality has always been augmented: Play and the promises of *Pokémon GO*. *Mobile Media and Communication*, *5*(1), 30–33. doi: 10.1177/2050157916677863

Simon, B. (2009). Wii are out of control: Bodies, game screens and the production of gestural excess. *Canadian Games Studies*, *3*(4), 1–17. Available at: http://journals.sfu.ca/loading/index.php/loading/article/viewArticle/65

Sjöblom, M., & Hamari, J. (2017). Why do people watch others play video games? An empirical study on the motivations of Twitch users. *Computers in Human Behavior*, *75*, 985–996. doi: 10.1016/j.chb.2016.10.019

Skalski, P., Tamborini, R., Shelton, A., Buncher, M., & Lindmark, P. (2011). Mapping the road to fun: Natural video game controllers, presence, and game enjoyment, *New Media & Society*, *13*(2), 224–242.

Smith, T. P. B., Orbist, M., & Wright, P. (2013). Live-streaming changes the video game. *Proceedings of EuroITV '13* (pp. 131–138). Como, Italy, 24–26 June.

Snider, M. (2020). Video games can be a healthy social pastime during coronavirus pandemic. *USA Today*, 28 March. Available at: www.usatoday.com/story/tech/gaming/2020/03/28/video-games-whos-prescription-solace-during-coronavirus-pandemic/2932976001/

Soriano, C. R. R., Davies, H., & Hjorth, L. (2019). Social surveillance and Let's Play: A regional case study of gaming in Manila slum communities. *New Media & Society*, *21*(10), 2119–2139. doi: 10.1177/1461444819838497

Sotamaa, O. (2002). All the world's a botfighter stage: Notes on location-based multi-user gaming. Paper presented at the *Computer Games and Digital Cultures Conference*. Tampere, Finland.

Sotamaa, O. (2010). When the game is not enough: Motivations and practices among computer game modding culture. *Games and Culture*, *5*(3), 239–255. doi: 10.1177/1555412009359765

Soute, I., Markopoulos, P., & Magielse, R. (2010). Head Up Games: Combining the best of both worlds by merging traditional and digital play. *Personal and Ubiquitous Computing*, *14*(5), 435–444. doi: 10.1007/s00779-009-0265-0

Statista (2019). *Fantasy sports revenue in the United States in 2018*. Available at: https://www.statista.com/statistics/820972/revenue-fantasy-sports-segment/

Statista (2020). *Cumulative video views of Felix Kjellberg's YouTube channel PewDiePie from August 2017 to January 2020*. Available at: https://www.statista.com/statistics/681092/pewdiepie-video-view-numbers/

Stauff, M. (2018). A culture of competition: Sport's historical contribution to datafication. *Tijdschrift voor economische en sociale geografie*, *21*(2), 30–51.

Stebbins, R. (2004). *Between Work and Leisure*. New Brunswick, NJ: Transaction.

Steinkuehler, C. (2020). eSports research: Critical, empirical, and historical studies of competitive videogame play. *Games and Culture*, *15*(1), 3–8. doi: 10.1177/1555412019836855

Stenros, J., Paavilainen, J., & Mäyrä, F. (2009). The many faces of sociability and social play in games. *MindTrek 2009*. Tampere, Finland, September–October.

Stockburger, A. (2007). From appropriation to approximation. In A. Clarke & G. Mitchell (Eds.), *Videogames and Art* (pp. 25–37). Bristol: Intellect.

Stuart, K. (2014). Zoe Quinn: 'All Gamergate has done is ruin people's lives'. *The Guardian*, 4 December. Available at: www.theguardian.com/technology/2014/dec/03/zoe-quinn-gamergate-interview

Stuckey, H. (2012). Mods and museums: Gaming the future of art. In E. McCrae (Ed.), *Game Masters: The Exhibition*. Australian Centre for the Moving Image. Wellington: Te Papa Press.

Surman, D. (2009). Complicating kawaii. In L. Hjorth & D. Chan (Eds.), *Gaming Cultures and Place* (pp. 179–93). London: Routledge.

Sutton-Smith, B. (1997). *The Ambiguity of Play*. London: Routledge.

Swalwell, M., Ndalianis, A., & Stuckey, H. (Eds.) (2017). *Fans and Videogames: Histories, Fandom, Archives*. London: Routledge.

Swink, S. (2008). *Game Feel: A Game Designer's Guide to Virtual Sensation*. New York: CRC Press.

Szulborski, D. (2005). *This is Not a Game: A Guide to Alternate Reality Gaming*. U.S.A: New Fiction Publishing.

Tacon, R., & Vainker, S. (2017). Fantasy sport: A systematic review and new research directions. *European Sport Management Quarterly*, *17*(5), 558–589. doi: 10.1080/16184742.2017.1347192

Takahashi, D. (2018a). YouTube game videos were viewed for 50 billion hours in 2018. *VentureBeat*, 8 December. Available at: https://venturebeat.com/2018/12/08/youtube-game-videos-were-viewed-for-50-billion-hours-in-2018

Takahashi, D. (2018b). App Annie: Mobile gaming widened market lead on PC and console in 2017. *VentureBeat*, 13 March. Available at: https://venturebeat.com/2018/03/13/app-annie-mobile-gaming-widened-market-lead-on-pc-and-console-in-2017/

Taylor, T. L. (2007). Pushing the borders: Player participation and game culture. In J. Karaganis (Ed.), *Structures of Participation in Digital Culture* (pp. 112–131). New York: Social Science Research Council (US).

Taylor, T. L. (2009). The assemblage of play. *Games and Culture*, *4*(4), 331–339. doi: 10.1177/1555412009343576

Taylor, T. L. (2012). *Raising the Stakes: E-Sports and the Professionalization of Computer Gaming*. Cambridge, MA: The MIT Press.

Taylor, T. L. (2018a). Twitch and the work of play. *American Journal of Play*, *11*(1), 65–84.

Taylor, T. L. (2018b). *Watch Me Play: Twitch and the Rise of Game Live Streaming*. Princeton, NJ: Princeton University Press.

Terdiman, D. (2004). Making wireless roaming fun. *Wired*, 4 December. Available at: www.wired.com/gaming/gamingreviews/news/2004/04/63011

Terranova, T. (2000). Free labor: Producing culture for the digital economy. *Social Text*, *18*. doi: 10.1215/01642472-18-2_63-33

Thomas, B., Close, B., Donoghue, J., Squires, J., De Bondi, P., Morris, M., & Piekarski, W. (2000). ARQuake: An outdoor/indoor augmented reality first person application. In *4th International Symposium on Wearable Computers* (pp. 139–146). Atlanta, GA: IEEE Press.

Todd, C. (2015). Commentary: GamerGate and resistance to the diversification of gaming culture. *Women's Studies Journal*, *29*(1), 64–67.

Trépanier-Jobin, G. (2017). Gender issues in video games. *Kinephanos: Journal of Media Studies and Popular Culture*, July, 24–53. Available at: www.kinephanos.ca/Revue_files/2017_Trepanier_En.pdf

Turkle, S. (1996). *Life on the Screen: Identity in the Age of the Internet*. London: Weidenfeld & Nicholson.

Turkle, S. (2012). *Alone Together: Why We Expect More from Technology and Less from Each Other*. New York: Basic Books.

Turner, J., & Thomas, L. (2013). The seventh 48-hour game making challenge. *IE2013*, Melbourne. Available at: https://eprints.qut.edu.au/64499/

Valente, L., & Feijó, B. (2013). A survey on pervasive mobile games. *Monografias em Ciência da Computação, Departamento de Informática*. Rio De Janeiro, Brazil. Available at: ftp://ftp.inf.puc-rio.br/pub/docs/techreports/13_07_valente.pdf

Van den Boomen, M. (2014). *Transcoding the Digital: How Metaphors Matter in New Media*. Amsterdam: Institute of Network Cultures Amsterdam.

Van Dijck, J. (2014). Datafication, dataism and dataveillance: Big data between scientific paradigm and ideology. *Surveillance & Society*, *12*(2), 197–208.

Van Maanen, J. (2006). Ethnography then and now. *Qualitative Research in Organizations and Management: An International Journal*, *1*(1), 13–21. doi: 10.1108/17465640610666615

Vella, K., Johnson, D., Wan Sze Cheng, V., Davenport, T., Mitchell, J., Klarkowski, M., & Phillips, C. (2019). A sense of belonging: *Pokémon GO* and social connectedness. *Games & Culture*, *14*(6), 583–603. doi: 10.1177/1555412017719973

Vierkant, A. (2010). *The image object post-internet*. Available at: http://jstchillin.org/artie/pdf/ The_Image_Object_Post-Internet_us.pdf

Villapaz, L. (2013). 'GTA 5' costs $265 million to develop and market, making it the most expensive video game ever produced. *International Business Times*, 9 August. Available at: www.ibtimes.com/gta-5-costs-265-million-develop-market-making-it-most-expensive-video-game-ever-produced-report

Vitores, A., & Gil-Juárez, A. (2016). The trouble with 'women in computing': A critical examination of the deployment of research on the gender gap in computer science. *Journal of Gender Studies*, 25(6), 666–680. doi: 10.1080/09589236.2015.1087309

Vygotsky, L. S. (1978). *Mind in Society: The Development of Higher Psychological Processes*. Cambridge, MA: Harvard University Press.

Wadeson, D. (2013). Gamertube: PewDiePie and the YouTube commentary revolution. *Polygon*, 6 September. Available at: www.polygon.com/features/2013/9/6/4641320/pewdiepie-youtube-commentary

Wagner, M. G. (2006). On the scientific relevance of eSports. In *International Conference on Internet Computing & Conference on Computer Games Development* (pp. 26–290). Las Vegas, Nevada, June.

Wajcman, J., Bittman, M., & Brown, J. (2008). Intimate connections: The impact of the mobile phone on work life boundaries. In G. Goggin & L. Hjorth (Eds.), *Mobile Technologies*. London: Routledge.

Walz, S. P., & Deterding, S. (Eds.) (2014). *The Gameful World: Approaches, Issues, Applications*. Cambridge, MA: The MIT Press.

Wawro, A. (2016). How did *Pokémon GO* conquer the planet in less than a week? *Gamasutra*. Available at: www.gamasutra.com/view/news/276955/How_did_Pokemon_Go_conquer_the_planet_in_less_than_a_week.php

WePC (2020). *Game statistics*. Available at: www.wepc.com/news/video-game-statistics/

Wesch, M. (2008). An anthropological introduction to YouTube. *YouTube*. Available at: www.youtube.com/watch?v=TPAO-lZ4_hU

Westecott, E., Stein, S., Cheryl, H., & Kashfia, R. (2019). In situ: Researching corporate diversity initiatives with game developers. In *DiGRA '19 – Proceedings of the 2019 DiGRA International Conference: Game, Play and the Emerging Ludo-Mix DiGRA*. Kyoto, Japan, 6–10 August. Available at: http://openresearch.ocadu.ca/id/eprint/2793/

Weststar, J., & Legault, M. J. (2016). *Developer satisfaction survey 2016: A summary report for the International Game Developers Association* (Developer Satisfaction Survey (DSS) series). Ontario: International Game Developers Association.

Whitson, J.R. (2019). The new spirit of capitalism in the game industry. *Television & New Media*, 20(8), 789–801. doi: 10.1177/1527476419851086

Wikipedia (2019). *Twitch.tv*. Available at: https://en.wikipedia.org/wiki/Twitch.tv.

Wilken, R. (2012). Locative media: From specialized preoccupation to mainstream fascination. *Convergence: The International Journal of Research into New Media Technologies*, 18(3), 243–247. doi: 10.1177/1354856512444375

Williams, D. (2004). 'Trouble in River City: The social life of video games'. Dissertation, Department of Communication Studies, University of Michigan, Michigan. Available at: https://netfiles.uiuc.edu/dcwill/www/research.html

Williams, D., Ducheneaut, N., Xiong, L., Zhang, Y., Yee, N., & Nickell, E. (2006). From tree house to barracks: The social life of guilds in *World of Warcraft*. *Games and Culture*, 1(4), 338–361. doi: 10.1177/1555412006292616

Willson, M., & Leaver, T. (Eds.) (2016). *Social, Casual and Mobile Games: The Changing Gaming Landscape*. London: Bloomsbury Academic.

Wilson, J., & Jacobs, J. (2009). Obsolete. *M/C Journal*, 12(3). Available at: http://journal.media-culture.org.au/index.php/mcjournal/issue/view/obsolete

Wingfield, N. (2014). Feminist critics of video games facing threats in 'GamerGate' campaign. *New York Times*, 16 October. Available at: www.nytimes.com/2014/10/16/technology/gamergate-women-video-game-threats-anita-sarkeesian.html

Wirman, H. (2014). Gender and identity in game-modifying communities. *Simulation & Gaming*, *45*(1), 70–92. doi: 10.1177/1046878113519572

Witkowski, E. (2009). Probing the sportiness of eSports. In J. Christophers & T. Scholz (Eds.), *eSports Yearbook* (pp. 53–56). Books on Demand.

Witkowski, E. (2012). On the digital playing field: How we 'do sport' with networked computer games. *Games and Culture*, *7*(5), 349–374. doi: 10.1177/1555412012454222

Witkowski, E. (2018a). Doing/undoing gender with the girl gamer in high-performance play. In K. Gray-Denson, G. Voorhees, & E. Vossen (Eds.), *Feminism in Play*. Basingstoke: Palgrave Macmillan.

Witkowski, E. (2018b). Sensuous proximity in research methods with expert teams, media sports, and esports practices. *MedieKultur: Journal of Media and Communication Research*, *34*(64), 31–51. doi: 10.7146/mediekultur.v34i64.97014

Witkowski, E., & Manning, J. (2019). Player power: Networked careers in esports and high-performance game livestreaming practices. *Convergence*, *25*(5–6), 953–969. doi: 10.1177/1354856518809667

Wolf, M. J. P. (Ed.) (2007). *The Video Game Explosion: A History from PONG to Playstation and Beyond*. New York: Greenwood Publishing.

Wong, D. (2017). The future of sports is digital, it's also Chinese. *Thatsmags*. Available at: www.thatsmags.com/beijing/post/20147/eSports-china

Wood, D. (2020). How to play *Pokémon Go* from home. *Tech Radar*. Available at: https://www.techradar.com/how-to/how-to-play-pokemon-go-from-home

World Economic Forum (2019). *The business case for diversity in the workplace is now overwhelming*. Available at: https://www.weforum.org/agenda/2019/04/business-case-for-diversity-in-the-workplace/

Wulf, T., Schneider, F. M., & Beckert, S. (2020). Watching players: An exploration of media enjoyment. *Twitch, Games and Culture*, *15*(3), 328–346. doi: 10.1177/1555412018788161

Xue, H., Newman, J. I., & Du, J. (2019). Narratives, identity and community in esports. *Leisure Studies*, *38*(6), 845–861. doi: 10.1080/02614367.2019.1640778

Yamazaki, I., & Gorges, F. (2012). *The History of Nintendo: 1889–1980: From Playing Cards to Game & Watch*. Houdan: Pix'N Love.

Yang, R. (2020). *Robert Yang*. Available at: https://radiatoryang.itch.io/

Yu, H. (2018). Game on: The rise of the eSports Middle Kingdom. *Media Industries Journal*, *5*(1), 88–105.

Zackariasson, P., & Wilson, T. L. (Eds.) (2012). *The Video Game Industry: Formation, Present State, and Future*. London: Routledge.

Zariko, Z. (2016). 'Screening embodiment: Let's Play video and observable play experience'. Master's thesis, RMIT University, Melbourne, Australia.

Zhang, G. (2019). '*Zhibo*: An ethnography of ordinary, boring, and vulgar livestreams'. PhD dissertation, RMIT University, Melbourne, Australia.

Zhang, G., & Hjorth, L. (2017). Live-streaming, games and politics of gender performance: The case of *Nüzhubo* in China. *Convergence*, November. Available at: https://journals.SAGEpub.com/doi/10.1177/1354856517738160

Zimmerman, E. (2013). Manifesto for a ludic century. *Kotaku*, 10 September. Available at: www.kotaku.com.au/2013/09/manifesto-the-21st-century-will-be-defined-by-games/Z

Zimna, K. (2014). *Time to Play: Action and Interaction in Contemporary Art*. London: I. B. Tauris.

# Index